15 March 1986 David

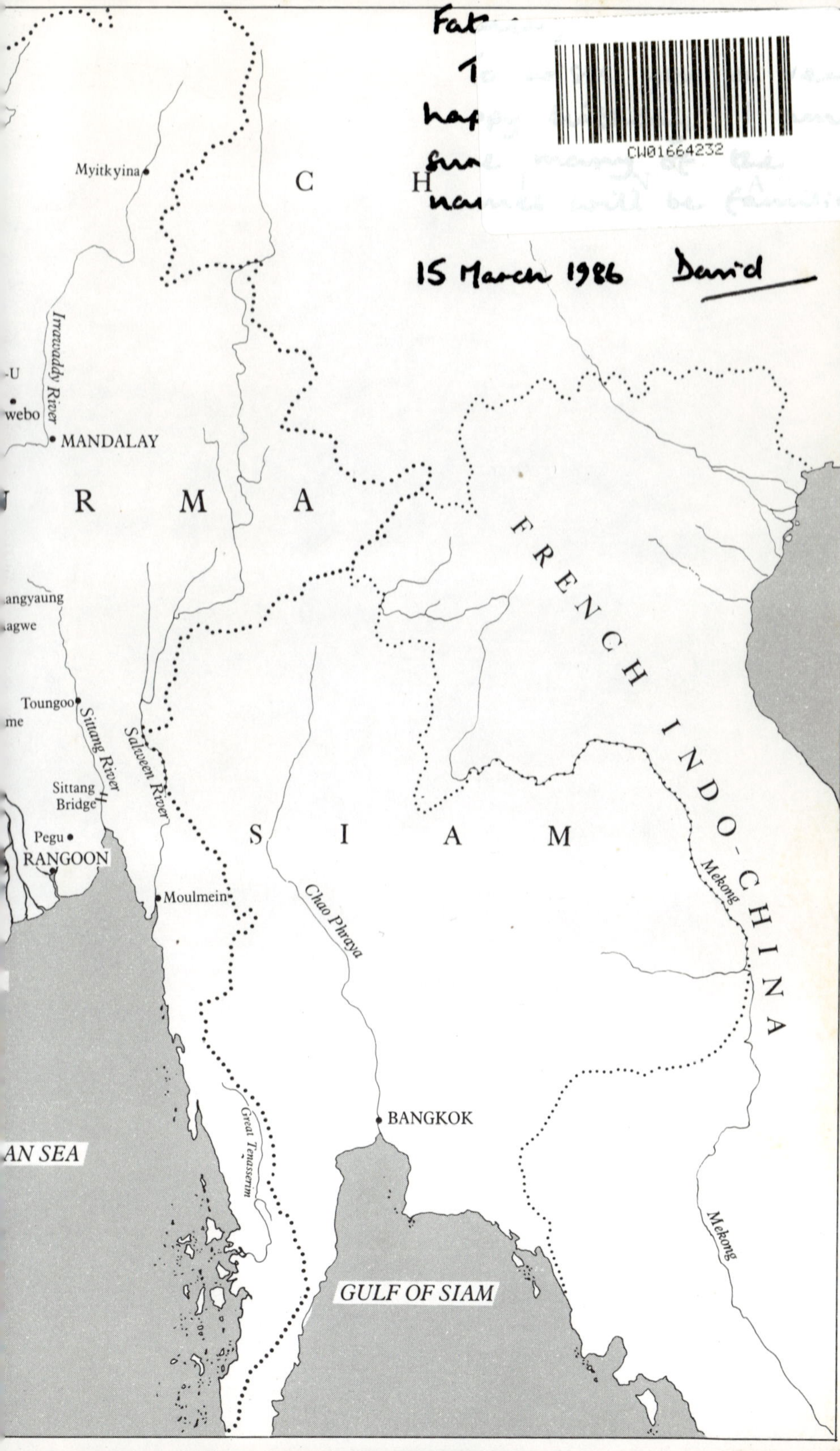

'A HELL OF A LICKING'

The Retreat from Burma 1941–2

By the same author

CHARGE TO GLORY
SCARLET LANCER
THE BARREN ROCKS OF ADEN
FROM SEPOY TO SUBEDAR (ED.)
BOKHARA BURNS
JOHN BURGOYNE OF SARATOGA
THE DUKE OF WELLINGTON'S REGIMENT
THE 16TH/5TH THE QUEEN'S ROYAL LANCERS
IMPERIAL SUNSET
GLUBB PASHA

A HELL OF A LICKING

The Retreat from Burma 1941–2

JAMES LUNT

COLLINS
8 Grafton Street London W1
1986

William Collins Sons & Co Ltd
London · Glasgow · Sydney · Auckland
Toronto · Johannesburg

BRITISH LIBRARY CATALOGUING IN PUBLICATION DATA

Lunt, James
A Hell of a Licking
The Retreat from Burma 1941–2
1. World War, 1939–1945—Campaigns—Burma
2. World War, 1939–1945—Personal narratives, British
I. Title
940.54′25′0924 D767.6

ISBN 0–00–272707–2

First published 1986

Photoset in Monophoto Plantin Light by
Ace Filmsetting Ltd, Frome, Somerset
Printed in Great Britain by
St Edmundsbury Press, Bury St Edmunds, Suffolk

for
Brigadier John Bourke
and
our comrades in
2nd Burma Brigade

'In the first place, no military commander in history made a *voluntary* retreat. And there's no such thing as a *glorious* retreat. All retreats are as ignominious as hell. I claim we got a hell of a licking. We got run out of Burma, and it's humiliating as hell. I think we ought to find out what caused it, go back, and retake Burma.'

Lieutenant-General Joseph W. Stilwell, US Army,
on his return to India from Burma

'We must be very careful not to assign to this deliverance the attributes of a victory. Wars are not won by evacuations.'

Winston Churchill on Dunkirk

ILLUSTRATIONS

CONTENTS

MAPS

ACKNOWLEDGEMENTS

This book is owed entirely to Brigadier John Bourke, my Commander during the Retreat from Burma in 1941–2. Although in his eighty-eighth year, his recollection of those difficult times is remarkably clear. He has read every chapter and I am greatly indebted to him for his advice and criticism. It has been a great pleasure to revive and strengthen a friendship which began forty-four years ago in Burma. I owe him my thanks but must make it plain that the opinions expressed are mine alone.

Those of us who took part in the campaign and still survive are all of us veterans. Nevertheless those I have been able to consult, either in person or in writing, have given me freely of their time. They include Major-Generals Sir John Winterton and Roger Ekin; Brigadiers Michael Calvert and S. J. H. Green; Mrs Nancy Scott; Colonel Peter Buchanan; Lieutenant-Colonel Humphrey Purton and Mr Richard Lewin. If by mischance I have omitted the names of others who have helped, I trust they will accept my apologies and take this as an expression of my gratitude.

I am particularly indebted to Dr Ralph Tanner who took part in the campaign as a young officer with the 2nd King's Own Yorkshire Light Infantry. He has put at my disposal the notes he made and the photographs he took. Even more importantly he has made available the English translation of the War Records of the 215th Infantry Regiment, Imperial Japanese Army. I must therefore include in my thanks Mr Kazuo Tamayama of Tokyo who so kindly made the translation for Dr Tanner. I have also to thank General A. C. Wedemeyer, US Army (retired), for replying so courteously and promptly to my letter.

For permission to quote from private papers and documents in their possession I have to thank the Trustees of the Liddell Hart Centre for Military Archives, King's College London; the Keeper of Documents, Imperial War Museum; the Controller of HM Stationery Office; the Director, National Army Museum; the Public Record Office; and the Director of the Historical

Section of the Ministry of Defence, Government of India. The Chief Librarian, Ministry of Defence (Central) Library and his staff are owed my thanks for the loan of books, as is also Miss Alexandra Ward, Head of the Historical Section of the Army Board.

I have to thank for permission to quote from private papers, Viscount Slim; Frances, Lady Smyth; Mrs Cowan; Mrs Field; Lieutenant-Colonel I. A. J. Edwards-Stuart; Mrs Davies; Mr Toothill; and the late Pat Carmichael from his *Mountain Battery*, probably the best subaltern's account of the campaign yet published. Dr Louis Allen has been kind enough to allow me to quote from *Burma: The Longest War 1941–45*, and Viscount Slim from his father's *Defeat into Victory*. I owe them my thanks.

Carol O'Brien, my publisher, has been as always a great support, and I also owe my thanks to Bruce Hunter, my agent, for his wise advice.

My old friend Major Charles Irwin is owed my thanks for reading the manuscript and for his trenchant criticism; as is my wife for reading the manuscript and bearing with me during the writing of it.

I have to thank Linda Jackman and Margaret Elliott for their assistance in the preparation of the manuscript.

My final acknowledgement must go to those comrades of mine, so many of them alas now dead, whose courage, humour and constant encouragement during the campaign made endurable what otherwise was an extremely uncomfortable time in my life.

Little Milton
Oxfordshire

JAMES LUNT

INTRODUCTION

'Let but the bugles of England play
Over the hills and far away.'
W. E. Henley

This is an account of a young man's first experience of battle; which, like his first experience of love, is likely to live long in his memory. His recollection of the many and varied incidents that went to make up the whole experience may not be precisely accurate, but the picture that lives in his memory is almost certainly a true one.

I have been encouraged to write this book by Brigadier John Bourke who commanded the 2nd Burma Infantry Brigade throughout the Retreat from Burma in 1942. He is now eighty-eight, somewhat crippled physically, but in spirit as indomitable as ever. He was my brigade commander, I was his staff captain, and we have been friends for forty-four years. A man of great humanity beneath a very conventional military exterior, his personal courage was an inspiration to me at times when my own morale was low. This book is in a sense my tribute to him.

It is said that the Duke of Wellington, when asked the test of a great general, replied: 'To know when to retreat and to dare to do it.'[1] British generals are certainly familiar with retreats, almost every war or campaign starting with one. There was Moore's to Corunna, Wellington's to Torres Vedras, French's to the Marne and Gort's to Dunkirk. The Retreat from Burma, however, was different from the others. It was just under 1000 miles in distance, and it lasted for five long and anxious months. Throughout, it was marked by a succession of disasters, any one of which might reasonably have been thought to have finished the campaign, but from which our troops recovered by some miracle and went on fighting and retreating.

Wellington was of course referring to tactical retreats, when a general withdraws his army in order to recover his balance, or to await reinforcements. This was not the case in Burma. We were made to retreat by our enemy. We had to dance to the Japanese tune. When we were back in India, Major-General D. T. Cowan, who commanded the 17th Indian Division from March 1942 until 1945, commented, 'Although withdrawal was the order of the day, we withdrew in our own time and in perfect order.'[2] But most of those who were in Burma with him, and who admired him as one of the finest fighting commanders ever produced by the old Indian Army, will find it difficult to agree. Our liveliest memories of the retreat are of confusion, disorder and near-escapes from disaster, all of which were brought about by the relentless pressure of the enemy.

The 2nd Burma Infantry Brigade was involved in the campaign from the day the Japanese crossed into Burma from Thailand and seized the important air landing ground at Victoria Point, in the extreme south of Tenasserim Province, on 13 December 1941. It was only a week after the Japanese had invaded Thailand by land and sea. From then onwards we were involved in the campaign until finally, after the longest retreat in the history of the British Army, the Brigade reached India on 25 May 1942. I had by that date been evacuated to India by air as a sick casualty, but Brigadier John Bourke, with what remained of the Brigade, marched out to India still as a fighting force. During the last stages of the retreat, while acting as flank guard to the retreating Burma Corps (BURCORPS), 2nd Burma Brigade actually marched 513 miles in forty days, during the hottest season of the year. It was a notable feat of endurance.

I had been serving in Burma on loan service from my British regiment to the Burma Rifles for nearly three years prior to the Japanese invasion. How I came to be there I shall shortly describe. However, the fact that I could speak the language and had acquired some knowledge of the customs and traditions of the Burmese people made the war in Burma a more personal matter for me than was probably the case for those newly arrived from India with their British and Indian units. I found it difficult to understand how it was that the whole elaborate edifice of

British power in Burma crumbled into ruins in less than six months. In the diary I kept in note form at that time, I express this bewilderment on many occasions. Clearly, it was something which troubled me a good deal.

All war is a puzzle, of course, its most puzzling aspect being man's resort to war in order to settle his differences or satisfy his ambitions. The Retreat from Burma is an example of what I mean. The Japanese had no more right to rule the country than the British. The Burmese had no desire to be ruled by either, as became clear when we retreated in 1942, and the Japanese in 1945. We devastated the country as we withdrew. We did the same when we went back. Tens of thousands of people died in a dispute over a country whose people only wanted to be left alone to rule themselves, as indeed they have done ever since Burma became independent again on 4 January 1948. It made me feel sick at heart to see the little country towns turned into flaming ruins, the columns of Indian peasants on their long trek back to India dying by the wayside from cholera, or cut down in their tracks by murderous Burmese gangs who hated the Indians above all others. It was a far cry from the Burma I had known before war came – the land of *The Lacquer Lady*,[3] as I prefer to remember it.

I went to Burma in March 1939; almost certainly by mistake. The previous August I had been serving in Amritsar with B Company of the 2nd Battalion of the Duke of Wellington's Regiment (the 'Dukes'). I was a second-lieutenant with only one year's service and aged twenty-one. The 'Dukes' were a good regiment in the solid county tradition of the British Army, recruiting from the West Riding of Yorkshire soldiers as fine as any to be found in England. But they, like me, were bored, although for different reasons. In their case most of them had been driven to enlist after long years on the dole. With few exceptions they were miners. Enlisted for seven years on the active list, and five years on the reserve, some had spent as many as six years in India, where the private's life was one of stupefying boredom for 75 per cent of the time. They longed to get back to 'civvy street' but the worsening international situation had led to a temporary postponement of their discharge dates.

Meanwhile Amritsar, in a shade temperature of 115° Fahrenheit, had little to commend it, particularly when we patrolled the fetid streets with memories of Dyer and the Jallianwallah Bagh to make us mind our business.[4] It was not a happy time for any of us.

But my boredom was different. We had too many subalterns in the 'Dukes' without enough to keep us occupied; I think there were seven officers in my company, including a couple on attachment prior to joining the Indian Army. That was my aim too, despite my father's opposition. He was convinced that India would become independent within ten years. I discussed my problem with a friend, staying a few days with me on his way to the 4th Gurkha Rifles depot at Bakloh, in the Punjab Hills. His name was Jack Masters, no hint then of the successful novelist he would eventually become.

Jack, who was older and more worldly-wise than I was, prided himself on speaking his mind. Although he agreed with me that life as a platoon officer in a British unit was terribly dull, he went on to damage my ego by saying he doubted whether I would get into a 'good' Indian regiment; by this I presume he meant the Gurkhas. Since British Service subalterns regarded themselves as being superior to their Indian Army equivalents, both socially and professionally, I thought Jack was shooting too much of a line. 'Why don't you try to join colonial forces?' he asked. 'Some corps like the Trans-Jordan Frontier Force? I think you would get on better with Arabs than Indians.' The thought had never occurred to me but I promised to think it over.*

Shortly after our conversation, a lengthy document from Army Headquarters landed on my desk; I was acting as the station staff officer at the time. It was the annual appeal for officers to serve on loan with the colonial forces for three or four years. In the days of empire there were a great many of them,

* We did not meet again for thirty years – when Masters was visiting New Delhi and I was serving on the British High Commissioner's staff. Masters was by then a very successful novelist. 'Did you ever get to the Arabs?' he asked, when I reminded him of the incident. I told him I had spent nearly seven years with them after the war. 'I always thought you would,' he said.

ranging from the King's African Rifles in East Africa to the Aden Protectorate Levies in South Arabia. After studying the list intently I followed Masters' advice and applied to serve with the Trans-Jordan Frontier Force, concerning which I knew absolutely nothing beyond the fact that they wore tall Astrakhan caps (*kalpaks*) like the Cossacks, rode horses and served in Palestine, not Trans-Jordan. When I showed my application to my company commander, a jovial Irish baronet, he laughed out loud. 'The CO will have a fit when he sees this,' he said. 'You are far too junior to be allowed to go. Anyway, it says you have to list three choices. You have only put down one.' Then together we searched through the list, adding as Numbers 2 and 3 the Burma Frontier Force and the Burma Rifles, neither of which meant anything to me, my knowledge of Burma being limited to Kipling's poem. Paddy Everard signed it, still laughing, and sent it off to battalion headquarters, located at Dalhousie in the Punjab Hills.

The Munich crisis followed soon afterwards, there was a serious internal security situation in Amritsar itself, and I forgot all about my application. War with Germany became the staple subject of conversation in our small officers' mess, most of us wondering whether we could possibly wangle a posting back to the 1st Battalion, stationed in Aldershot, in order to be in the hunt from the very beginning. When December came our tour of duty in Amritsar came to an end and we returned to the battalion, about to leave for Kohat on the North-West Frontier, where we were to brush up our training in mountain warfare against the Pathan tribesmen.

On a cold January morning we marched out from Kohat, picketing the hills on either side of the track as we went. Mine was Number 9 picket, the last to go up and come down. Although we were supposedly in 'friendly' territory, no chances were being taken against surprise. Throughout a broiling hot afternoon my platoon of some twenty bloody-minded Yorkshire soldiers squatted among the boulders on our hilltop, watching the rest of the battalion constructing a perimeter camp a thousand feet below us. Then, at long last, the red flag was waved nine times and we came hurtling down the hillside, carefully avoiding the re-entrants for fear of ambush. It had been a long, hot and thirsty day.

Arriving in camp, I was disturbed to learn that the adjutant wanted to see me – *immediately*! He was a very strong-willed officer who had found frequent cause to find fault with my military conduct and I wondered what had occasioned this latest summons to his presence. I almost ran to the tent serving as Battalion Orderly Room and gave him my best salute. Without looking up, he pushed a paper towards me. 'Don't ask me why,' he began, 'but some outfit called the Burma Rifles seems to want your services. Ever heard of them?' I had to plead ignorance. 'Well, you have forty-five minutes to make up your mind whether you want to go,' he said. 'The CO feels he can dispense with your services in the running of this battalion. If you decide to go,' he went on, 'the contractor's car is leaving for Kohat within the hour and he can run you in. But don't be late!' And then he dismissed me.

The message from Army Headquarters in New Delhi was to the effect that *if* I was willing to volunteer, I was to report to the 4th Burma Rifles (4 BURIF) in Mandalay as soon as possible. I remembered that I had included the Burma Rifles in my list of preferences when I had applied to second to colonial forces way back in August, but I had no idea who they were or what they did. I sought out my company commander who was drinking whisky in the mess tent and discussing tiger-shooting.

'Mandalay, eh?' he mused. 'Never been there. Somewhere in Burma, I believe. Knew some Burma Rifles once. Played polo against them in Singapore. Nice chaps, I thought. If I were you, I'd go, Jimmy. Far better than running into debt in New Delhi where the CO says we shall be going next. But watch out for the Burmese women. I'm told they're damned good-looking.'

Little wiser than I had been beforehand, I returned to the adjutant. 'Made up your mind?' he asked. 'Well, sign here at the bottom of the page before you change it! Go and pack your kit, make sure you settle your mess bill, and then go with the contractor to Kohat. The station staff officer will fix up your ticket. The CO's out on a recce so you won't see him before you go. Good luck – and keep in touch.'

On the face of it this may seem to have been a remarkably casual way to dispatch a young officer to what was virtually *terra incognita* where the battalion was concerned. Having myself been responsible for secondment policy in my last appointment in the army, I can state categorically that it could never happen today. There were, however, some extenuating circumstances. Firstly, we had more than enough subalterns, with others in the pipeline; I could easily be spared. Secondly, as I discovered later, my commanding officer was a firm believer in his officers serving for a period with what were then known as 'colonial forces'. Thirdly, we were shortly due to move to New Delhi where our duties would principally be ceremonial. My colonel probably reckoned that I would come to less harm in Mandalay than in Delhi among the fleshpots. But whatever his reasons for letting me go, I have always been grateful to him.

Three weeks later, having collected my kit and disposed of my cocker spaniel and my pony, I boarded the British India steamer, SS *Karagola*, at Calcutta, and set sail for Rangoon. It was 3 March 1939, two weeks before Hitler marched into Czechoslovakia and the world began to slide helter-skelter into chaos. Almost as a foretaste of what was to come, the Bay of Bengal was frightfully rough and I was very seasick. Just as well, perhaps, because I felt very homesick for the 'Dukes', with whom, as it happened, I was never to serve again . . .

CHAPTER ONE

Uneasy Burma

'It was taken for granted that the Burmese enjoyed having the British in Burma as much as the British enjoyed being there.'

Imperial Sunset.[1]

Burma is different! This was the first impression received by the visitor on landing at Rangoon after the passage across the Bay of Bengal from Calcutta or Madras. The streets might be teeming with Indians (most of them Tamils from southern India, who accounted for two-thirds of Rangoon's population of half a million) and yet by no stretch of the imagination could Rangoon be mistaken for an Indian city. It was so much more colourful: the flowers, the birds, and above all the Burmese themselves.

Bengal might be lush but southern Burma was even more so, and just as humid. Rangoon's gardens bloomed with tropical profusion – bougainvillea, poinsettias, laburnum and tall delphiniums of piercing blue. The Golden Mohur trees flamed like candles against the green foliage, while high above this pageant of colour towered the great bulk of the Shwe Dagon Pagoda, its golden cupola reflecting the sun's rays like some vast twinkling diamond.

The Burmese themselves were a happy-go-lucky, cheerful people, usually smiling behind the huge cheroots smoked by young and old alike, irrespective of sex. They had none of the subservient, hang-dog appearance of the Indian poor, weighed down by their constant struggle against poverty and disease. The Burmese looked well-fed and opulent, flamboyant in both manner and dress. Their women in trim white bodices and brightly coloured ankle-length skirts (*tameins*), their long black hair sleeked back in a tight bun, with a flower stuck in it, were not like the shy, downcast Madrassi girls who shuffled past; instead they sat behind their stalls in the marketplace, cracking jokes with European males as they drove the hardest of bargains.[2] Their men, too, were equally colourful, their cotton *lungyis* brightly-coloured, topped usually by a white shirt, and on their heads a basketwork skullcap round which was twisted a strip of coloured cloth. They were much tattooed and looked as if they enjoyed a drink, which they did, and gambling also, which they did even more. A jolly crew, until they were crossed or became panicky, when they could be both treacherous and brutally cruel. Jekylls and Hydes, each one of them.

Rudyard Kipling's poet's eye marked this contrast between India and Burma during his briefest of visits to Rangoon. But he did not venture far from the city, which probably accounts for the geographical inexactitudes in his poem 'Mandalay'. This was a pity because Rangoon was hardly the real Burma – this lies much farther to the north, where the Kings of Ava ruled for so long over this smiling, prosperous land until we came and dispossessed them.

It required three wars and sixty-two years before the British became masters of all Burma, but the country remained throughout our rule the uneasiest of all our imperial possessions, an Ireland in Asia. No Burmese worth his salt ever became truly reconciled to foreign rule, a fact which those of us who served there found hard to believe since our rule was on the whole beneficent, bringing many material improvements to the people as a whole. We built the roads and railways, developed a flourishing traffic along the country's two great rivers, the Irrawaddy and Chindwin, exploited Burma's many indigenous resources – oil, minerals, timber and rice – instituted the rule of law, put down highway robbery (dacoity), the Burmese favourite pastime, introduced an excellent system of education, respected the Buddhist religion, and protected the hill tribes (Chins, Kachins, Karens and Shans), whom previously the Burmese had shamefully exploited. Most important, perhaps, we stood between the Burmese and their Chinese neighbours in the north who had long claimed Burma as a tributary and Burma's northernmost provinces as *China irredenta*.

To set against these advantages of British rule, obvious even to the most ardent Burmese patriot, there were however several oppressive disadvantages. First and foremost was the fact of foreign rule when the Thais, their cousins to the east, were their own masters. Next, and probably worse, had been the influx of Indians into the country in the wake of their British overlords. It had been Indian soldiers who had played the principal part in conquering Burma for the British, for subjugating it thereafter, and for keeping the peace once the fighting was over. In their train had come tens of thousands of Indian coolies, to work in the docks, to build the roads and railways, to crew the Irrawaddy Flotilla Company steamers, to sweep the streets, to man the civil police force, to pull the rickshaws, drive the cabs, and do all the other menial tasks the Burmese preferred to leave to others. Worst of all had been the moneylenders, buying up the profligate Burmese landowners, cornering the rice market, building great mansions in cities like Rangoon, Bassein and Moulmein. As if to add insult to injury, Burma was not administered as a British colony in its own right, as it might be like Malaya, but as a mere province of British India, by a Lieutenant-Governor subservient to a distant Viceroy and his Council, not one of whom was a Burmese.

Finally, and equally irksome, the exploitation of Burma's great wealth was hardly at all in Burmese hands. Great trading combines like the Bombay-Burma Trading Corporation and Steel Brothers controlled the timber (and there were smaller firms too); the mines and the oil were British-controlled; Indians and Chinese handled the rice trade; the Chinese were the entrepreneurs. The dentists were mostly Japanese, some said to be doubling up as spies. Even the head office of the Irrawaddy Flotilla Company was in Glasgow, its board of directors, master mariners and chief engineers British to a man, the vast majority of them Scotsmen of a particularly tough and enduring breed.

Burma is a large country, as big as Spain, traversed from north to south by the Irrawaddy, 1500 miles long from its sources in the wild mountains on the border with China, and discharging into the Bay of Bengal through a mass of tributaries, beside one of which stands Bassein, Burma's second port. The Irrawaddy is navigable for 800 miles from the sea to Bhamo, in the far north of Burma, and it has throughout history been the country's principal artery of communication. Fifty miles west of Mandalay it is joined by the Chindwin, rising in the mountains on Burma's border with India, itself navigable by special shallow-draught vessels for 400 miles. At the confluence of these two great rivers, between the towns of Myingyan and Pakokku to east and west, there is a vast sheet of water three miles or more wide during the monsoon floods.

Besides these two great rivers, there are two others flowing from north to south. One, the Salween, as mighty as the Irrawaddy but navigable only at its mouth where it enters the Gulf of Martaban, rises in China and for part of its course marks Burma's border with Thailand. It flows through terrifying deep gorges in its early reaches, while its mouth extends from shore to shore for as much as three miles. Moulmein, Burma's third port, stands on its eastern bank; Martaban, on the far bank, serves as Moulmein's railhead for Rangoon. Eighty miles west of Martaban the River Sittang also enters the Gulf of Martaban; it will figure prominently later in this narrative. The Sittang rises in the Karen Hills, its course of some 250 miles lying wholly within Burma. Sluggish in the dry season, it flows at four knots or more during the monsoon and is a formidable obstacle; though unnavigable to all but country craft there are numerous local ferries throughout its course. These are only Burma's main rivers. There are innumerable others, many as wide as the Thames at Oxford, wider still during the monsoon, as well as thousands of *chaungs*, dry watercourses in the hot season that become raging torrents in the monsoon, when large parts of Burma are transformed into one huge swamp.

The British first arrived in Burma, uninvited, in 1824. A Burmese army under Bandula, Burma's greatest soldier, had invaded Manipur and Assam, providing the East India Company with a *casus belli* it was not unwilling to accept, trade usually following the flag in the Company's experience. But first a commander for the expeditionary force had to be nominated, and as was to be expected Britain's greatest soldier, the Duke of Wellington, had to be consulted. 'Send Lord Combermere,' he said. The staff were astonished. 'But, Your Grace,' they exclaimed, 'we always thought you considered his Lordship to be a fool.' 'So he is – and a damned fool,' replied the Duke, 'but he can take Rangoon.' Fortunately they disregarded the great man's advice and chose instead a run-of-the-mill Company's general, Sir Archibald Campbell, most of his troops being drawn from the old 'Coast Army' of the Madras Presidency. There were also four British regiments. The high-caste *sepoys* of the Bengal Army having an aversion to crossing the sea, the 47th Bengal Native Infantry mutinied rather than do so. General Paget dealt with the matter summarily. The ringleaders were tied to and then blown from the muzzles of the guns; the rest of the regiment was disbanded. There were no further attempts at mutiny.

The campaign was not the walkover originally anticipated. At one stage it came very close to disaster, disease killing far more of the combatants than bullets. The Burmese were brave if somewhat temperamental enemies, placing as much faith in charms and tattoos as in their marksmanship, which left much to be desired. The heart went out of them after Bandula's death at Donabyu and a treaty was eventually agreed in 1826. Rangoon was returned to the Burmese but the coastal provinces of Arakan and Tenasserim were ceded to the East India Company, Moulmein becoming the principal trading station and garrison. An uneasy peace followed for twenty-five years.

The Second Burmese War from 1852 to 1853 was almost entirely due to the intransigence of the Court of Ava, as the Burmese Government styled itself. The British occupation was fiercely resented and there were frequent clashes along the border. This brought about another confrontation with the East India Company and its imperious pro-consul in Bengal, the Earl of Dalhousie. An expeditionary force was assembled under General Godwin who captured Rangoon on 12 April 1852, storming the Shwe Dagon Pagoda during the action. Only seventeen were killed and 124 wounded but hundreds more died from the fevers and cholera that followed. Dalhousie was not satisfied with the result and the war was renewed until finally the Burmese gave in. They lost their southern province of Pegu, and also Rangoon, thereby cutting themselves off from the sea. It hardly made for good relations.

The Burmese King Mindon moved his capital to Mandalay and was wise enough to appreciate that it never paid to quarrel with the British. Nevertheless he, like all his subjects, bitterly resented the loss of Pegu and Rangoon. A wise and enlightened ruler, he managed to keep the peace, *faute de mieux*, despite the depredations of his soldiers who behaved more like *banditti*. Theebaw, a younger son, succeeded Mindon. He took the wise precaution of butchering every relative who might have had a claim to the throne. Much under the thumb of his Queen, Supalayat, more beautiful than wise, Theebaw sent embassies to Italy and France, and then proceeded to quarrel with the powerful Bombay-Burma Trading Corporation, which had a virtual monopoly in timber extraction. War inevitably followed.

General Prendergast assembled a strong force at Thayetmyo on the Irrawaddy, embarked it on six vessels of the Irrawaddy Flotilla Company, already a power in the land, and sailed upstream to Mandalay. There was a brisk encounter at Minhla but thereafter it was quite literally plain sailing all the way to Mandalay which was entered on 28 November 1885. Poor Theebaw and Supalayat, deserted by their court and palace guards, were sent downstream on board the Flotilla steamer *Thooreah*, and then across the Bay of Bengal to Coonor in the Nilgiri Hills to live out the rest of their lives in exile. Upper Burma was annexed by the British Crown on 1 January 1886. Theebaw's palace was named Fort Dufferin in honour of the Viceroy, who promptly added 'and Ava' to his title as a witness to posterity. It had been a very neat and tidy campaign.

But the fighting was far from over. Theebaw's soldiers, with their belief in talismans and fears of spirits (*nats*), may have been no match in the open field for General Prendergast, but it became a different story in the mountains and jungles where they found refuge. For more than five years after their King's departure they continued to harass the British and their *sepoys*. Small columns of 200–300 men were regularly involved in running battles with Burmese guerrillas. The 'Subalterns' War', as it came to be called in the pages of *Blackwood's Magazine*, was a war of ambush, long marches, dawn attacks and the crossing and recrossing of formidable rivers – a struggle as much against disease, the climate and the terrain as against the elusive Burmese gangs. Nearly sixty years later we were to encounter the same conditions, and to die from the same diseases. When, finally, the Burmese abandoned the struggle and made their peace with the British, much of the credit was owed to Brigadier-General Sir George White, VC, who went on to win fame nine years later as the defender of Ladysmith against the Boers in South Africa.[3]

King Theebaw had not been a popular ruler and the fact that so many young Burmans took to the jungles to fight on his behalf was evidence of their hatred of foreign rule. That Burma was to be governed as a province of the Indian Empire was hardly calculated to reconcile the irreconcilable. The Burmese looked down on Indians just as the Bedouins of Arabia despised the cultivators in Doughty's *Arabia Deserta*.[4] Besides, Delhi was a long way from Rangoon, and India was where ambitious men came to notice, not Burma. Some very able men from the Indian Civil Service and Indian Police did choose to make their careers in Burma, but there were few of them. In the early days certainly, and almost until the end in the frontier areas, officers on deputation from the Indian Army to the Burma Commission did most of the district work. Burma is naturally prosperous, and once law and order had been established the country began to flourish – although opposition to foreign rule never died.

Despite being outwardly friendly, the Burmese nurse a chronic suspicion of all foreigners. Culturally Burma has been the bridge between the two ancient civilizations of India and China, the Burmese preferring to keep themselves to themselves. They fear the Chinese, dislike the Indians, and keep a wary eye on the Thais whom they rightly suspect of wanting to acquire Tenasserim, Burma's southernmost province. Devout Buddhists, they are nevertheless intensely superstitious, believing profoundly in soothsayers and spirits. They have no caste prejudices like Hindus but are nevertheless much under the sway of their priests (*pongyis*) whose saffron-coloured robes are to be seen wherever Burmese happen to congregate. With shaven heads, and clasping their begging bowls, the *pongyis* are a familiar sight every morning as they visit the houses and huts of the faithful to beg the day's meal. They never come away empty-handed.

British Burma was divided roughly into the Upper and Lower halves of the country, Mandalay being the chief city in the north, Rangoon in the south. The south was the rich rice-growing area, the country's main cash-crop. It was hot, humid and wet from May to October. The north was much drier, almost desert round the oil-fields at Yenangyaung, but it was from Upper Burma that the timber and oil came, the rubies and precious stones, and the minerals from Mawchi in the Karen Hills. Tenasserim, the long tongue of land in the south-east which almost joins Burma with Malaya, was where tin was mined and rubber cultivated. To the west was the Arakan, separated from the rest of Burma by virtually trackless, jungle-covered, razor-backed hills, which looked as much to Calcutta as it did to Rangoon for its markets. Burma's size, not easy to judge from the ordinary map, soon became apparent when one sought to travel in the country. It sadly lacked all-weather roads, the railway was single-track and only metre gauge, there were few airfields and fewer still planes, and the Irrawaddy remained, as it had done throughout the centuries, the most reliable, if somewhat time-consuming way of getting around the country.

This large country was under-populated, so much of it being mountainous or jungle. The 1941 Census showed a population of around seventeen million, ten million of them Burmans who lived mainly in the central part of Burma, between Mandalay and the Bay of Bengal. They were a curious mixture of kindliness and savagery, usually docile but easily roused to a frenzy. Brave as individuals, they disliked discipline and saw no shame in running away in order to fight another day. By and large they were literate, compared with most other Asian peoples, and much addicted to political intrigue. With few exceptions their political leaders were venal, self-seeking and corrupt. If it was difficult to dislike the average Burmese, it was just as difficult to trust him. He was completely his own man.

There was more than a little arrogance in the Burmese

character, a sense of superiority that was at its worst when dealing with the minorities amounting to seven millions or more. Four million of them were Karens, a brave, likeable and intelligent people, many of whom had embraced Christianity, chiefly of the American Baptist creed. The home territory of the Karens was the wild, jungle-covered hills lying between the Sittang and Salween rivers, but there were even more of them living in the Irrawaddy delta, Bassein being mainly a Karen town. Their staunch Christianity brought them into frequent conflict with the Burmese, who had persecuted them abominably in the past, as they were to do again in the future. The Karens in consequence were very pro-British, although we left them to their fate without a backward glance the moment it became expedient for us to do so. I am grateful that I have never had to meet any of my old Karen friends again: I could not bear to look them in the eye.

East of the central plains, stretching as far as the Salween border with Thailand, and north as far as Yunnan, was the land of the Shans, a rolling, smiling country of red earth and small villages nestling alongside gentle streams, their banks overgrown with wild rose hedges. For administrative purposes there were the Southern and Northern Shan States, their chief towns Taunggyi and Lashio respectively, but they were divided traditionally into a series of minor principalities, semi-independent and ruled over by hereditary *sawbwas* (or minor rajahs). Theirs was a beautiful country, mild in climate for much of the year, inhabited by a kind and gentle people whose women were renowned for their beauty. Men, women and children alike bathed together in their crystal-clear streams, a kind of garden of Eden. There were about two million of them, administered not by the central government but by officials of the Burma Frontier Service. There were Shans too living west of the Irrawaddy, along the banks of the Chindwin, great handlers of elephants, or *oozies* as they were known.

In the far north-east, high up in the tangled mountains, lived the Kachins, animists for the most part, who bore some resemblance to the Gurkhas. They were brave, loyal and hospitable, but sadly addicted to opium. They had all the hillman's contempt for the plains dweller and bore little love for the Burmese. Between them and the Chins, mountaineers too who lived in the huge mountain massif west of the Chindwin and south of the Indian border, there were the Nagas, head-hunters until recent times and as fine a people as any on this earth. Nagaland lies within the Indian frontier, although the Nagas have long claimed their independence. Ursula Graham Bower's *Naga Path* is one of the finest tales of heroism yet recorded.[5] The Kachins were among the first of the Burmese hill tribes to take service under the British, originally in the Burma Military Police, although from 1917 onwards they were enlisted into the Burma Rifles. They were great smugglers and an attractive people, perhaps the most charming of the races we enlisted. When everything went sour towards the end it was the Kachins who stood by us the longest.

Westward, beyond the Chindwin, was the great massif of the Chin Hills, a tangled mass of knife-edged ridges and almost bottomless valleys, covered in jungle, riddled with fevers of every kind, drenched throughout the monsoon with torrential rainstorms, policed by the Chin Hills battalion of the Burma Frontier Force who wore their long hair tied neatly in a top-knot. The Chins were darker in colour than the Kachins, bigger men on the whole, inclined to be dour, and very careful with their money. They were sub-divided into Haka, Falam and Tiddim for recruitment purposes, had an amazing capacity for Mandalay rum and were practically omnivorous. My orderly, Go Chin Tawng, would sit for hours under a tree waiting to bring down an unsuspecting tree-rat with his bow and arrow.

Chins, Kachins and Shans probably totalled five millions at most, to which could be added one million Indians, 500,000 Chinese, and a few thousand Japanese and Malays; even some Thais in Tenasserim. Burmese was not their mother tongue, although most of them could speak it. There were a bewildering number of dialects. The Burmans and Shans were Buddhists, the Karens mostly Christians, the hill tribes animists although the missionaries were making significant inroads among them. But Burma was a homogeneous country on the whole, unlike India, and even the Tamil coolies in Rangoon could make a fist at speaking Burmese, difficult though it was to read.

West of the lower reaches of the Irrawaddy, extending to the shores of the Bay of Bengal, was another range of jungle-covered mountains, the Arakan Yomas, remote, virtually roadless, more swamp and bamboo than cultivable land. At Akyab, an island off the coast, there was an airfield, another link on the route from Calcutta to Singapore. There was a track across the Arakan Yomas which started at Prome and ended at Taungup on the Bay of Bengal after crossing a steep pass, soon to be marked by the skeletons of those Indians who chose this difficult route in their flight from Burma.

It was hard to believe that a handful of foreigners coming from thousands of miles across the sea had conquered this vast and very beautiful land. Bands of young Burmans, tattooed to make them invulnerable to British bullets, fought for years to defeat the invaders. One of their leaders, Po Thit, a native of Shwebo, birthplace of Alaungpaya who had founded the dynasty of Ava, had taken to the jungle when King Theebaw's bodyguard fled. Po Thit, a junior officer in the bodyguard, remembered the King reviewing his troops only the day before they abandoned him to the British. But Po Thit made amends for his cowardice by spending the next five years living like a wild animal, as he described it, several times wounded and many more times debilitated by fever.

In the end it became hopeless. 'If you can't beat them, you must join them,' he told his followers. Po Thit made his submission to the District Commissioner in Shwebo and after a decent interval was allowed to join the Burma Police. He rose to the rank of Chief Inspector before retiring full of honours to the handsome house he had built himself beside the moat surrounding Fort Dufferin in Mandalay. There he taught British officers the Burmese language, among them myself, dispensing regular cups of tea made all the more welcome by the very beautiful granddaughter who waited upon us.

As a learned man we addressed him as *Saya*; he called us *Thakin* (master). Aged eighty or more, his temper was inclined to be irritable, particularly during the long, hot afternoons when counting up to one hundred in Burmese invariably made me drowsy. It is not an easy language and I have never been a linguist. But if Po Thit never succeeded in making me an interpreter in Burmese, he taught me a great deal about his country's history, his people's customs and their aspirations. He taught me for the first time that God was not necessarily an Englishman; that not everyone could be expected to regard the British Empire in quite the same light as I did myself; and that there was a great deal more discontent in Burma than one would ever have imagined possible from the everyday talk in the European clubs and officers' messes.

Po Thit paid credit where credit was due. The British, he said, had made the land safe, where before they came highway robbery was common, villages were burnt down in pursuit of family feuds and murder was commonplace. Arbitrary arrest at the whim of the King or of some court favourite or governor no longer need be feared. He need no longer fear for his beautiful granddaughter who in Theebaw's time might have been swept away to the palace, there to be done to death in hideous fashion by a jealous Supalayat. All this had been due to the British, who could be rude and boorish when drunk, but for whom honest dealing was an article of faith – more than could be said for their lackeys, the Indians! He had liked most of his British superiors, had shared their sense of humour. 'When Smith *thakin* was DSP in Mogaung,' he told me, 'we always laughed at the same things.'*

And yet . . . and yet . . . why were the British in Burma? What right had we to rule over a people who had ruled themselves for at least as long as the British had done in their own islands? The sooner we left, the better for all of us, although he expected he would lose his pension. He was a gruff old man, blunt to the point of being rude, but when I miraculously passed the colloquial examination in Burmese he threw a small party in my honour. We drank a toast in Mandalay rum, a potent liquor when taken neat. 'We pray you will never forget us,' he said, raising his glass, 'nor the language you have studied with such diligence whenever you were awake. Come back often to our country where you will be our honoured guest, the more so if we are free to rule ourselves in our own fashion, as we did before

* DSP = District Superintendent of Police (a gazetted officer).

you British came.' At the time it made very little impression on me, but three years later, after war came, I remembered it vividly.

Another incident that occurred about the same time has also returned to mind. On the road from Mandalay to Madaya there was a small monastery (*pongyi kyaung*) shaded in a grove of mango trees. I had come to know the Abbot, possibly through Po Thit, and visited him from time to time. He was a charming, cultured man, speaking perfect English although we invariably conversed in Burmese. He used to greet me warmly and we sat there in the warm sunlight, sipping tea and gossiping until it was time for him to attend to his devotions. On one occasion I used a word, in my ignorance, which obviously angered him. His face darkened as he said, in English, 'Please, never use that word again in my hearing! It reminds me that you British are the masters – we Burmese the servants!'

I was astonished. 'Don't you like us?' I asked. 'You have always spoken well of the British to me.' His anger passed, he smiled. 'Yes, I like you well enough, better than say the French or the Dutch. But the Burmese are perfectly able to rule themselves and we do not require the British to do this for us. The sooner you go, the better it will be for both the British and the Burmese.'

Writing history from hindsight is an error many of us commit. It would therefore be wrong of me to pretend that in 1939, at the age of twenty-two, I sympathized with those of my Burmese friends who sought to see the backs of us. There were those in Britain who believed sincerely that we had run out of time where the British Empire was concerned, but I was certainly not to be numbered among them. However, it did cross my mind from time to time to wonder if we were as well-liked as we seemed to assume that we were. *Saya* San had led a rebellion against us in 1930 that required two years, and many additional troops, to subdue. There had been ugly riots in Rangoon in 1938, and in Mandalay some months later. 'The relations between British and Burmese were friendly and pleasant,' we are told, 'and the riots were never directed against the Government, but against the Indian community which the Burmese could not tolerate.'[6]

At a lunch party some time after my discussion in the *pongyi kyaung*, the wife of a senior official said much the same. The Burmese got on remarkably well with the British, she assured me: it had been different in India where her husband had been recently stationed. 'It's the Indians they dislike, not us,' she said. It was not the impression I had received either from *Saya* Po Thit or my *pongyi* friend.

The fact remains, however, that our everyday relations with the Burmese were friendly and easy. There was no evident racial superiority. The fact that Burmese women attended mixed social gatherings was a refreshing change after India. Intermarriage may not have been encouraged but it carried with it no social stigma. Whereas in India the treatment of the vast majority of Anglo-Indians was disgraceful, the same was not true in Burma. I had many Anglo-Burman friends. Out in the villages we were always made to feel welcome. There were few restrictions on our coming and going, although in districts where dacoity was prevalent, we were supposed to contact the local constable (for all the good he would have been). Out in the jungle my main fear was elephants, not people. We drove the main roads in perfect safety, by day and night, and in early 1941 my wife drove on her own the 500 miles from Maymyo to Rangoon without a second thought. It helped, of course, to be able to speak the language.

In the forty-six years that have passed since first I set foot in Burma, I have served in some thirty countries. Apart from Jordan in 1952 and 1953, I can think only of Burma before war came as a place where one felt as safe as once used to be the case in London (alas, no longer). I never carried a weapon, locked no doors and never bothered to insure any of my property. Once, inadvertently, I left a bag in the rack of my compartment on the Rangoon–Mandalay mail. It was delivered to me in person by the stationmaster, no less, a charming Anglo-Burman who insisted on my checking the contents before he was willing to hand it over to me.

Unhappily, however, there could be no doubt regarding the unpopularity of the Indians. *Saya* Po Thit told me on more than one occasion that he would never forgive us for introducing so many of them into his country. Racism, it would seem, is not only founded on colour. Burma was administered as an Indian province from 1862 until 1937. The Burmese themselves had little say in their own affairs. When, in 1919, the British, by the Government of India Act, went some little way towards introducing responsible government in Indian provinces (dyarchy as it was termed), Burma was excluded. There was such resentment that the Government relented. Burma was brought into line with the other Indian provinces. A Legislative Council was introduced consisting of 103 members, 84 of whom were elected. At the same time the Crown made it clear that the ultimate aim was to be self-government within the Commonwealth, but no time limit for this was as much as hinted at. The Burmese were not content.

In 1935, in the teeth of Winston Churchill's opposition, another Act was passed by Parliament. This separated Burma from India – to universal rejoicings. But the Secretary of State for India merely added 'and Burma' to his statutory title, giving him little or no time for the overall supervision of Burma's particular problems. However Burma was to be provided with two Houses and a Council of Ministers. The House of Representatives, with 123 seats, was to be elected for five years. There was also to be a Senate, half elected by the House of Representatives, the other half appointed by the Governor (an elevated title for the previous Lieutenant-Governor). He was provided with reserve powers for a whole host of tricky subjects, regarded as being beyond the capacity of the elected representatives to resolve. These included foreign affairs, defence, the currency, control and appointment of the European bureaucracy, and the right to declare war or peace. The Governor was also entirely responsible for administering the hill areas, where the local inhabitants harboured the deepest suspicions of their former Burman masters. As a Burmese friend described the new constitution to me at the time, it was like being given the key to the door at the age of twenty-one, only to find the locks had been changed the moment one tried to unlock the door. Nevertheless, even he had to admit that the new constitution, despite its faults, had severed the long-hated link with India.

CHAPTER TWO

Before the Battle

> 'The country was a military backwater and the command was usually held by a General Officer whose last post it was to be before retirement.'
>
> *India-Pakistan Official History*[1]

It is almost certainly true to say that the British held Burma for more than half a century by bluff, rather than by force of arms. There were at various times, such as during the 1930–2 Rebellion, several battalions of Indian troops in Burma, in addition to those recruited in Burma itself, but for most of the time between the two world wars two battalions of British infantry alone constituted the hard core of Burma's defence against both external and internal enemies. One battalion, the 2nd King's Own Yorkshire Light Infantry (2 KOYLI) was in the north at Maymyo, with one company detached in Mandalay; the other, the 1st Gloucestershire Regiment (1 Glosters), was at Mingalodon, seventeen miles outside Rangoon where the aerodrome was situated, with a company on detachment in the city itself. Neither unit approximated to war strength, amounting together to perhaps 1200 all ranks, deficient in mechanical transport, mortars, light machine guns and anti-tank weapons; their rifles, the Lee-Enfield Mark IV, had rendered sterling service at Mons and Ypres in 1914. The soldiers were all long-service regulars, some of whom had been overseas for seven years and more, many of them marrying into the country. Some of them wore medal ribbons awarded for service between 1914 and 1918.

Prior to Burma's separation from India in 1937, Indian infantry had also served in Burma, but the new Burmese Government was anxious to see the back of them. All that remained in 1939 was a field company of Madras Sappers & Miners, waiting to hand over to a Burmese field company that was in the process of being formed, and a battery of Indian Mountain Artillery. These were the mule-transported 3.7″ 'screw-guns' of Kipling's poem, served by Indian gunners under the command of British officers on loan from the Royal Artillery. The only other artillery were four 18-pounders of First World War vintage, crewed by volunteers from the Burma Auxiliary Force (BAF), part-time soldiers like Britain's Territorials, most of them Anglo-Burmans with a sprinkling of British and Burmese. Their principal task was to fire salutes on appropriate occasions, such as on the arrival and departure of distinguished visitors.

Since Maymyo in the north is about as far from Rangoon in the south as San Sebastian in Spain is distant from Seville, it is almost as if Napoleon had sought to hold Spain with a battalion of infantry in each city, supported in the rest of the Peninsula by a force of locally-raised native troops of mixed race, organization and efficiency. Yet such was the country's apparent tranquillity that one writer has commented: 'The vast majority of the inhabitants of Burma never saw a soldier throughout their lives, and only occasionally a military policeman on treasury guard or on riot duty.'[2] That says a great deal for the forces of law and order in a country as large as Burma.

The pacification of Burma had in the main been carried out by Indian troops; partly by regular battalions, some of them raised specially for service in Burma,[3] and partly by battalions of para-military police, largely Gurkha in composition,[4] with a mounted infantry element of Sikhs and Punjabi Mussalmans whose large frames sat rather incongruously on sturdy Burmese 'tats' of barely thirteen hands. There were at one time as many as thirteen or fourteen Burma Military Police (BMP) battalions, commanded usually by a major on secondment from the Indian Army, who might have three or four subalterns or captains to assist him. Each British officer had the powers of a magistrate; every soldier the powers of arrest of a village constable. The BMP's exploits figure largely in *Blackwood's* 'Tales of the Outposts', their relations with the ordinary civil police ranging from good to indifferent, according to the personalities concerned. They owed allegiance to an inspector-general (usually a brigadier from the Indian Army) who would, if he were wise, turn a blind eye to the eccentricities of some of his subordinates, one of whom, it is said, invariably fed passing guests on python and monkey stew, washed down by a rice wine of such potency that it required a week to recover. It was, he swore, a certain cure for malaria, if not for cirrhosis of the liver (from which he eventually died).

There is a tale, doubtless apocryphal, of one such worthy whose proud boast it was that he had never taken a day's leave in fifteen years; he feared lest his vegetable garden would go to rack and ruin during his absence. As the years passed he grew madder and madder until he became convinced he had been turned into a *nat*. There came a year when the monsoon was late, the crops failed, and the major's vegetables withered on their stems. From far and wide the villagers came to beseech him to do something to avert the inevitable famine. One night, after an unduly heavy libation of rice wine and to the consternation of the forest officer he was hosting for the night, he announced his intention of spending the night under an umbrella in a bamboo copse close by, the favoured haunt of a notorious rogue elephant. Nothing would dissuade him from this foolhardy undertaking. In bright moonlight they set him up, squatting on his camp bed, umbrella raised against the dew, and left him. At midnight the thunder rolled, the lightning flashed, and the rain came down in torrents.

Came the dawn and the villagers rolled up their *lungyis*, splashing contentedly through the paddy fields, now knee-high in water. Sadly. however, the rogue elephant had come during the storm and kneaded the major into a bloody pulp, only the umbrella lying untouched by his side. He was to receive only a few lines of obituary in his regimental journal – the 17th Cavalry's as I recall – but the villagers did not forget him. They set up a shrine in the bamboo grove, the major's effigy crowned with a *topi*, and clutching, as was indeed appropriate, an umbrella. I wonder if it is still there?

Besides the BMP, there were three infantry battalions of indigenous troops, first raised during the First World War as the 70th Burma Rifles (70 BURIF). As such they formed part of the Indian Army, seeing service in Mesopotamia, Aden and Egypt without achieving much distinction. Composed originally of Burmans, Karens, Kachins and Chins, the Burman element displayed a disposition to drink unwisely and gamble their pay away. When the Indian Army was reorganized into 'large' regiments of several battalions in 1922, 70 BURIF were re-numbered 20 BURIF, taking their place as the junior line infantry regiment in the Indian Army. Recruitment of Burmans was abandoned, the unit becoming the 1st, 2nd and 3rd Battalions of 20 BURIF. A fourth battalion, numbered 10th, served as the Depot and Training Battalion, located in that delectable hill station in the Shan States, Maymyo.

20 BURIF differed in no way from the other infantry regiments in the Indian Army. The more senior officers were those who had chosen to remain in the army after the war had ended in 1918. The junior officers had passed through Sandhurst. Each battalion consisted of four rifle companies, two of Karens and one each of Chins and Kachins. All had their different characteristics but were refreshingly free from the religious differences that divided Hindu from Mussalman in other Indian regiments. Nor were there dietary problems; pork being as welcome as beef; Chins and Kachins were even less choosy, python, monkey and even squirrel making a welcome addition to the menu. There can have been few soldiers serving the British Crown who were as easy to handle, and certainly none smarter when on ceremonial duties. The *lingua franca* was Urdu, as in the Indian Army, although many of the British officers learnt Burmese and the several tribal dialects.

There was something about Burma that, like Ireland, brought out the eccentricity often to be found deep-down in the British character. In July 1940 I happened to be convalescing from an appendicitis operation in the hill station of Kalaw, in the Southern Shan States. My host, a major who had retired from the army in those parts and who had taken to himself a Shan wife, excused himself midway through the meal, seized a shotgun, and went outside where he blazed away into the night. Returning, he excused his conduct by the presence of spirits who were particularly powerful at that time of the year. 'They won't come back in a hurry,' he said cheerfully, his wife apparently unaffected by this strange behaviour. Somerville and Ross would have found themselves entirely at home in that household.[5]

The truth was of course that where Britain was concerned Burma was a purely commercial enterprise. Admittedly it provided a glacis where the defence of India was concerned, just as Poland does in the case of Russia, but landward invasion of India via Burma was virtually a strategical impossibility. There were no roads linking the two countries, and the border was a range of high mountains covered by impenetrable jungle and suffering from the highest rainfall on earth. The only possible invaders were the Chinese, their country torn apart by the ambitions of rival and warring warlords. There was, where Burma was concerned, a *dolce far niente* that India's 'guardians', much troubled by Mr Gandhi and his movement for *'Swaraj'*, were only too happy to leave undisturbed.

Perhaps Air Chief Marshal Sir Robert Brooke-Popham, the British Commander-in-Chief Far East from 1940–1, was not so far wide of the mark when he wrote:

> I can only suggest three things that are, at any rate, worthy of investigation. First a tendendancy [sic] among Englishmen to regard themselves as naturally superior in every way to any coloured race, without taking steps to ensure that this is always a fact. Secondly, a failure to develop a sympathetic understanding with the Burmese, to know what they were really thinking all the time, what were their particular difficulties and aspirations. Thirdly, the fact that the majority of non-official Englishmen in Burma were more concerned with making money and getting high dividends from their investments than of benefiting the native population.[6]

Burma in 1939 was under the military control of India, Army Headquarters being located in New Delhi. The General Officer Commanding (GOC) was appointed by the Commander-in-Chief in India, advised by the Military Secretary, and was invariably a senior officer in the Indian Army. His summer headquarters was located in Maymyo; in the winter months he accompanied the government to Rangoon. His staff, ludicrously small, was headed by a colonel, concerned almost entirely with administrative and financial matters. A lieutenant-colonel (GSO I) handled Operations, confined largely to internal security and liaison with the police. There was no Intelligence organization worth the name, nor any money with which to establish agents in such neighbouring countries as Thailand, Indo-China and China. Japan might have been *ultima Thule* for the little that was known about it. The CID of the Burma Police kept the military informed of such matters as they thought might interest them, and there was of course the usual plethora of government committees that met as much to exchange views as to achieve anything more positively useful.

The Governor was Vice-Admiral the Honourable Sir Archibald Cochrane, a son of the Earl of Dundonald and descendant of that quarrelsome naval commander who had contributed so brilliantly to the achievement of Chile's independence from Spain. His senior military adviser was Major-General D. K. McLeod, an uncommonly nice man who after service in the Guides Cavalry and various other staff appointments in India was serving out his last four years on the active list as GOC Burma. Their principal task, as both men saw it, was to complete Burma's severance from India as laid down in the Government of India Act passed by Parliament in 1935.

Where Cochrane was concerned, this meant that he had to work in conjunction with a Burmese Prime Minister, initially U Ba Maw, a congenial rascal, and then U Pu, a more solid citizen. In McLeod's case he had to 'Burmanize' the army, cutting it adrift from the Indian Army and providing Burma with its own indigenous defence services. India was nothing loath in removing its troops but it requires time to build an army. The Burma Sappers & Miners were resurrected, the depot of the Burma Rifles converted to a fourth active battalion, and the Burma Rifles battalion formerly garrisoning Taiping in Malaya was brought back to Burma. But this meant only four active battalions of Burma Rifles to support the two British battalions in the maintenance of internal security. Reluctantly, the Government of India agreed to leave the Indian Mountain

Battery in the country until Burma could raise its own artillery.

One possible accession of military strength were the BMP battalions scattered round Burma's periphery. Most of them were reconstituted as the Burma Frontier Force (BFF), their task being to 'watch and ward' along the borders. There were six such battalions, a seventh being raised in 1940 specifically for aerodrome defence,[7] armed with rifles and Lewis guns, and reasonably mobile with their mules and ponies. The BFF was under the direct control of the GOC, but not its administration. The three remaining battalions of BMP, one in Mandalay and two in Rangoon, were responsible to the Inspector-General of Police. Indians and Gurkhas predominated in both forces.

It was intended eventually that Burma's links with the Indian military establishment would be completely severed. As part of this policy officers from the British Service began to be seconded to the Burma Army during 1938. By the time I arrived in March 1939 there were about a dozen of us serving in the Burma Rifles, captains and lieutenants, and one or two with the BFF. Our Indian Army seniors looked on us as beings from another world, ignorant of the language, unaware of the customs, and for the most part more trouble than we were worth. In my case I was allocated to a squad of recruits, newly arrived from the Chin Hills, and introduced to the mysteries of 'Rifles' drill of which we, as a rifle regiment, were unconscionably proud. Once 'passed off the square', I was put in charge of the band, all of them Gurkhas under the baton of a Goanese, who always wore a suit and a Homburg hat; presumably it was assumed that if I could not speak Urdu, I did at least know the tune of 'Colonel Bogey'.

In the course of a military career that by no stretch of the imagination can be termed conventional, and extending over thirty-five years, 4 BURIF in Mandalay live in my memory as a relic of a bygone age. We shall certainly never see their like again. I recall us debating throughout one long morning on 3 September 1939 the most suitable 'walking-out dress' for the Chin Company. It was, it may be recalled, the day we declared war on Germany. Close order drill delighted my commanding officer (a veteran of Mons), as balletomanes might rejoice in

Swan Lake, and when even his enthusiasm had been satiated, then hockey took its place. I can recall no tactical instruction of any kind other than the construction of perimeter camps during our annual battalion training in the Shan States, the North-West Frontier being separated from us by the width of the subcontinent. We attacked in line up the gentle slopes, the commanding officer galloping to and fro as he adjured us 'to keep our dressing'. Afterwards, during the critique, he told us that British officers should always lead the line, waving their walking sticks. I wonder what the Japanese were being told round about the same time? Perhaps they did not carry walking sticks?

They gave me command of the Signals Platoon for a time. We had flags for semaphore, signalling lamps for morse, and even heliographs. Lord Roberts, returned to earth, would have found nothing changed since he marched from Kabul to Kandahar. Our field telephones worked only fitfully, the cable dating back for the most part to Palestine in 1918. The only excitement I remember during that battalion training early in 1940 was when the commanding officer's horse ran away with him and threw him into a wild rose bush.

I did enjoy the additional responsibility after a year as a platoon commander in the 'Dukes'. Once I had acquired a smattering of the language I was given command of the Chin Company (A) and promoted automatically to Lieutenant. A few months after being given the Signals Platoon to oversee I was put in charge of the Vickers Medium Machine Gun Platoon. I liked the soldiers, particularly the Karens. The Chins were inclined to be clannish, feuding among themselves, the Kachins were delightful, but the Karens I found the most friendly of all.

When I joined 4 BURIF at the beginning of March 1939 we were stationed in Fort Dufferin in Mandalay. This had formerly been the Palace of the Kings of Ava, surrounded by salmon-pink walls twenty feet high, one and a quarter miles long, backed by embankments seventy feet wide at their base. Beyond the walls was a moat, 200 feet wide and choked with lotus, spanned by four bridges, north, south, east and west. Within the walls were the decaying remnants of Theebaw's ornately painted teak palace, a polo ground and an apology for a golf course, our regimental lines, a military hospital, the Upper Burma Club, and a criss-cross of geometrically laid out roads beside which stood a series of two-storeyed bungalows, brick below, wooden above, each in a large compound with the servants' quarters and the stables tucked away in the farthest corner. The roads were shaded by Neem trees, Mandalay being oppressively hot from May until October; outside the walls, along the road skirting the moat, there was a line of Golden Mohur trees, flaming brightly at the right season of the year.

During Theebaw's reign this vast enclosure had been packed tight with bazaars, barracks for the royal bodyguard, houses for the court officials, audience chambers and so on. Under the British it had become strangely empty, rather like Wellington Barracks when compared with the bustle of Buckingham Palace Road beyond. The city itself, a honeycomb of streets narrow or broad, lined with shops and stalls, thronged with people, tri-shaws being pedalled furiously, decrepit cabs drawn by under-fed horses, all pulsating with life and noise, made a strange contrast with our imperial decorum within the walls. There was a busy railway station and marshalling yard, since at Mandalay the railway bifurcated, one line running north-east up the Shan plateau to Lashio on the border with China; the other crossing the Irrawaddy by the great Ava bridge before turning north via Shwebo to Myitkyina in the Kachin Hills, 250 miles beyond.

On the southern outskirts of the city, which had a reputation for turbulence, were the lines of the Mandalay battalion of the BMP, whose mounted infantry company provided impecunious subalterns such as myself with the opportunity to learn polo at little or no expense. The Irrawaddy itself was a mile or so to the west, a vast expanse of water more than a mile wide, and along the bank beyond was the line of the Sagaing Hills that turned every colour in the rainbow in the rays of the setting sun, every summit crowned by a white pagoda erected by the pious to the greater glory of the Lord Buddha.

North-east of Fort Dufferin, overlooking us from every angle, was Mandalay Hill, a great rock 800 feet high, honeycombed with temples and pagodas, where *pongyis* of every age and description dwelt on the charity of rich and poor alike. Only once did I climb the hundreds of steps to the summit, accompanied by a *pongyi* who told me he was eighty-one. I felt every day of his age by the time I arrived, gasping, at the top. From there the view was superb, the entire city and fort at our feet, the long line of the Irrawaddy stretching far into the distance, while for miles around were the flat fields of paddy, green at that time of the year, and teaming with the snipe for which Mandalay was famous. To the east were the jungle-covered foothills of the Shan plateau, and away beyond them the mountains, purple in the sunlight. I little thought that afternoon in October 1939 that five years later General Pete Rees's 19th Indian Division would have to fight every foot of the way up this great rock to plant the Union Jack above the spot where I was sitting and chatting so amicably with my *pongyi* guide.

The Burma Rifles suffered from a drawback that was in no way their fault. In the Indian Army every battalion expected sooner or later to serve on the North-West Frontier against the tribesmen. There, reputations were made or lost while real bullets winged their way overhead. In Burma, unfortunately, there was no such test of military worth. One critic has written:

> The men were recruited from the hill tribes and were excellent material. Turning these fellows into regulars, however, seemed to have deprived them of their martial qualities. They had been made to shave their heads like Gurkhas* so that they all looked alike. On parade they were extremely smart, but they had become too civilised. They had forgotten their jungle lore – had indeed been encouraged to put it behind them – and their knowledge of infantry tactics was rudimentary, for, after all, there was nowhere for them to practise them. Unlike the Gurkhas and the Indian Army, their reputation in military circles was not high and this I could well understand, for they never had to do anything like fighting Pathans, and had become very soft.[8]

Unduly harsh? Probably. There was nothing wrong with our soldiers. The best of our senior officers spent most of their time in the outposts, learning the tribal dialects, recruiting our

* Not in 4 BURIF.

soldiers, working as Intelligence officers. They were men like L. G. Wheeler, E. H. Cooke and J. H. Green for whom garrison life in Maymyo, Mandalay and Mingalodon had little appeal. Those content to pass their time in the humdrum activities of peacetime garrison duties were not all of the same calibre. One of them told me he had not come to Burma to waste time learning the language, but rather to shoot snipe. Another complained that he was compelled to spend too much time on the parade ground when his main aim in life was to shoot a tiger.

There were seldom more than nine or ten British officers present with the battalion. Two of these, the adjutant and the quartermaster, were the commanding officer's staff officers. Then there was the commanding officer and his second-in-command, both officers in their latter forties with long service in the Indian Army. This left no more than six or seven majors or captains to command the rifle companies and carry out the other necessary regimental duties. The administration was largely in the hands of the Governor's Commissioned Officers (GCOs) – Viceroy's Commissioned Officers (VCOs) in Indian Army units – who still retained their Indian ranks, viz: *subedar-major*, *subedar* and *jemadar*. All had twelve or more years' service and were powers in the land, none more so than the *subedar-major* who was the CO's right-hand man and adviser in all matters affecting the well-being of the soldiers. Although with the exception of some of the Karens lacking in education, they took a tremendous pride in their job and taught me all that I know about the management of men.

As can be imagined, they relieved the British officers of most of the chores of administration; but since few of us were able to converse with them with any degree of fluency, a very great deal had to be taken on trust. I had been nearly a year commanding my company before it dawned on me that an unduly high percentage of Chins from the Haka area were being promoted to the detriment of those from other areas in the Chin Hills. Discreet inquiries showed that my *subedar*, Hram Lai, was a minor chieftain from Haka.

There were no Burmans enlisted, apart from a few clerks. This had been decided in 1927, by arbitrary decision on the part of Army Headquarters in India, although it was bitterly opposed by experienced officers like Major Enriquez of 20 BURIF. The argument ran that the Burmans did not take kindly to discipline and were inclined to run amuck when drunk. They also made a practice of pawning their equipment to pay off their gambling debts. The most unfortunate consequence was to separate the Burma Rifles from the rest of the population, making them as much an army of occupation as the two British battalions. The fact that Rangoon University was provided with an OTC, and there were two Territorial battalions of the Burma Rifles (11 and 12 BURIF) did nothing to remove this sense of alienation where the Burma Rifles were concerned.

Soon after my arrival in Burma I started to agitate for transfer to the BFF whose role had much more appeal than garrison duties in Mandalay, Maymyo and Rangoon. It operated in what were termed columns in the jungles and mountains on the border with India, China and Thailand; a column consisted usually of a company of Gurkhas, Kachins or Kumaonis, with a platoon or more of mounted Sikhs or Punjabi Mussalmans. Unfortunately they had few British officers, nearly all of them from the Indian Army. When these efforts failed, I applied to return to my British regiment, convinced I was doomed to see out the war on Mandalay's parade ground, but one short, sharp interview with General McLeod showed me the error of my ways. 'You can speak Burmese, can't you?' he asked. I agreed. 'Well, there are not many other officers in the Duke of Wellington's Regiment who can do that,' he said, 'and you are much more use to us here than you could ever be commanding a platoon in France. So don't let me hear any more of this nonsense. Good day!'

I returned to Mandalay convinced the war had passed me by, and that my military future had come to a blinding halt. It was 13 November 1939, my twenty-second birthday.

CHAPTER THREE

The Japanese Invade Burma

'Where was I when the war was on?
I can hear a faint voice murmur.
Where was I when the war was on?
In the safest place – in Burma.'

Music hall song of the 1920s

However true that song may have been between 1914 and 1918, it was to be proved horribly wrong from 1941 onwards. But none of us would have thought so had we been asked, as 1939 was succeeded by 1940. There was at that time a considerable debate in progress regarding who was responsible for Burma's defence. After her separation from India, Burma became responsible for her own defence, forming a Defence Department for this purpose. But strategically Burma was an outwork of India, and a vital link between that country and Malaya. Successive Commanders-in-Chief in India argued that Burma's defence should be India's responsibility, a view rejected by Burma's politicians whose principal aim it was to sever all connection with India.

The British Chiefs of Staff never wavered in their view that Burma should be under command of the Commander-in-Chief in India, but in the end politico-strategic considerations swayed the balance. In August 1940 Burma was removed from India Command and placed under the newly-established Far East Command with headquarters in Singapore, under Air Chief Marshal Sir Robert Brooke-Popham. In his Dispatch on the Burma Campaign of 1942, Wavell wrote: '. . . The cardinal mistake seems to me, however, to have been in placing Burma in the Far East Command, instead of under India.'[1] This view was endorsed by General Sir Alan Brooke (Chief of the Imperial General Staff) when he minuted on 29 September 1942: 'I agree with General Wavell that Burma should never have been separated from India. I succeeded in getting it transferred back before ABDA Command* was formed, but was unable to convince the Chiefs of Staff in Washington.'[2]

There can never be certainty in war, but it is as near certain as anything can be that if the organization is wrong from the start, nothing short of a miracle will pull you through. This was certainly the case where Burma was concerned. The Far East Command was predominantly an Air-Sea one, the first priority being protection of the great naval base at Singapore. Burma's strategic significance was that the airfields constructed down the length of the Tenasserim peninsula constituted the air reinforcement route, particularly for fighters, between India and Malaya. An additional consideration, of great significance where the Americans were concerned, was that Rangoon was the port of entry for the vast quantity of war *matériel* being supplied by the USA to Chiang Kai-shek, without which it seemed unlikely that he could continue the struggle against the Japanese. There were more than twenty Japanese divisions fighting in China, the Americans having no wish to see them made available for employment elsewhere.

Singapore had mesmerized British naval strategists since the 1920s.† It has never been possible to prove whether its possession was vital to British interests in the Far East since, when the moment arrived, we lacked the resources to defend it. Nevertheless, it must surely be admitted that by its surrender, after pro-

* The American-British-Dutch-Australian Command (ABDACOM) was established by the Combined Chiefs of Staff in Washington (with Roosevelt's and Churchill's blessing) on 30 December 1941. Wavell was the popular choice as Supreme Commander. He set up his headquarters in Java, his Command including Burma, Malaya, the Philippines, the Dutch East Indies and the approaches to northern Australia. He took over on 5 January 1942.

† Their Lordships at the Admiralty were so convinced of the requirement to make Singapore a great naval base that in 1928 they did a deal with the Air Staff, agreeing to support the RAF's claim to take over the defence of Aden in exchange for the RAF's support over Singapore. The army, nothing loath to give up its most unpopular overseas garrison, thought it had come well out of the horse-trading.

claiming for so many years its near-impregnability, British prestige suffered a blow from which it has still to recover.

The desirability of keeping China in the war as a fighting ally was more Roosevelt's brain-child than Churchill's. The British considered the Chinese to be in a more-or-less perpetual state of confusion, riddled by internal jealousies, corrupt and incompetent. On the other hand the Americans, and Roosevelt in particular, considered they enjoyed some special relationship with Chiang Kai-shek and his talented, American-educated wife. This delusion was to persist until Mao Tse-tung destroyed it. Brigadier-General Frank Dorn, a Chinese-speaking US officer with many years' experience in China, believed that his President's Sinophile attitude derived from the exploits of Roosevelt's grandfather, who made a fortune in China. In Dorn's opinion it was emotion more than anything else that attracted Roosevelt to Chiang: '. . . because of what was considered to be American self-interest – as well as because of sentimentality – the so-called government of China had to be kept in the war as an active ally. A political and economic mess . . . China had to be perpetuated in the mistaken belief that it could and would help the United States defeat Japan.'[3]

Churchill almost certainly shared the views of his Chiefs of Staff on the Chinese. But he was far too shrewd a politician not to attach the utmost importance to Roosevelt's opinion. Indeed, in his letter to Wavell acquainting him of his appointment as Supreme Commander of ABDACOM on 30 December 1941, Churchill strongly emphasized the importance of China in Roosevelt's eyes, and exhorted Wavell to bear it in mind. It was a thousand pities that Wavell, with so many pressing problems on his mind, failed to follow Churchill's advice.

Chiang Kai-shek, having lost half his country, was holed-up in Chungking, dependent almost entirely on the ceaseless flow of munitions pouring into Rangoon from the USA. The flow far exceeded the capacity of the American Lease-Lend officials to transport them north along Burma's single-track metre gauge railway to Lashio, 120 miles from the Chinese border. The Burma Road, that miracle of engineering which like the Pyramids owed almost everything to human muscle power, ran from the frontier for more than 1500 miles across some of the most rugged mountains in the world, crossing and recrossing two of the world's greatest rivers, the Salween and Mekong, as well as innumerable tributaries. Day and night the trucks thundered past, making travel along it a torment. On the one occasion that I saw the road I marvelled that men, working like so many industrious ants, could create such a miracle of engineering. It was my first encounter with the Chinese, for whom I have ever since had the greatest respect.

At Lashio, almost a Chinese-American town, we were told that a railway was under construction. I do not know whether it was ever completed. The Burmese police inspector who acted as my guide was opposed to the railway, claiming that the Chinese would then move in and take Lashio from the Burmese. I asked him whether he preferred the Chinese to the Indians. 'Oh no, the Indians every time,' he said. 'We know how to deal with them. Beat a few of them up and the rest run away. You cannot do that to the Chinese. There are far too many of them.'

Spending that night in the Lashio Club which seemed to be almost entirely full of Americans, most of whom were drunk, I met an interesting character whose name, he said, was Hank. He had little use for the British Army, he told me; we spent most of our time running away from either the Germans or Italians. But the RAF was in a different category altogether. Then he told me he was a major in the USAAF, serving in General Claire Chennault's American Volunteer Group (AVG), for which he was being paid the equivalent of a Brigadier-General's salary in the USAAF. It was the first time I had heard of the AVG.

Apart from that short visit to the Burma Road in January 1940, and an attempt to catch a *mahseer* (fish) at the junction of the two turbulent rivers that come together at 'the Confluence' twenty miles north of Myitkyina to form the Irrawaddy, I cannot recall that the war in Europe disturbed in any way the even tempo of my days with 4 BURIF in Mandalay. My friend Hamish Mackay, a true fighting soldier,* has since complained

* Major (later Brigadier) Hamish Mackay, began his army career in the Madras Pioneers, transferred to the 4th Gurkha Rifles, and spent many years

bitterly to me that throughout 1940, and for most of 1941, 'we wasted our time in Burma preparing for the kind of war we were never likely to have to fight'. Hamish was right, of course, but no man is a prophet in his own country.

We travelled north in February to Kangyi, north of Maymyo, where we practised the kind of North-West Frontier drills appropriate should the Burma Rifles ever be let loose against the Afridis, or the Faqir of Ipi join forces with U Ba Maw to fight for Burma's independence. It was suggested that we should carry out some field firing, but come the day we were limited to twenty rounds per rifle which made it all seem pointless. It was playing at soldiers – no more, and no less.

It has to be remembered that Burma was at the very bottom of a priority list for equipment that had acquired crisis proportions with the return of the virtually naked British Army from Dunkirk. The Middle East was first priority after the Home Army; India was next; then Malaya. If anything was left, it had to be divided between Burma and West Africa. We had to make do with what we had already got, and that amounted to very little. Even mules were in short supply. There were plenty in Yunnan but hardly anyone could converse with their owners. There were some 13-pounder horse artillery guns in the Rangoon arsenal, 'galloping guns' that had won distinction at Mons, and a few anti-aircraft pieces. But Burma's arsenal was virtually bare. They took from us our 12-bore shot guns, ostensibly to arm the Home Guard who were supposed to defend our hearth and homes. I never saw mine again. I have a shrewd suspicion they were employed to hasten me on my way out of the country. More important, perhaps, we were short of sandbags, barbed wire and the means of erecting it. Engineer stores in general were in lamentably short supply. There seemed to be plenty of horseshoes, as I recall, but an absence of horses for the fitting of them. There were also plenty of *topis*. It was a mad, mad world.

In March 1940 I was sent to the Small Arms School at Saugor

in Burma, first with the BMP and then with the Burma Rifles. He was awarded the DSO commanding a company of the 5th Burma Rifles, and a bar when commanding a battalion of the 4th Gurkhas. He was a 'proper soldier' in every meaning of the word. His wife, Meisha, was just as brave.

in India. Apart from the fact that the students slept six to a room, the war was little in evidence. But once back in Mandalay I did notice a change. An Officers' Cadet School had been opened in Maymyo and we had three new subalterns. These emergency commissioned officers – ABROs (Army in Burma Reserve of Officers) as they were called – were probably unmatched anywhere else in the Empire. Mostly they were 'teak wallahs', employees of the timber firms that dominated so much of Burma's commerce; or they worked for the Burmah Oil Company, the great mining companies, the Irrawaddy Flotilla Company, the other commercial concerns, the forests or the police. They spoke the language, knew the people, were mature in their judgements and accustomed to using their initiative. No British army at any time in its long history has had less reason to quarrel with the quality of its junior officers. British, Anglo-Burman, Anglo-Indian, or in a few instances Burmese, they were material of the highest class.

To say they took kindly to our old-fashioned ways in the Burma Rifles would be an exaggeration. They had given up their chosen civilian careers to fight the enemy, not to practise close order drill. At that time the British Army was chiefly employed in chivvying the Italians in the Western Desert. Desert warfare was all the rage. We had precisely four 30-cwt trucks in the battalion with which the commanding officer insisted we practise 'leaguering drill' as if Sidi Barrani was just round the corner. I had just been appointed adjutant and found it awkward when one of our newly-joined officers took me to one side, inquiring solemnly whether I thought the CO was 'barmy'.

To balance this influx of exceptionally gifted junior officers, from mid-1940 onwards we began to lose more and more of our experienced GCOs and senior NCOs. In the Burma Army, as in the Indian, it was the junior commissioned officers, *subedars* and *jemadars*, on whom so much depended. Week after week, month after month, we saw our most experienced soldiers depart to help form new units. Those who replaced them were young and inexperienced, some of them little better than recruits just 'passed off the square'. This 'milking of regular battalions' to form new ones was probably inevitable in the circumstances, since Burma had no other reinforcements at that time, but it did incalculable damage from which we were to suffer in the years ahead.

The Burma Rifles was not a long-established regiment and we had few reservists. The taboo against enlisting Burmans had to go and both 5 and 6 BURIF, formed from the existing four regular battalions, were given Burman companies. The civil police came up with a battalion, 7 BURIF, roughly 50 per cent Burman and Karen, and the balance Indians settled in Burma. Best of all, perhaps, the Burma Frontier Force provided 8 BURIF, all of them Sikhs and Punjabi Mussalmans, who had no need to fear comparison with the best of the old Indian regiments. In less than a year we had doubled the size of the Burma Rifles at the cost of halving our efficiency. The two territorial battalions, the 11th and 12th, were also embodied and had to be provided with a permanent staff. The 13th and 14th battalions were raised in the Shan States, again requiring permanent staff to train them in the rudiments of the military art (they did not prove apt learners), and there was the inevitable mushrooming of headquarters, all requiring clerks, defence platoons and the like. Half Burma seemed to be in khaki, ill-fitting and badly pressed.

Most serious of all was the drain on our two British units. They had to provide instructors for the Cadet and other schools of instruction, many of their NCOs were commissioned, some of them (including officers) were returned to England to fill ranks depleted after Dunkirk, others were sent to the Middle East to form pioneer companies etc. The KOYLIs could muster barely two full rifle companies, the Glosters little better, and yet these would be our 'thin red line' if ever things got desperate, or internal security got out of hand.

General McLeod, as he watched the gradually ascending strength graph on the wall of his office, could have found little to comfort him. He came to visit my company in Mandalay one day in May 1940, saying he wished we could find more time for jungle training. 'That's where we shall have to fight, Lunt,' he said, but I never came across a directive to that effect. They were all concerned with the use of the sun compass in the desert, and how to immobilize vehicles. Since we had only three or four vehicles, the matter seemed purely academic. I did take my company out in the jungle for a week's training (it was the only time I have eaten – and enjoyed – python), and it taught me a lot. Major E. H. Cooke, one of the best of the original Burma Rifles, came out to spend the week with me. He made me a stew of delicious mushrooms, taught me the name of every bird and butterfly we saw, and also taught me how to swim mules across torrential rivers, a skill unlikely to be of much use in temperate climes. Poor 'Cookie'; only in Burma would he have found his *métier*, and only perhaps in the Burma Rifles where eccentricity was part of everyday life. Eventually he made his way out of Burma after incredible hardships which undoubtedly shortened his life, leaving an account of his odyssey in the National Army Museum[4] which I hope that one day someone will write up. I have met three remarkable men in my life – Cookie, Hugh Boustead and Wilfred Thesiger – and the world would have been a poorer place without them. Perhaps I should add Freya Stark as another for whom hardship and rough living added salt to life.

During that long, hot summer of 1940, when the news from Britain grew worse and worse, a young Burman friend, an artist, used to come and commiserate with me. A student at Rangoon University, he had joined the OTC, the better he claimed to learn how to drive us out of the country when the time arrived! He said this with such charm that I could hardly take offence. However he left me in no doubt that the majority of his fellow-students were members of the Thakin Party, extreme nationalists with little time for U Saw, the then Prime Minister. He also told me that the temporary closure of the Burma Road to China, to which the British Government had agreed under duress in the aftermath of Dunkirk, should never be reopened. The Chinese, he said, were acquiring far too much influence in Rangoon with the help of their friends, the Americans. I reported most of this conversation but without appearing to evoke much interest.

It was the closure of the Burma Road that first brought home to me the possibility of war with the Japanese. When in July

1940 the Japanese occupied north Indo-China, extending their influence throughout the country to include Thailand by March 1941, the prospect of war with Japan came closer. Not that we seemed to know much about them other than that they had defeated the Russians in 1904 but had failed to defeat the Chinese despite fighting them since 1937. My friend the Japanese dentist, with whom I continued to play golf, assured me that the Japanese liked the British, although they were not so keen on the Americans. He also told me in a revealing aside that he did not think much of the Burma Rifles. 'They are not brave soldiers. But your Navy,' he went on, 'the best in the world.' Soon afterwards he left Mandalay and I have often wondered since whether he was a spy.

While General McLeod and his overworked staff officers were struggling all hours of the day and night to make bricks without straw, the Japanese Imperial Headquarters were methodically making plans for the war they were sure was coming. The basis of that plan was the conquest of the Dutch East Indies, to make certain of the oil supplies Japan so desperately lacked, and which were now denied to them by America's embargo. As a shield for the annexed Dutch colonies, Japan would also need to seize the Philippines and Malaya, Singapore providing the base for her South Seas fleet. Indo-China was already in the bag, Thailand quiescent, but Burma did not really enter into the scheme of things, other than for the seizure of the Tenasserim airfields. Later it might be profitable to capture Rangoon, thereby sealing off the supply route to China, but at the outset Burma was very much a secondary theatre of operations.

Field-Marshal Terauchi was in overall command of the Japanese Southern Army with his headquarters in Saigon. The XVth Army (consisting initially of only the 55th Division), commanded by Lieutenant-General Shojiro Iida, was to concentrate in Indo-China prior to moving to Bangkok in the latter part of December 1941. Its primary task was to act as right flank guard to the main Japanese forces moving south by land and sea into Malaya; as part of this role General Iida intended to cross into Burma to seize the airfields at Tavoy, Mergui and Victoria Point. Once this had been accomplished he could turn his attention to Moulmein, which was much more strongly defended. At some later stage the 33rd Division, then still engaged in central China, would be moved south to reinforce Iida's XVth Army.

There was time enough to perfect these plans. There were Japanese agents scattered throughout Burma, Thailand and Malaya. In Burma itself the Thakin Movement were willing helpers. There was, it is true, a shortage of accurate maps, but many were stolen, flown to Japan, and translated into Japanese. The Prime Minister himself, U Saw, was believed to be in collusion with the Japanese.* As for the Imperial Japanese Forces, they were among the most battle-experienced in the world. Their soldiers, peasant conscripts for the most part, were tough, hardy and fanatically patriotic. Their officers, no less devoted to their Emperor, imbued by a warrior tradition that ranged from fantastic bravery to almost insensate savagery, were complete professionals for whom duty to one's country and Emperor was the one and only overriding consideration. With the possible exception of the Zulus, or the Sudanese at the Atbara, the British Army had seldom encountered such a formidable opposition.

Although military organization is for the uninitiated more boring than illuminating, it may help to outline here the chief differences between the British and the Japanese. In both armies the principal formation tactically and administratively was the division, consisting in the British case of three brigades, and in the Japanese of three regiments; each brigade/regiment contained three battalions, from 600–800 strong. Each division contained three or four artillery regiments, field or mountain in calibre which could either be employed as a whole for maximum effect, or be detached to support individual battalions or regiments. Every division also contained its own organic engineer,

* U Saw was arrested by the British in December 1941 on evidence showing him to have been in seditious correspondence with the Japanese. He spent the rest of the war in internment. He was both corrupt and vain but doubtless, according to his lights, a Burmese patriot. The Thakins thought little of him. He was sentenced to death and executed (in January 1948) for his part in engineering the assassination of Aung San, the Burmese leader, on 18 July 1947.

transportation, medical, signals and supplies services. The Japanese division was slightly larger in size than the British, from 12–14,000 men, and it was common to detach an infantry regiment (or battalion) for a special mission, giving it the name of its senior commander, viz: the Awabe Detachment. Japanese infantry battalions had organic infantry cannon companies, something like heavy mortars, which they employed very skilfully, although their marksmanship with rifles was poor. They used the bayonet a great deal and their officers invariably carried swords – for use, not merely for effect.

The commander of a Japanese division was a lieutenant-general, his chief of staff often a major-general. Additionally the divisional infantry as a whole would be commanded by a general, sometimes of the same rank as the divisional commander, but more usually a major-general. In the British Army a major-general commanded a division, his chief of staff being a colonel or lieutenant-colonel. When two or more divisions were grouped under one command, the British term was corps (as in Burma Corps), under a lieutenant-general; the Japanese equivalent was army (as in XVth Army).

In Burma during 1942 both the Japanese and British employed reconnaissance troops to scout ahead of the main bodies; they were usually mounted on local ponies or mules, although the Japanese often used cycles and cycle trishaws where the terrain was suitable. The Japanese had only a few tanks, lightly armoured and mechanically temperamental. The British from March onwards employed two tank regiments, equipped with the US Stuart light tank ('Honey'), 37 mm main armament and two .30 Browning machine guns. Though mechanically reliable, it had a very limited radius of action and there was no high explosive shell for its main gun. The British also employed a certain number of tracked Bren gun carriers, providing no overhead cover and mechanically unreliable. The British were weak in mortars, which the Japanese handled well; the British artillery, on the other hand, was streets ahead of the Japanese both in accuracy and in skill of handling. Sadly, there was not enough of it.

Our Intelligence regarding the Japanese was lamentable. In

a comment on the lack of Intelligence organization in Burma, the War Office was later moved to comment: 'This lack was not peculiar to Burma. It is fair to say that throughout the British Empire the necessity for an Intelligence system was realized by Service Headquarters but the various Governments concerned were not prepared to spend the money to make it effective.'[5]

Even when military attachés in foreign capitals, such as Lt-Col Lovat Fraser of the 8th Punjab Regiment in Tokyo, drew attention to the formidable quality and admirable training of the Japanese soldier, hardly any one, either in New Delhi or London, saw fit to draw conclusions from such a report. The truth is that it takes years and years and a great deal of money to establish an effective Intelligence organization with sufficient authority to arouse interest in the highest circles in government.

Such information as we received filtered back in dribs and drabs from forest officers and elephant drivers (*oozies*) whose ability to differentiate a battalion from a company, or an armoured truck from an armoured car was no better than the average uneducated peasant or civilian official. Over the border in Thailand, however, in Raheng where the Japanese intended to establish the main jumping-off point for their invasion of Burma, experienced Japanese agents had been at work for many months. It was said that Bangkok was full of Japanese officers in civilian clothes, surveying the bridges, calculating the capacity of the railway line to Malaya, but the main concentration seemed to be north of the Mekong, where the transports from Japan were discharging their cargoes regularly in the sheltered waters of Cam Ranh Bay. One Intelligence report I recall reading reported that the Japanese suffered from bad eyesight due to their diet of seaweed, which meant their bombers might find difficulty in recognizing their targets: 'Shoot down the leading plane and the remainder would be at sea'. That never turned out to be my experience when at the receiving end.

As I recall it was our general expectation during the summer of 1940 that the Japanese, having established themselves in northern Indo-China, would take steps to cut the Burma Road by invading the Northern Shan States. Since we were certainly in no position to prevent this, we contented ourselves in Mandalay with helping to form 5 BURIF, due to move early in January 1941 to Meiktila, sixty miles south of Mandalay. In October, however, General McLeod paid us a visit that lives long in my memory. In the course of a reception to which the world and his wife had been invited, certain officers were bidden by the ADC to a room where McLeod proceeded to take us into his confidence. Nearing sixty, with a white moustache, bronzed face and very tired eyes, he was the first general officer I had found until then to be in the least degree '*sympathique*'. War with Japan was very much on the cards, he told us. Were that to happen, they could deploy overwhelming force against us. He anticipated no reinforcements. We might delay their advance – no more than that. Recently married, my first thought was for my wife, but we were pledged to the utmost secrecy . . . it was an uncomfortable secret to carry around with one.

CHAPTER FOUR

Moulmein

'By the old Moulmein Pagoda,
Lookin' eastward to the sea.'
'*Mandalay* by *Rudyard Kipling*

Early in January 1941 the Commanding Officer bustled into my office. His parent regiment was a battalion of 13 FFRif whose long service against the Pathan tribesmen had given them a sense of superiority denied to such 'down-country' regiments as the Burma Rifles. It was his avowed intention to bring home to us that 'there was a war on', and the sooner we acknowledged the fact the happier we should all be. As our splendid *Subedar-Major*, a Chin named Mang Tung Nung, remarked to me after their first meeting, 'The Colonel *Sahib* eats too many chillis with his curry – they make him hot-tempered.'

'We are being mobilized,' the CO announced, almost dancing with excitement. 'When?' I asked. 'Today, of course. Recall everyone from leave, sharpen bayonets and issue mobilization kit.' I imagined the Japanese had crossed the Indo-China border and were advancing on Lashio. At the time we formed part of the Maymyo Infantry Brigade, Burma's only field formation; I assumed we were to entrain with the rest of the brigade for the north. 'Nonsense,' he said, 'we are going to Moulmein.' That was about as far from the Burma Road as it was possible to imagine, so war could not immediately be in the offing. But he went on to explain that a second infantry brigade was to be formed in Tenasserim, to protect the airfields in that part of Burma, and we in 4 BURIF were to form the nucleus of the new brigade that was to be formed around us.

Moulmein is an attractive town extending for about two miles along the east bank of the wide estuary by which the Salween River enters the Gulf of Martaban. Its great pagoda, immortalized by Kipling, looks *west*ward, rather than *east*ward, to the sea, which is some ten to twelve silt-laden, muddy miles farther west. Once the principal British garrison in southern Burma, its only military representation in January 1941 was a platoon of BMP and an aerodrome guard of less than a company from the Kokine battalion of the BFF. It was an important rice and timber port, isolated from the rest of Burma by the Salween estuary, 7000 yards wide, on the far side of which was the small town of Martaban, containing a railway station, some rudimentary marshalling yards, a PWD bungalow, and a local population to be numbered in hundreds rather than thousands. Between Moulmein and Martaban the Irrawaddy Flotilla Company operated a variety of ferries, some stern-wheelers, some operated by paddles. The Salween was navigable by ocean-going cargo steamers as far as Moulmein, beyond which launches operated on the Ataran and Gyaing rivers, tributaries of the Salween. From November to March the climate was equable, from May to June blindingly hot, and from then onwards subject to a torrential monsoon, turning paddy fields into lakes and *chaungs* into violent, and virtually uncrossable, torrents.

As battalion Adjutant it was of course part of my duties to organize our move from Mandalay to Moulmein. Only then did it become clear to me that Burma's communications were truly appalling. In this connection I cannot do better than quote from General Smyth's description of his line of communications:

> The long line of communications from Moulmein northwards towards Bilin and Sittang . . . was an absolute nightmare . . . From Moulmein northwards there was a somewhat antiquated steamer ferry service over the 7000 yards of open water which lay between Moulmein and Martaban. From the railhead at Martaban a good metal road and single track railway ran back through Thaton over the Bilin River to Kyaikto. Thence a dusty unmade track led to the Sittang river railway bridge . . .[1]

Smyth might have added that road and railway were skirted to the east by thick bamboo jungle; westwards, between railway and the seashore, were rice fields, brick hard in summer, swamps during the monsoon, and intersected by numerous tidal creeks. The railway bridge at Sittang, nearly half a mile in length, was unusable by motor vehicles. Beyond, the line of rail ran along a high embankment for fifteen miles to Waw, where an all-weather road connected it with Pegu, twelve miles farther on. The 250-mile journey from Rangoon to Moulmein took from twelve to fifteen hours, longer during the monsoon when land-slips were common.

'Never be in a hurry in Burma,' a senior police officer advised me one night in the Upper Burma Club. 'It results in ulcers and won't get you promotion.' There was in fact little point in trying to speed things up. From Moulmein there was a good road as far as Amherst, where sandy beaches and waving palm trees stretched for miles and miles. But Amherst was only forty miles from Moulmein and there the road ended. A wood-burning, antiquated railway joined Moulmein with Ye, 150 miles farther south, where it was necessary to cross the broad Ye river by *sampan*.[2] A fair to moderate road then took one to Tavoy, an important tin mining centre with a small airfield. Tavoy was a small port in the same latitude as Bangkok and about sixty miles from the Thai border.

Mergui was the next airfield, a Somerset Maugham sort of place where tin miners, remittance men, collectors of *bêche-de-mer*, and other less reputable characters contrived to make a living. Saturday nights at the Mergui Club were occasions to remember: one British officer, incensed by the continuous racket, fired his pistol through the floor of his bedroom, necessitating his removal to less rowdy surroundings. There was a road of sorts from Mergui to Tavoy, liable to regular interruption during the rains, and numerous tracks led through the dense jungle across the mountains into Thailand. Travel by launch was the only certain way of getting around the district which included Victoria Point, Burma's southernmost post, separated from Malaya, 350 miles to the south, by Thailand's Kra Peninsula. Victoria Point had an airfield too.

This long, narrow peninsula was divided from Thailand by a range of malaria-infested hills, the Dawnas, the haunt of tiger, leopard and even the occasional rhinoceros. Much of the jungle was bamboo, impenetrable except by cutting, favoured by a particularly vicious breed of ant whose bite raised great weals on arms and legs. The local inhabitants lived mostly in the flat country, growing rice or working in the tin mines. There were among them a fair number of Karens, particularly around Moulmein. Militarily it was indefensible without a great many more troops than we had available; and apart from the airfields, that were in any event a hostage to fortune, it might reasonably have been asked whether there was any point in trying to defend Tenasserim when all the advantages lay on the side of the enemy.

From Moulmein to Myawaddy on the Thai frontier was about 100 miles, nine tenths of it through thick jungle intersected by deep *chaungs* traversed by rickety bamboo bridges. There were at least two wide rivers, crossable only by ferry with a capacity of two trucks at a time. My CO and I spent one exhausting day traversing this route in the dry season; in the monsoon we would have done better to have remained at home. There was a launch service from Moulmein to Kyondo, from where a reasonable road of about fifteen miles took one to Kawkareik, head of the Sub-Division. From there a mountain road wound over the Dawnas to the highest point, Sukli, from where, on a clear day, Thailand could be seen ten to fifteen miles to the east. If one had had to choose, from a Staff College point of view, the least desirable terrain in which to fight a battle, Kawkareik and its immediate environs would have had my vote every time. I have a feeling, however, that the planning staff in Army Headquarters believed we were taking counsel from our fears. Planning staffs so often do.

Moulmein, on first arrival, had much to commend it. There was a very small European community, mostly 'teak wallahs' and government officials whose hospitality was princely. The Amherst beaches were entirely unspoilt and we spent every weekend picnicking there. We were accommodated in tents just outside Moulmein while a camp was being built for us some miles down the Amherst road. The surrounding countryside was either flat paddy fields or rolling, bush-covered hills, growing higher and more densely jungle-covered to east and south.

Since it was the dry season most of the district officials and 'teak wallahs' were out on tour but the Provincial Commissioner, Colonel Pelly, and his wife entertained us handsomely. Their lovely house, on the mile-long ridge running from north to south above the town itself, was one of several situated among the trees. There was also a fine pagoda and a handsome statue of Buddha standing high above the ridge. Apart from the town's sole hotel, soon to be known as 'dysentery hall', the 4th Burma Rifles regarded Moulmein as a considerable improvement on Mandalay. There was even a handsome park, lying between the foot of the ridge and the town proper, where the soldiers could play football, and I, as Adjutant, could drill the battalion to the delight of the townspeople.

It was 6 March 1941. Shortly afterwards a new Brigadier arrived and established a headquarters to be known as Tenasserim Area. His name was John Bourke and he had come directly from Waziristan on the North-West Frontier where he had been commanding the 4th battalion of the 8th Punjab Regiment (92 Punjabis). An Anglo-Irish bachelor of medium height and ruddy complexion, we treated him with some suspicion at first. Having begun his service with the Connaught Rangers in France in 1915, he had subsequently joined the Guides Infantry in the Indian Army, exchanging to 92 Punjabis in 1922 when the Guides lost two of their battalions. He was essentially an infantry officer with a sharp eye for the pretentious and inefficient. I doubt whether he was wholly satisfied with what he found in us, but his bailliwick extended so far – from Moulmein to Victoria Point, and eastwards to the Thai border – that he was compelled more-or-less to leave us to our own devices. My own Commanding Officer, argumentative by nature, found considerable satisfaction in complaining about matters great and small to Brigadier Bourke's newly-established headquarters staff, adding greatly thereby to my labours.

Elsewhere in Burma, too, things were beginning to happen. The 13th Indian Infantry Brigade under Brigadier A. C. Curtis arrived from India in April 1941 and was moved into the Southern Shan States. It was the considered view at the time that the Japanese, were they to invade Burma, would do so from that direction. General McLeod discounted the prospect of a major advance against Moulmein, reckoning that only one infantry brigade could be supported on the axis of an advance from Raheng-Kawkareik-Moulmein. 'But I do not regard the land threat very seriously,' he reported. 'Air attack by Japan from Siamese aerodromes is the big danger.'[3] He was wrong. Both the 55th and 33rd Japanese Divisions entered Burma by this route.

This was only made possible of course by the endurance and ruggedness of the Japanese soldier, coupled with the boldness and ruthlessness of Japanese planning – an unknown quantity where most of us were concerned. 'From the start of the war with Japan,' wrote Major E. H. Cooke, 'the general attitude of those with whom I came in contact seemed to indicate a very great under-estimation of Japanese strength. Some parties seemed to look upon them in the light of a troublesome hill tribe and they held this belief right up to the fall of Singapore and the direct threat to Rangoon.'[4]

Under-estimating the fighting qualities of one's enemy has been a recurring factor of military history. The Israelis fell into this error *vis à vis* the Egyptians at the outset of the Yom Kippur War; more recently still, the Iraqis did not achieve the walkover they expected in Iran. In the Japanese case I think we had great admiration for their Navy, but thought their Army had made very heavy weather of their war in China. The 'warrior ants', Slim's later description of the Japanese infantrymen, had yet to be encountered in battle. Moreover, in the Japanese Army the infantry were the *élite* arm of the service, a fact that took a long time to register in British military circles.

None of this was made apparent in the various Intelligence summaries circularized before war came upon us. A Chinese merchant who gave a dinner for us in Moulmein warned me solemnly that the Japanese were very good soldiers indeed. He had seen them in action in Manchuria and clearly had no desire to repeat the experience. I have long felt that the Japanese have never been given sufficient credit for the brilliance of their military planning and the success of their operations, until they allowed that success to go to their heads and outran their capacity to hold on to their gains. Their soldiers did quite literally defend their positions to the last man and the last round, proving themselves some of the most formidable fighters in the history of warfare. God alone knows how much it would have cost us to storm their home islands.

We were too busy settling ourselves into Moulmein to bother with such imponderables. The monsoon was only a few weeks away and our hutted camp was slow in construction. 2 BURIF had moved to Mergui, 6 BURIF to Tavoy, but we had no artillery of any kind and virtually no engineer stores to erect defences. On paper, however, our strength looked greater. The former Maymyo Brigade had now been converted into the 1st Burma Brigade under Brigadier G. A. L. Farwell, moving into the Southern Shan States in July 1941. It had two battalions of the Burma Rifles and the KOYLI, at most 250 strong. What was more, we were now formed into a division, the 1st Burma Division (1 BURDIV), under Major-General Bruce Scott, who had formerly commanded the Maymyo Brigade. He moved his headquarters to Toungoo in central Burma; his responsibilities extended from Mergui in the south-east to Lashio in the north. His division lacked artillery, engineers, signals, transport and provost staff; there were no light aircraft, helicopters or other modern means for covering great distances rapidly, but Bruce Scott found time to visit all his units at some time or another. If ever a man commanded a 'paper tiger', Scott did.

No one would ever have thought it. He radiated confidence. A handsome, young-looking man, he had won his spurs during the First World War with the Punjabis, transferring thereafter to the 6th Gurkha Rifles.[5] Always alert and cool, he was at the same time friendly and relaxed. Had Bruce Scott's fate taken him to the Middle East rather than to Burma he might well have risen to the highest rank. He had the temperament to take the rough with the smooth, and, as he was to demonstrate on more than one occasion later, he had a remarkable capacity to recover his equilibrium after surviving experiences that would have destroyed a lesser man.

We had also acquired a new Governor. Sir Reginald Dorman-Smith, an MP and former Minister of Agriculture, arrived in

May 1941 to succeed Cochrane. Aged forty-one, he had served with the Indian Army in the First World War and looked more like a soldier than a politician. He came down to visit 4 BURIF in July and I was pleasantly impressed. I fancy his sympathy with the Burmese desire for self-government carried no weight with Churchill, but that was all in the future.

Dorman-Smith was followed by Wavell, moved by Churchill from the Middle East to India Command, an unwise decision taken despite the advice of General Dill (then CIGS) who felt that Auchinleck was the right man for India and that Wavell, after so long and hard an innings, deserved a complete rest. It is a great pity that Dill was overruled. Wavell visited Burma and Malaya in October 1941 and was horrified. He expressed himself as disturbed by the paucity of troops, lack of air defences, apathy, lethargy and general absence of drive. His first move on his return to India was to send the 16th Indian Infantry Brigade (under Brigadier J. K. Jones) to Burma. His impressions of the Far Eastern scene as a whole were unhappy in the extreme. Of Malaya, he wrote: 'My impressions were that the whole atmosphere in Singapore was completely unwarlike, that they did not expect a Japanese attack . . . and were very far from being keyed up to a war pitch . . . As regards Burma, I was horrified by the complete lack of organization, of military intelligence, and of planning generally to meet any Japanese attack.'[6] He described Lieutenant-General D. K. McLeod as 'a nice old gentleman', and followed this up by a signal to the CIGS (Dill) emphasizing the need to return Burma to the responsibilities of the Commander-in-Chief India rather than leave it under the Commander-in-Chief Far East Command. This was finally agreed by the War Cabinet on 12 December 1941, five days after the Japanese struck at Pearl Harbor.

The 16th Indian Infantry Brigade disembarked in Rangoon in November and were moved to Mandalay. There, according to Edwards-Stuart, then commanding a company in 4/12 FFR, they spent a pleasant three weeks. 'The war had not yet affected this part of Burma, and the Upper Burma Club and the race meetings flourished as usual. Training in jungle warfare was carried out in rather a half-hearted manner, owing to very little direction being given on the subject. We were to pay the cost of this later.'[7]

I am not sure we were much better off in this respect in the Burma Rifles, although we had in our Karens, Chins and Kachins men to whom the jungle was home. It is easy to be wise after the event but until war came in 1939 the ambition of every Indian Army officer was to serve on the North-West Frontier; from 1940 onwards it was the Western Desert of Egypt, or Abyssinia, where fighting was in progress. This set the pattern, not helped by the fact that mechanization of transport was in full cry, although in jungles trucks are more likely to be an embarrassment than the reverse. The truth was that we forgot the basic virtues of the infantry soldier, so well exemplified by the 'Old Contemptibles' at Mons in 1914, to shoot straight, harbour our ammunition and to march and march and march and still be fit to fight.

During those months before war came to Burma in 1941 I can only recall two occasions when my battalion actually practised jungle warfare. On the first, just before the monsoon broke, we practised a battalion advance to contact. Two companies advanced in line through the thick undergrowth, the other two companies advancing three or four hundred yards behind them. Battalion headquarters was in the centre of the square, and I, as Adjutant, was mounted on a horse, a signaller running beside me, unrolling telephone cable as he ran. This enabled me to communicate with the battalion second-in-command who was bringing up the rear, also on a horse. The CO, who detested horses, darted from company to company, usually coming to rest with D Company whose commander he disliked and with whom he was for ever conducting some kind of argument. The entire business reminded me of the 'Grand old Duke of York, who had ten thousand men . . .'

At the end of August, when the monsoon was tailing off, 4 BURIF was moved to the Thai border at Sukli, at the crest of the Dawnas. There we lived in perpetual mist and went down like ninepins with malaria. The CO decreed we should practise a night attack through jungle in which tigers were not uncommon, elephants not infrequent. The bamboos grew in great clumps, making it virtually impossible to move in a straight line, and much of the time we were clambering down and up steep-sided streams. Having previously taped a forming-up area we set off an hour before first light, marching by compass bearing on our objective, a small hillock on which someone had stuck a Union Jack.

The Chin and Kachin companies were in front, the Karens bringing up the rear. Again I was in the centre, this time on foot with the CO, who was in the vilest of tempers. The second-in-command was way behind in the rear, complaining bitterly that he had malaria. Bayonets were not to be fixed but each man carried his *dah* (jungle knife), and magazines were charged with five rounds per man, lest we encountered a charging elephant.

After about twenty minutes of slithering, slipping and falling in the wet and uneven ground, it began to rain – in torrents. Simultaneously there was an unmistakable growl, followed by the sound of rifle bolts being opened and rounds entering the breeches. As one man, the leading line of Chins and Kachins turned inwards, the Karens behind following suit, as the CO dashed forward shouting 'Stop! Stop!' in his best Hindustani. Should the tiger break cover, since tiger it unmistakably was, one half of the battalion would be shooting at the other. The animal, more frightened than angry, went bounding down the middle of the column, taking a swipe at the CO as it passed him (or so he told us afterwards), and then disappeared. The bugler was ordered to sound the 'stand fast' and I was sent off to ascertain how the second-in-command had fared at the back of the column. I found him emerging from a stinking buffalo wallow in which he had taken refuge as the tiger came charging towards him, but none the worse otherwise for his ordeal. We practised no more night attacks. My Chins always told me that they were much more afraid of bears than tigers.

Soon after the tiger incident, which grew with the telling, I was posted away from 4 BURIF to be Staff Captain at the Headquarters of Tenasserim Area in Moulmein. I was lucky to go when I did because within weeks the battalion was virtually decimated by malaria. Mepacrine was still in an experimental stage, many soldiers refusing to take it lest it impair their virility.

My CO never forgave Brigadier Bourke for wafting me away, my early days in the headquarters being spent drafting emollient replies to what seemed at times to be letters verging on the insubordinate.

Hindsight makes the writing of history easy (if inaccurate), but I do not think that most of us serving in Burma at that time anticipated attack by the Japanese. Doubtless the few in possession of information from ULTRA were under no illusions but I could detect no quickening of the tempo as October followed September. We were gradually building up the strength of the Moulmein garrison, 7 and 8 BURIF being earmarked to join Tenasserim Area, soon to be restyled the 2nd Burma Infantry Brigade. To improve our mobility a quantity of mules from Yunnan, accompanied by their drivers who spoke no word of any understood language and who were sodden with opium, were sent down to us from the north. I cannot recall them being of the slightest use.

In a telegram to the Chiefs of Staff, dated 13 August 1941, the Commander-in-Chief Far East said: 'Should war break out between Britain and Japan I consider that owing to present shortage of AA weapons and fighters, bombing of Rangoon would constitute greatest danger to Burma Road.'[8] General McLeod's view also was that air attack represented the greatest danger. But all we had at Mingalodon (Rangoon's airfield) were sixteen obsolescent Buffalo fighters. At Toungoo and Magwe in Central Burma the AVG was equipped with P. 40 (Tomahawk) fighters, all under Chiang Kai-shek's control and employable only with his authority. Without them the campaign might well have ended earlier than it did.

I believe it to be true that from the outset those of us who fought in Burma in 1941–2 were acutely aware of our vulnerability to air attack. The influence of air power on ground operations seems to me to be a lesson we are in grave danger of forgetting, as a consequence, I imagine, of our planes roaming at will throughout the European skies from OVERLORD onwards. We should be better advised today to recall the times when the distant hum of an airplane meant almost automatically the enemy. It is not an experience I should choose to relive.

There is something sinister about the slide into war. I was not in Britain during the summer months of 1939 when event followed event until war seemed inevitable. But during October and November 1941 the tempo of life in Burma seemed to quicken. My responsibilities were primarily administrative and I was not therefore involved in the forward planning that occupied so much of the time of my Brigadier and his Brigade Major, Charles Appleby. But the logistic problems of providing for units scattered the length of Tenasserim, preparing to receive the 16th Indian Infantry Brigade that was due to arrive in December, and conveying across the Salween and storing everything from artillery shells to cans of bully beef, kept me more than fully occupied.

The lack of good communications between our scattered units was a major headache. Radio communications, poor though they were, were reserved for operational traffic. I had to use the civil system, much of it *en clair* and subject to long delays. The Japanese had agents in every post office, goods yard, printing press, and also, I suspect, in the police. They knew all they wanted to know about our movements. We knew next to nothing about theirs. They were extending airfields in Thailand, strengthening bridges, improving roads to take heavier traffic. I never once set eyes on a report to this effect, although I assume there must have been some.

There was so much to do that I sometimes wonder nowadays how we managed to get through it all. As a Brigade Commander in Aden from 1961–4 I had four experienced staff officers for Operations,[9] five administrative staff officers, and a host of other hangers-on. In our headquarters in Moulmein, with war about to break upon us, there was the Brigadier, his Brigade Major, me, and Micky Merton who doubled up as Intelligence Officer and Mess Secretary. There was also the odd Warrant Officer, liaison officer and, of course, the chief clerk. Nor were we lavishly provided with transport. The Brigadier had his staff car (jeeps had yet to come in), while there were four or five pick-up trucks for the rest of us to use, whenever we could lay hands on one. I seem to remember we did requisition some civilian cars, but not until after the outbreak of hostilities and then only after filling in dozens of forms in triplicate.

Charles Appleby eventually worked himself into a state of complete exhaustion. Later in the war he commanded 2/1 Punjabis with distinction and was awarded the DSO. Micky Merton, whom we used to call 'Mert', was his chief assistant. He had at one time skied for Cambridge before joining the timber firm, Foucars, in Burma. He married a Burmese lady, 'Minnie', and had several children by her, his intention being to settle in Burma after the war. He was building himself a house in Maymyo for the purpose. Speaking fluent Burmese, completely imperturbable, several years older than me, he found the ways of the regular army beyond all understanding. He seldom saw eye to eye with Appleby and carried on an amicable feud with the Brigadier whose taste in food frequently ran counter to Merton's own. He had to leave his wife behind when we retreated from Burma, but it is pleasant to be able to record that she and he were reunited in 1945. By then he had been awarded the Military Cross and Bar for his services behind the Japanese lines. My only complaint against him was that he smoked the strongest-smelling Burmese cheroots. Other than that he was brave, humorous, a wonderful companion and the nicest man one could hope to meet.

On 30 November 1941 Headquarters Tenasserim Area was redesignated Headquarters 2 Burma Brigade. At the same time units were warned that the proclamation of a state of emergency was imminent. Men were to be recalled from leave. Telephones were to be manned by officers at all times. War was imminent. That was certain. What was less certain was, were we prepared for it? There follows the opinion of an official historian, written admittedly with the advantage of hindsight:

> To sum up, the Burma Army had had a very short existence dating as it did only from the separation of Burma from India in April 1937. The rapid expansion from 1938 lowered rather than raised its efficiency. From October 1940 peace-time expansion became merged with war-time expansion. The Headquarters staff was totally inadequate. The Army Headquarters combined within itself the functions of a war office, general headquarters

> and subordinate headquarters. The organization or the lack of it clogged the whole machine . . . The force, such as it was, was quite unprepared for war. None of the units was trained for jungle warfare and was therefore tied to roads and mechanical transport. But much of the blame attaches to the higher command which grossly underrated the strength and efficiency of the Japanese and the scale of attack on Burma. Nor did the reinforcements arrive in time or to the full extent promised. 'Shuffle and reshuffle was the order of the day and commanders did not know from day to day of what their commands were composed.'[10]

Can any of the above be denied by those of us who were present at the time? But could it not be repeated for campaign after campaign in British military history? When has the British Army ever been trained and prepared for the wars its politicians have decided it must fight? Under Marlborough in the Low Countries? Under Wellington in Spain? Under French at Mons, Gort in France or Wavell in the Far East? Burma was to prove no different from anything that had gone before. Nor has the fault always lain with the generals.

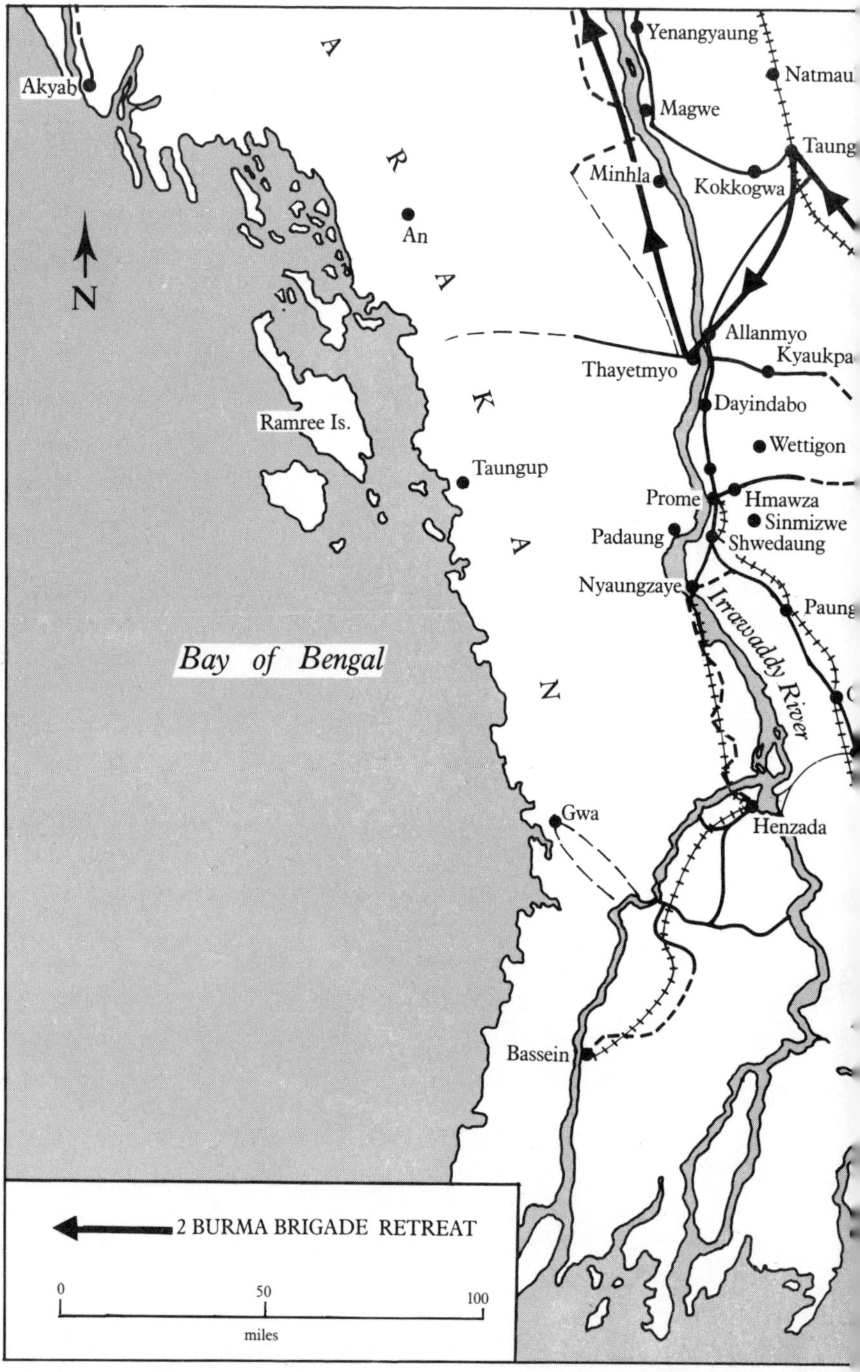

Akyab
A
R
A
K
A
N
An
N
Ramree Is.
Taungup
Bay of Bengal
Gwa
Bassein
Yenangyaung
Natmau
Magwe
Taung
Minhla
Kokkogwa
Allanmyo
Thayetmyo
Kyaukpa
Dayindabo
Wettigon
Prome
Hmawza
Sinmizwe
Padaung
Shwedaung
Nyaungzaye
Paung
Irrawaddy River
Henzada
2 BURMA BRIGADE RETREAT
0
50
100
miles

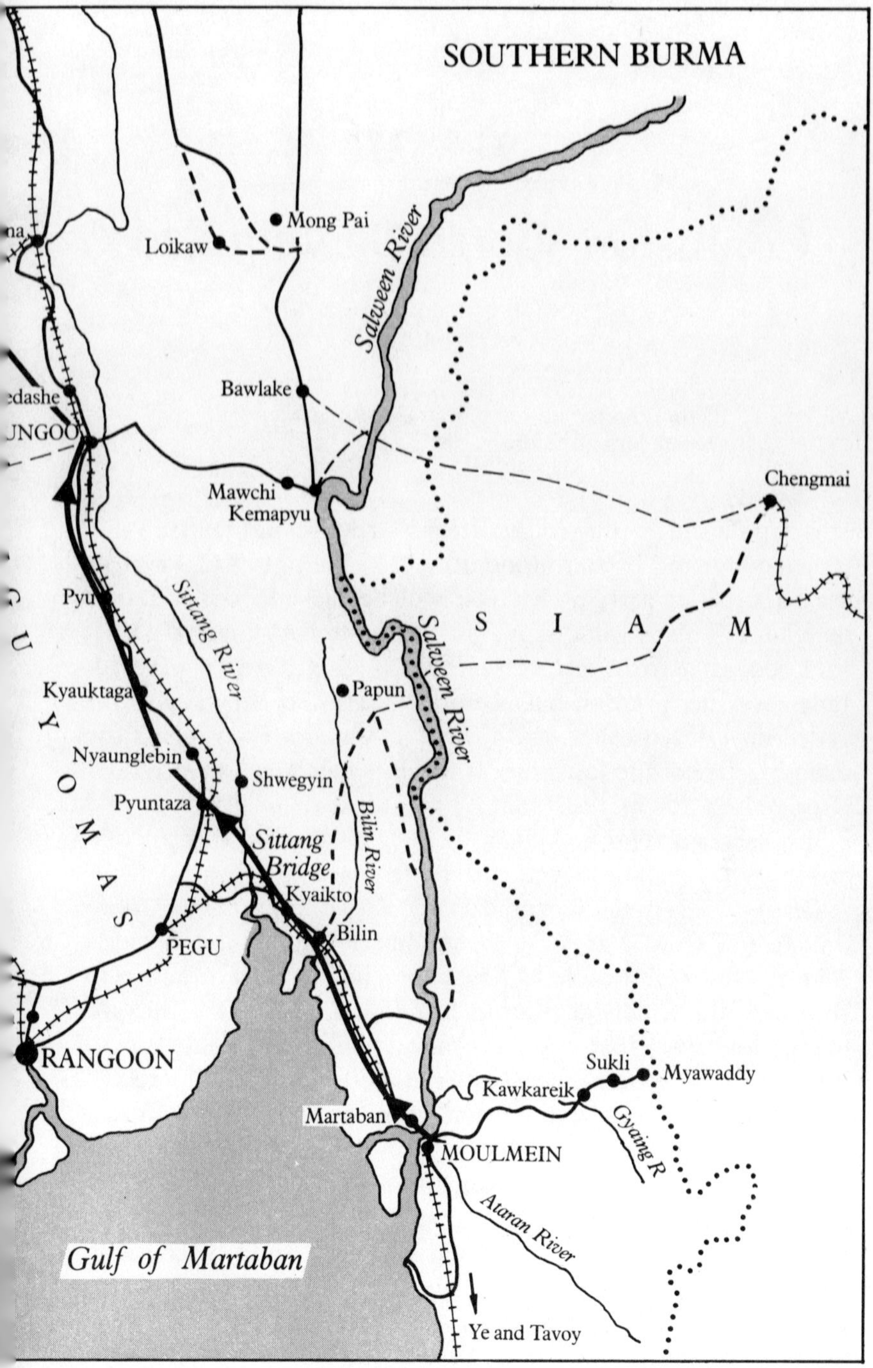

SOUTHERN BURMA
Mong Pai
Loikaw
Salween River
Bawlake
edashe
UNGOO
Mawchi
Kemapyu
Chengmai
Pyu
Sittang River
S I A M
Salween River
Kyauktaga
Papun
Nyaunglebin
Shwegyin
Pyuntaza
Sittang Bridge
Bilin River
Kyaikto
Bilin
PEGU
U Y O M A S
RANGOON
Sukli
Myawaddy
Kawkareik
Martaban
Gyaing R
MOULMEIN
Ataran River
Gulf of Martaban
Ye and Tavoy

CHAPTER FIVE

Confusion Worse Confounded

'If the trumpet give an uncertain sound, who shall prepare himself to the battle?'

I Corinthians xiv. 8

It is a great misfortune in the British Army to find yourself in a senior command or staff appointment at the outset of a war or campaign; it is certain that you will be sacked, sooner rather than later. This is what happened to Lieutenant-General D. K. McLeod, after three testing years as GOC in Burma. War with Japan was declared on 9 December 1941, and Burma was invaded on 11 December, the airfield at Victoria Point being the first objective of the Japanese. It was evacuated on 13 December after only a token resistance. The sub-divisional officer and police sergeant who had stuck to their posts were thrown into prison by the Japanese, and starved to death.

On 15 December, responsibility for Burma having been transferred from Far East Command to India, the General Staff in New Delhi cabled a new appreciation of the situation in Burma to the Chiefs of Staff in London. The principal recommendations were that: (i) the maximum air force should be put into Burma as soon as possible; (ii) defences should be erected at all crossing places from Thailand; (iii) mobile guerrilla forces should be organized immediately; (iv) two divisions should be transferred from India to Burma at the earliest possible date; and (v) – possibly the most important of the lot – 'Staff conversations with the Chinese should be held at an early date with a view to formulating a strategic plan for the future and examining the possibilities of immediate Chinese action against the Japanese forces now in North Thailand.'[1]

It is to be assumed that Wavell, as Commander-in-Chief in India, agreed with this appreciation, and that in essence it summed up his views.

However, even to this admirer it must seem that Wavell's sharp intelligence and quick perception had been dimmed by his long, hard years in Cairo, although his capacity for air travel under the most arduous conditions had, if anything, increased. On 21 December he arrived in Rangoon to confer with the Governor and General McLeod, discovering little to his satisfaction. Then he set off for Chungking the next day for a meeting with Chiang Kai-shek. Before doing so he telephoned General Hutton, his Chief of Staff in New Delhi, telling him he had decided to replace McLeod and asking for a nomination for his successor. The general proposed by Hutton turned out to be on the sick list. Wavell made up his mind quickly. 'I'm afraid it will have to be you, Tom,' he said. 'Get here as quickly as you can.' Hutton did as he was told, and like many before him and, no doubt, many to come, found he had been handed a fine can of worms.[2]

Wavell was hardly the most communicative of men; nor was Chiang Kai-shek, where the British were concerned. Their meetings were not sparkling occasions, despite the glamorous presence of Madame Chiang, nor were relations improved by Wavell's rather less than enthusiastic acceptance of Chiang's offer of help. Chiang had immediately offered to send his Vth and VIth Armies to Burma, but Wavell only accepted at once the VIth Army, already on the Yunnan-Burma border, less one of its divisions.[3] Wavell has since been much criticized for this apparent failure to close with Chiang's offer, but in fact his reasons for not doing so were perfectly sound. In the first place he had been promised substantial reinforcements, to include one British and two British-Indian divisions, two East African brigades, and possibly an Australian division. He believed that Burma should be defended by imperial troops, if at all possible. Secondly, he must undoubtedly have known of Burmese suspicions of China's long term ambitions in North Burma, to which were added his own of the fighting capabilities of the Chinese. And finally, he knew that the Chinese were almost totally deficient in any kind of logistic support. He had no wish to increase the GOC's already acute logistic difficulties by adding to them the requirement to supply the Chinese. As seen at the time, his decision made sense.

Wavell's journey back to India via Rangoon was not without incident. He flew in an aircraft with Chinese markings, the crew being American. They left early on Christmas Day and lost their way, Wavell himself surmising they were heading for Bangkok, then in Japanese hands. The pilot promptly turned west, arriving over what he presumed to be Akyab, where he landed. It was in fact Moulmein. The airfield defence platoon, from the Kokine battalion of the BFF, very nearly fired at the plane during its approach, and Brigadier Bourke, who happened to be at the airfield at the time, walked over to the plane to discover who the visitors might be. He was astonished to find Wavell, who asked for something to eat. He was provided with sandwiches and then took off for Mingalodon, landing there a short head in front of the strong force of Japanese planes which bombed Rangoon that day. Wavell just had time to find himself a slit trench before the bombs came hurtling down. It proved to be an apt curtain-raiser for the series of disasters that plagued Wavell from the beginning to the end of his conduct of operations against the Japanese.

On 27 December, the day after Wavell's return to India, Lieutenant-General Thomas Jacob Hutton arrived in Rangoon to take over command from McLeod. After my one meeting with Hutton, on 6 February 1942, I wrote in my diary that he looked 'more like a head gardener than a general'; his personality made no impact on me. He was born in 1890 and commissioned into the Royal Artillery in 1909. He served with the field artillery during the First World War, winning the Military Cross and Bar in command of a field battery. Thereafter he had served almost exclusively on the staff, apart from 1938–40 when he commanded the Western (Independent) District at Quetta. He had then taken up the post of Deputy Chief of the General Staff at Army Headquarters in New Delhi, later becoming Chief of the General Staff (CGS) to Auchinleck and Wavell successively. On Hutton's shoulders had rested the main responsibility for the expansion of the Indian Army and his reputation as a staff officer was of the highest. But the fact remains that he had not been in close contact with troops for more than twenty years.

Hutton was a humble man. He was to record later that '. . . before the Sittang disaster I had little opportunity to see much of the troops under my command or even to get to know my brigade commanders.'[4] This, for Montgomery, would have been an appalling admission and it is certain he would never have made it. The army had moved on since Hutton had commanded his field battery in 1918, and the soldiers expected to know something of the general on whose nod they would be committed to battle. The fact that he was thoroughly decent, determined to do the best he could for them, shared their hopes and fears and bore like Atlas on his shoulders the awesome burden they shared together, meant nothing unless they knew his face, trusted his judgement. His undoubted personal courage, his devotion to duty, his loyalty to Wavell who had saddled him with such an impossible task, meant nothing in the end. He was truly an unknown general.

He assumed command of the Burma Army on 28 December 1941. He was to last for exactly two months. McLeod left for India and retirement, his only recognition promotion to Lieutenant-General. In Hutton's view, McLeod's most important contribution had been the preparation of the Rangoon Evacuation Scheme in conjunction with the Governor and his advisers, Mr T. L. Hughes of the Burma Civil Service playing a prominent part. The scheme, which related largely to civilians, provided for three stages: Stage 1, the evacuation to India or up-country of all non-essential military and civilian establishments and personnel; Stage 2, the evacuation of all remaining personnel, civil and military, who were maintaining essential services in Rangoon; Stage 3, the demolition of the oil refinery and the docks, and the evacuation of the personnel concerned with them. Hutton considered that Stage 1 turned out to be completely successful but that Stages 2 and 3 were delayed too long, owing to Wavell's intervention.

It is interesting that Hutton should have taken such a keen interest in evacuation plans so early in his command. The vital importance of Rangoon to the Anglo-American aim of keeping China in the war does not seem to have been sufficiently appreciated by the War Cabinet and Chiefs of Staff in London. Lieutenant-Colonel W. E. V. Abraham, who paid a liaison visit to Burma in early March on behalf of the Commander-in-Chief Middle East (Auchinleck), was quick to spot this:

> The fundamental reason for the loss of Rangoon was our failure to appreciate quickly that as soon as Singapore ceased to be of value to us as a naval base (which was after the first week or two of the Jap war) the holding of Singapore became very much less important than the holding of Rangoon and Burma. Had this been appreciated it would not have been possible for troops to have been poured into Singapore at the expense of Burma, especially 18 Div.[5]

Against this paragraph Auchinleck had pencilled, 'Right!'

Rangoon's importance was certainly appreciated by the Governor, and by Hutton also; indeed Hutton titled the monograph he was later to deposit in the Liddell Hart Archives in King's College London: *Rangoon 1941–42, A Personal Record.* But he had other considerations in mind, as Abraham was quick to note:

> A contributory factor [to the loss of Rangoon] was the failure of the command in Burma to appreciate that the holding of Rangoon was fundamental to the effective protection of Upper Burma and the Burma Road to China. Since last December the feeling of Burma Command – never put on paper in so many words – has been, (a) we shall try to stop the Japs wherever we can at MOULMEIN, on the SALWEEN, on the SITTANG, etc, BUT (b) we shall make sure of getting our forces back in such a way as to be in a position, if we fail to hold Rangoon, to form a defensive line farther north.[6]

Abraham went on to say that this had formed the basis for fighting the campaign since the previous December, although it had never been discussed with higher authority, nor had the GOC, remarkably, ever received a directive to the effect that his plans should be based on 'the vital necessity of holding Rangoon'. In Abraham's view, had this been the case, Hutton's plea for more troops would have been received with much more sympathy, particularly in the case of the 18th British Division, which would not have been diverted from Burma to Singapore.

Whether this would have made much difference to the course of the campaign is a matter of opinion. I believe it would not have done. It was only after we had trained our soldiers better, mastered the problem of jungle warfare, gained control of the air, and acquired a more offensive fighting spirit, that we were in a position to take on the Japanese on equal terms – and defeat them.[7]

Hutton knew of course of the promised reinforcements in the pipeline. 18th Division, under Major-General Beckwith-Smith, was already embarked and steaming from the UK to Rangoon. 17th Indian Division was to embark for Burma in mid-December. 14th Indian Division, less a brigade, 63rd Indian Infantry Brigade, two East African brigades, three British infantry battalions then serving in India and, last but not least, 7th Australian Division, were all intended for Burma. In the event only 17th Division, 63rd Brigade and the three British battalions ever got there; in the case of 17th Division *less two of its brigades*.

Soon after Japan's entry into the war, Churchill hastened to Washington to confer with Roosevelt, at long last an *official* ally. There they decided to set up the unified Command in the south-west Pacific known as ABDACOM.* General Wavell, with American support, was appointed Supreme Commander as from 30 December 1941; General Sir Alan Brooke, later Field Marshal Viscount Alanbrooke, had become CIGS on Christmas Day that year, the day Hong Kong was surrendered to the Japanese. Much against the newly-appointed CIGS's better judgement, Burma was included in ABDACOM, although remaining for purposes of administration under India Command. 'A fine baby you have handed me,' Wavell signalled to the CIGS before setting out on another of his marathon air journeys, this time from New Delhi to Bandoeng in Java. After his departure there was a hiatus in the Command arrangements

* See page 52.

in India until General Hartley, then one of the Army commanders, was appointed to officiate as Commander-in-Chief. A strong hand at the wheel of India Command was therefore lacking for several weeks, crucial weeks where the Burma Army was concerned since Wavell had gone to Java and Hutton, his CGS, to Rangoon. This probably accounted for the feeling in the Burma Army that in India the urgency of their requirements was insufficiently understood.

The Japanese had carried out two heavy air raids on Rangoon, on 23 December and on Christmas Day, which provided some of us with an idea of the shape of things to come. The enemy lost heavily at the hands of the RAF and the AVG, mostly at the latter's, but inevitably many of their planes got through and set Rangoon ablaze. The result was the virtual paralysis of the city as its terror-struck inhabitants departed for the countryside. Everything, from the disposal of nightsoil to the dispensing of dangerous drugs, came to a grinding halt. Then, and only then, were the more comfortably situated of Rangoon's merchant princes, British, Indian, Burmese and Chinese, brought face to face with the unpalatable fact that what went on below stairs, however remote from everyday notice, had a profound effect on the living style of those who dwelt above stairs. Although some labour did eventually begin to trickle back, nothing was to be quite the same again. The Indian coolies on whom so much depended began in their tens of thousands to leave on the long trek for India, mostly by Prome and Akyab via the Taungup track, while the Burmese departed for their villages, leaving the way open for the *lu-zoes* (criminals) to reap whatever harvest they could. The RAF and AVG struck back at the Thai airfields from which the Japanese were operating, often with success, but the weight of numbers favoured the Japanese until it came to be the case that every time we heard a plane overhead, we immediately assumed it to be the enemy's. It did not help morale.

On the day when the Japanese made their first air raid on Rangoon I was in Martaban, in the marshalling yards across the Salween from Moulmein, engaged in the transhipment of ammunition. We had already experienced the Japanese bombing technique, which was remarkably effective. The enemy flew in a very tight formation, escorted above by fighters, and at a given word of command, presumably from their leader, they dropped all their bombs in a wide carpet. Although the bombs were small compared with those dropped on Hamburg by the RAF, they nevertheless exploded with deafening effect, and almost simultaneously. It was very alarming. Therefore, as soon as we heard the noise of approaching planes, rather like the sound of an Underground train approaching through the tunnel, we at once downed tools and dived into the nearest slit trench. But no bombs fell. As we clambered out sheepishly, the noise above dying away in the distance, I was confronted by the stationmaster, an Anglo-Burman, who had remained at his desk throughout. 'If a bomb has got your name on it, you'll get it, whatever you do,' he told me severely. However, he failed to explain how one ascertained whether or not it had.

I used to feel horribly exposed while crossing the Salween on an Irrawaddy Flotilla Company's paddle-steamer, making only a few knots against the current. On one occasion the *serang* panicked, throwing the wheel so hard that we ended up broadside to the stream, almost turning turtle. The cause was a plane passing overhead, which turned out to be an RAF Lysander bringing Major-General J. G. (Jacky) Smyth to Moulmein where the headquarters of 17th Indian Division was in the process of being set up early in January 1942.

That was the first time I met General Smyth, who had been awarded the Victoria Cross when serving with the 15th (Ludihana) Sikhs in France in 1915. He added a Military Cross later, on the North-West Frontier. Smyth was a bright, perky and friendly little man, with a wonderful ability to put young officers like me at their ease. There was no 'side' about him; he was neither grimly taciturn like Wavell, nor curiously unimpressive, like Hutton. He was alert, relaxed and willing to listen, even to a 25-year-old junior staff captain like me. He had been one of the Indian Army instructors at Camberley Staff College, a distinct feather in his cap (his successor was Slim), where the Commandant at the time had been General Dill, later to be CIGS. Smyth was in Britain on leave when war broke out and through Dill's help managed to wangle a posting to the BEF in France, where eventually he commanded a Territorial Army infantry brigade. This was at the least unusual for an officer in the Indian Army. Later, he was recalled to India by Auchinleck, another patron, to be groomed for the command of one of the newly-formed divisions. My Brigadier, a contemporary of Smyth's, knew him well, and liked him. But there were some in the Indian Army, a very closed shop, who considered Smyth to be too ambitious, and something of a showman. This was, of course, before the days when Monty (and Patton) made showmanship an acceptable part of a general's *persona*. Smyth was forty-eight years old, and I thought him tremendous.

Although we were not to know it at the time, nor would it have been easy to detect, Jacky Smyth was not a fit man. He had only left hospital the previous October after a serious operation for anal fissure. The wound was still open when he arrived in Moulmein. He had originally been appointed to raise the 18th Indian Division[8] and could reasonably anticipate six to nine months working up before his division was sent overseas. By then he expected to be fully fit again. But on 4 December, shortly before Pearl Harbor, he was ordered to take over command of 17th Indian Division, whose commander had fallen sick. It was this division, intended originally for Iraq where it could complete its training, that was abruptly switched to Burma, but not before two out of its three infantry brigades had been taken away and sent to Malaya.

17th Indian Division, whose divisional sign caused it to be known to all and sundry as the 'Black Cats', eventually came to be the most experienced in battle of all the infantry divisions in Slim's XIVth Army. It fought throughout the war from January 1942 onwards in Burma, acquiring a reputation that led to its selection as part of the Commonwealth Occupation Force in Japan after the Japanese surrender. But when first it arrived in Burma early in January 1942, it was a division only in name. As Major-General H. L. Davies has written, it 'was a very young unit, only partially equipped and completely untrained as a division. Having been earmarked for the Middle East it was on a mechanized basis and its battalions had no experience of jungle warfare.'[9] Only 46th Indian Infantry Brigade (Brigadier R. G.

Ekin) remained of its original 44th, 45th and 46th Brigades, and it was hopelessly deficient in field artillery and sappers.

It had been more or less decided by General Hutton, prior to Smyth's arrival in Burma, that 17th Division would be responsible for the Tenasserim front, with its headquarters in Moulmein. With this in mind the leading elements of the headquarters staff began to arrive early in January, my diary being full of complaints about their inadequacy – 'they seem to mill around all day, getting in everyone's way, without accomplishing anything, other than to create confusion'. To make matters worse, and to my Brigadier's unconcealed fury, they displaced Headquarters 2 Burma Infantry Brigade from our comfortable camp, constructed originally for 4 BURIF (now on the Thai border), and compelled us to find other accommodation in Moulmein itself. But since we now formed part of 17th Division, we had to put a good face on it.

There was one other so-called division in Burma, 1 BURDIV, of which we had previously formed part. Its task was to watch the approaches from Thailand through the South Shan States, for which purpose it had under command the 1st Burma and the 13th Indian Infantry Brigades, with divisional headquarters in Toungoo. BURDIV was in an even worse situation than 17th Division in terms of artillery, sappers and logistic support, and was even more widely dispersed.

Smyth was later taken to task by the Military Secretary at Army Headquarters in New Delhi for his failure to comply with mobilization regulations which required that every officer and soldier proceeding on active service should be passed fit to do so. Clearly, had Smyth been examined by a doctor, he would not have been allowed to accompany his division to Burma, but it is inconceivable that a man like Smyth, a holder of the Victoria Cross, would have chosen such a way out of his predicament. The Military Secretary must have known that Smyth had been in hospital earlier in the year and should have taken steps to check up on his physical fitness before allowing him to go. However, the fact that Smyth had in effect disobeyed mobilization regulations was used as the reason for withholding from him the honorary rank of Major-General when he was retired from the

Indian Army a year later. This can only be described as vindictive.

Hutton, who had preceded Smyth in Burma by only two weeks, had prepared his appreciation of the situation which he forwarded to Wavell on 10 January. He was assisted by his Brigadier General Staff, Brigadier H. L. (Taffy) Davies, a brilliant staff officer. Their joint effort proved to be uncannily correct in its conclusions. Discounting the view previously held that the Japanese would only be able to deploy three divisions in Burma, they argued that this figure could be increased very quickly, provided the approaches from Thailand were improved; nor did they rule out the possibility of seaborne landings. They believed the Japanese would attack on as broad a front as possible, moving very lightly equipped and living off the country. Since they would be planning for a rapid decision before the onset of the monsoon in mid-May, their attack would be carried out simultaneously with that on Malaya, selecting the shortest route to their objective, Rangoon, by way of Moulmein in the south, and Toungoo in central Burma. Heavy air attacks on Rangoon could close the port; similarly, air attacks on road/rail communications could seriously affect the Burma Army's mobility. That army was short in artillery, tanks, sappers, mechanical transport, and infantry for internal security duties. It was also deficient in a whole range of warlike stores, e.g. barbed wire, sandbags and field telephone cable. The militarizing of the railway, PWD and Post & Telegraph was essential, but the shortage of suitable military staff made this impossible. 'Even with the foreseeable reinforcement, that is up to the period mid to end March, our operational resources are so limited as to preclude anything except a defensive attitude possibly combined with very local offensives,' the report concluded.[10]

Every opportunity should be taken to bring the Chinese into battle as soon as possible, Chiang Kai-shek having already offered to make his Vth and VIth Armies available for this purpose. Hutton also urged that further shipments of American Lease-Lend material to China should be halted until the existing congestion in the port could be cleared, at the same time requesting that some of this material urgently required by Burma Army could be utilized for the defence of Burma. The current weakness in troops dictated a defensive strategy, concentrating on such vital areas as Moulmein and the Southern Shan States, until the arrival of the reinforcements already promised would permit Hutton to undertake offensive operations. Hindsight has shown that this appreciation was entirely realistic, but it was unlikely to appeal to Wavell when it landed on his desk in faraway Java. Not only did he underrate the Japanese as soldiers; he also considered that it was the lack of an offensive spirit among his own subordinate commanders which was contributing to our defeat.

'Burma was lost before the first shot was fired,' wrote Professor Raymond Callahan. 'Neither the trained troops nor the aircraft to hold it were available.'[11] This cannot be gainsaid, unfortunately, but the War Cabinet and Chiefs of Staff in London were hardly to blame for the fact. As we have seen, they had to dole out exiguous resources with parsimonious hands, and if any crumbs were left at the end of the process, Burma, if lucky, might get them. This does not, however, excuse the inability of the commanders on the spot to agree a coherent strategy. Wavell, remote in his headquarters in Java, had his attention chiefly directed on Malaya and Singapore, convinced that a more determined attitude would stop the Japanese in their tracks.[12] Hutton, who was after all Wavell's own choice for the job, took a more realistic view, but still insisted that the Japanese must be held as far away from Rangoon as possible. Although he knew as well as anyone else that Tenasserim was wide open to Japanese attack, it nevertheless contained the airfields linking Burma with Malaya, and must therefore be defended. It was also a vital area for Burma's modestly equipped but surprisingly efficient Observer Corps, on whose prior warnings the air defence of Rangoon so heavily relied.

CHAPTER SIX

The First Shocks

'We had a choice of difficulties.'
Wolfe at Montmorenci Falls,
2 September 1759[1]

At the end of November the Brigadier called me into his office and inquired if I knew anything about Operation YACHT. I did not. Apparently it was a plan intended to destroy a couple of bridges on the railway line linking Thailand with Malaya near a place called Parachuap-Khirikan. The operation had been planned for some time and was under the overall command of Lieutenant-Colonel Dennis O'Callaghan, OC, 2 BURIF at Mergui. The troops who were to carry out the operation were Frontier Force Column 2 (FF2), commanded by a remarkable character, Major S. W. A. Love, whose nickname 'Bwana' told of long years of service with the King's African Rifles before fate brought him to Burma. He was a splendid character, unorthodox in thought, word and deed, who must have been a sore trial to any regular-minded adjutant whenever he returned to his parent regiment, the Worcestershires.

During 1941 the BFF had raised several columns, numbered eventually from 1–8, mainly Indian in composition although they did include Chins, Kachins and Karens. FF2 was almost entirely Gurkha. Their transport was chiefly mule and pony but Love, by various means, had acquired a couple of launches. Love had two British officers, Captains E. J. Stephenson and J. O. V. Edwards.

As soon as the news of Japanese landings in Malaya reached Rangoon, Army Headquarters ordered us to implement YACHT between 12 and 16 December, Victoria Point having been captured by the enemy on 13 December. Love divided his force into three columns and set off through thick jungle and across very rugged country towards the railway. Edwards unfortunately ran into the Japanese, losing his radio set and the message he had just been deciphering. He fought his way out, losing fifteen men killed or captured, but the Japanese now knew there were other troops in the area. They carried out an intensive air reconnaissance while Stephenson's column searched vainly for the bridge they were intended to demolish; it later transpired that it did not exist, the column's map being out of date. Stephenson was forced to withdraw, as indeed was Love with his column, having accomplished nothing. The official history castigates the entire operation as 'needless and blundering', the more so because shortly after FF2 had set out, a message was received in Mergui from Rangoon cancelling YACHT since the enemy were already in possession of Parachuap-Khirikan. By then, however, it was too late to recall Love to Mergui.

It was not the end of a sorry episode. Midway between Mergui and Victoria Point, at Bokpyin, was a police post. The Japanese occupied it. Love, returning by launch from his abortive sally into Thailand, was ordered by O'Callaghan to drive them out. A launch carrying some mortar bombs for his mortars failed to rendezvous with Love who then attacked the police post with rifles and hand grenades. It stood on a hill 147 feet high and was well defended. Nevertheless, although the anticipated RAF support failed to materialize, some of Love's men got close enough to lob grenades into the post before being forced to retreat. Love was killed, his second-in-command was wounded. The column then withdrew to Mergui through the jungle. Two days later a company of 2 BURIF from Mergui easily recaptured Bokpyin, which was hardly worth the loss of an officer as valuable as 'Bwana' Love.

The news of this unfortunate affair reached us in Moulmein on the day when Lieutenant-Colonel F. C. Simpson, senior Operations Staff Officer (GSO I), at Headquarters 17th Indian Division was paying his first visit to our brigade headquarters. I remember John Bourke telling him that we would never be able to operate efficiently in the jungle until we had good radio communications, and the sooner he made that clear to headquarters in Rangoon the better. Bourke also told him that we ought to be a 'damned sight better moving about in the jungle than we are, considering the length of time the British had been in Burma'. How right he was, but how long it took for the message to sink in.

General Hutton had yet to arrive to take over from General McLeod, but when he did it was clear that the air reinforcement route to Singapore had been well and truly scuppered. It had never made sense to us in 2nd Burma Brigade; how could we possibly be expected to defend airfields two to three hundred miles apart, with virtually no land communications between them? But both the Governor and McLeod were worried out of their wits at the prospect of air attacks on Rangoon, and rightly so; they wanted to keep the Japanese air force as far away from that city as possible.

That war is an option of difficulties is one of the oldest of clichés; nevertheless it remains true. Compared with Wolfe's difficulties as he advanced on Quebec, Hutton's would prove incomparably the greater. He would be under great political pressure from the Governor to hold the Japanese as far away from Rangoon as possible; Air Vice-Marshal Stevenson, the Air Officer Commanding, would be singing the same tune. Wavell, far away in Java, would be preaching the advantages of offensive action. The Chiefs of Staff in London, prodded in turn by Churchill and acting under continuous reminder by Roosevelt, would dispatch telegram after telegram reminding him of the requirement to keep the supply chain to China running without interruption. And Hutton might have found it easier to deal with what was a virtually insuperable problem had his views been agreed with by the two officers upon whom he principally relied.

The first of these was Major-General Jacky Smyth. Hutton had told him that Headquarters 17th Indian Division was to be established in Moulmein and that all the necessary stores, tentage, equipment etc. was being shipped there for the purpose as rapidly as could be arranged. As we have seen, the 17th Division had originally consisted of the 44th, 45th and 46th Infantry Brigades, organized for desert warfare in Iraq. Raised early in

1941, all its units contained a very high proportion of untrained soldiers, complicated further by the fact that a large number of the British officers spoke little Urdu. The 44th and 45th Brigades were sent to Malaya, to become prisoners of war; only the 46th Brigade ended in Burma.

Smyth, having seen his division so summarily dispersed, was summoned to Delhi on 28 December 1941 where Wavell told him he was to take his headquarters and remaining brigade to Burma where he was to form a new 17th Division. He gave Smyth the impression that anything that might happen in Burma would be no more than a normal difficulty, most of the rest of their conversation being devoted to pig-sticking, a sport Wavell had taken up with great enthusiasm. 'The General Staff will tell you the form,' he said, shaking Smyth's hand. 'Look after Burma for me.'[2]

Smyth's father, who had been a member of the ICS, had at one time been District Commissioner in Moulmein, and as such was an old friend of Pelly, the Provincial Commissioner in Tenasserim. There were drinks that night at the Pellys' and as a very humble fly on the wall I sat nursing my whisky and listening to my elders and betters discuss the situation. 'This is a crazy place to defend,' said Smyth. 'They'll bomb us to hell, just like Dunkirk.' When Pelly protested, Smyth brushed him aside. 'Will your Burma Rifles fight, Paddy?' he asked Bourke. 'I'm not sure,' Bourke replied. 'The 4th Burma Rifles at Kawkareik are at fifty per cent strength from malaria. The 7th and 8th have just arrived here; they were only raised earlier this year – from the Police and Frontier Force. The 2nd battalion in Mergui aren't bad, but I don't reckon much to the 6th in Tavoy. And we have no artillery.' He added he would feel happier with a good British or Indian battalion to provide us with some stiffening.

I also remember Bourke saying that he thought his brigade would have been better employed on the frontier, at Kawkareik and on the Dawnas. We knew the ground and had good contact with the locals. 'But for some unknown reason they've sent "Jonah" with 16th Brigade up to the frontier, leaving us to defend Moulmein.'

'From the start of the campaign,' Smyth recorded, 'General Wavell had been insistent that my 17th Division should fight as far forward as possible and this objective was passed on literally by General Hutton.'[3]

A study of the map showed there were three distinct river lines between Moulmein and Rangoon. The first was the Salween, 7000 yards wide, tidal, and on the direct route from Thailand into Burma. Above Moulmein it flowed through hilly, densely jungle-covered country, hard to defend, although there were local ferries at various places. At a conservative estimate it would require a full division, with its complete complement of field and medium artillery, to defend Moulmein; even then its largely wooden houses could be razed to the ground by air attack, while the surrounding coastline was wide open to seaborne landings. 'They say we are going to turn the place into a second Tobruk,' I wrote in my diary. 'They must be crazy!' I remember John Bourke telling me that he could not understand why we were still bringing stores across the Salween. 'Jacky Smyth wants to get us all back behind the Sittang as soon as he can,' he said.

Fifty miles west of the Salween was the River Bilin. Rising in the Karenni Hills it flowed through jungle-covered hills until reaching the coastal plain near the town of Bilin. From there it meandered through the paddy fields, marshy at its mouth on the Gulf of Martaban but no obstacle except during the monsoon. I waded across it often when jungle-fowl shooting in March 1941. Quite a good road ran along the foot of the hills, this being an area for growing rubber, and Thaton, the district headquarters, was a sizeable market town. For much of the way the railway from Martaban ran parallel with the road, raised on an embankment against the monsoon floods.

Fifty miles farther west still was the Sittang, one of Burma's larger rivers, entering the Gulf of Martaban via a large estuary, much of the banks being boggy. The railway bridge was about half a mile long, single tracked and unusable by vehicles. Just above the bridge there were a couple of primitive ferries. The Sittang was 500–600 yards wide with a current of three or four knots. Farther upstream the river was broader and more easy to swim. But below the bridge there was a tidal bore, rising as high as forty feet.

For some reason unknown to me the PWD had not bothered to construct an all-weather road either from Kyaikto, eighteen miles east of the bridge where the road from Martaban ended, or on the west bank of the Sittang to join up with Pegu, twenty-five miles away on the main Mandalay–Rangoon highway. Presumably there was no good economic reason for such an expensive undertaking, particularly as the railway already existed, but we were to pay dearly for this failure in the future.

I remember Montgomery telling us at the Staff College that a general must make up his mind how he intends to fight the battle, and then, against all opposition, insist on having his own way. Poor Smyth was no Montgomery. From the outset he was convinced that the Sittang provided by far the best position on which to hold the Japanese until the anticipated reinforcements had been landed at Rangoon. He put in a strong bid to do so, never ceasing to press his view on Hutton, both verbally and in writing. Of course it would mean abandoning Tenasserim and Moulmein, but what use were they, anyway? The air bridge to Singapore had been breached, neither Tavoy nor Mergui could hold out against determined attack, and defending Moulmein was as good a way as any of handing over to the Japanese a brigade or more of soldiers on a plate.

But Smyth was overruled. Personalities matter a great deal in war (as they do of course at other times), and it is hard to avoid the conclusion that Hutton and Smyth did not much care for each other. Hutton was a hard-working, earnest, conscientious type of man, perhaps a little dull but eminently reliable. Smyth, on the other hand, was inclined to be cocky, extremely self-confident, adept at getting men to work for him and to enjoy doing so. A Victoria Cross sets a man apart, whether rightly or wrongly, and Jacky Smyth's military career so far had included little of the humdrum, and a great deal of the more exciting.

In a letter to Maurice Collis, author of *Last and First in Burma*, Smyth wrote on 11 November 1955: 'Davies told me something extremely interesting . . . that was that it was the Governor of Burma who was so strongly against my plan to concentrate behind the Sittang because that would have brought the Japanese so close to Rangoon that it would have fatally weakened the morale of the people of Burma.'[4]

I wonder. Brigadier Taffy Davies may not have been an unbiased witness. Field-Marshal Slim has written of him: 'Taffy Davies was something more than a brilliant staff officer; he was a character in his own right.'[5] After serving Hutton first as his BGS (Brigadier General Staff, or in modern parlance, Chief of Staff), he went to Slim in the same capacity when Slim was appointed the commander of Burma Corps. A tall, thin, emaciated Welshman, he combined driving energy with a first-class tactical brain. Although loyal to Hutton as his senior staff officer, his sympathies were wholly with Smyth. His military vision was clearcut and uncluttered by the kind of compromises that in war lead inevitably to disaster. Later, when Smyth was engaged in bitter argument with the official historian concerning the disaster at the Sittang, Davies came down uncompromisingly on Smyth's side.

Hutton was as strongly opposed to a premature withdrawal to the Sittang as the Governor was. 'It is obvious,' he was to write later, 'that if he [Smyth] had been left a free hand he would have scuttled back across the River Sittang as quickly as possible, after perhaps a token resistance on the Bilin River.'[6]

Hutton's arguments for fighting as far forward of Rangoon as possible can be easily summarized:

(a) The road and railway from Rangoon to China ran immediately west of the Sittang. Once the Japanese reached the Sittang all aid to China must cease, with serious implications for Anglo-American relations.
(b) Rangoon's air warning system depended very largely on Observer Corps in Tenasserim. Without prior warning the airfield at Mingalodon and the port could not be defended.
(c) Considerable reinforcements, possibly a British and/or Australian division were expected. Bombing of the port, and the consequential flight of labour, would seriously dislocate disembarkation.
(d) If Rangoon had to be evacuated, the main line of withdrawal would be up the Sittang Valley. This route was vital for the backloading of stores and personnel.

(e) If the reinforcements promised by Chiang Kai-shek were to arrive in Burma it was essential to retain his confidence, never strong where the British were concerned. He might easily construe a premature withdrawal from Tenasserim as evidence of Britain's lack of will to fight.

These were cogent arguments, endorsed by the Governor, which made sense to Wavell when cabled to his headquarters in Java. They carried much less weight with those of us in Moulmein hastily staking out a defensive perimeter with hardly any barbed wire, virtually no sandbags and insufficient picks and shovels to equip a single battalion.

What Hutton does not disclose, when arguing in favour of holding as far forward from Rangoon as possible, is that he was under the strongest pressure from Wavell not to yield an inch of ground. Wavell believed that much of the cause for the failure to hold the Japanese in Malaya was lack of offensive spirit, coupled with a tendency 'to look over one's shoulder', a fault he ascribed to senior and junior commanders alike. He was determined to prevent this from happening in Burma. He made this plain on many occasions to Hutton, who naturally did his best to comply. Wavell, unfortunately, not only underrated his enemy, but overrated his own troops. They would be all right in time, but needed hard training before they could be compared with the veterans of the Western Desert and Abyssinia.

The fact has to be faced that from the very outset of the campaign, Wavell, Hutton and Smyth were at loggerheads. Wavell, 2000 miles away, with almost impossible problems to deal with, could only manage to visit Burma four or five times during the campaign, and then only for forty-eight hours at most. He could hardly have been more out of touch had he been in London. Hutton and Smyth, although outwardly on good terms, wrangled and argued behind the scenes. Not surprisingly, this affected the staffs as well. Considering the appalling difficulties facing Hutton and Smyth, it is doubly unfortunate that almost from the very beginning they were at cross purposes.

On arrival in Moulmein, Smyth took under command the 16th Indian Infantry Brigade (under Brigadier J. K. Jones), then moving forward to the Thai border near Kawkareik, about fifty miles east of Moulmein. The brigade consisted of the 1/9 Jats, 1/7 Gurkha Rifles and 4 BURIF (my old battalion). 2nd Burma Brigade also came under 17th Division. It consisted of 7 and 8 BURIF, two companies of 3 BURIF and the 4/12 FFR, together with 12th Mountain Battery. Brigade headquarters was in Moulmein. We also commanded 6 BURIF in Tavoy, and 2 BURIF in Mergui, but the former scattered like chaff before the wind when the Japanese attacked Tavoy on 18 January; this made it necessary to evacuate 2 BURIF from Mergui by sea between 20 and 22 January.

Smyth had few illusions about the practicability of holding Moulmein, or of the battle-worthiness of his Burma Rifles battalions. How much of the latter was due to his discussions with his senior commanders, like Bourke and Jones, and how much to his own observations, is hard to determine. Certainly Brigadier Bourke never concealed from me his view that the Burma Rifles in no way compared with the average Indian battalion. Smyth held the view, which he pressed on Hutton, that the Burma Rifles, apart perhaps from the 8th battalion (composed entirely of Sikhs and Punjabi Mussalmans), should be employed only for reconnaissance.

Hutton did not dissent from Smyth's view but said it would be politically unacceptable to do as Smyth advised; moreover, without the Burma Rifles battalions, 17th Division would be even weaker in strength. However, he did agree with Smyth that Moulmein was not the place for Smyth's headquarters, and on 23 January the divisional headquarters, which had been established in Moulmein with the utmost difficulty, packed up and departed for Kyaikto, with an advanced headquarters at Thaton. 'Order, counter-order and disorder,' I commented in my diary, adding, 'No one, including the Brigadier, knows whether we are to stay here, or to follow HQ 17 Div. Yesterday we were leaving; today, it seems, we are staying.'

To add to our difficulties, the means of communication with both higher and lower headquarters were totally inadequate. The newly formed Burma Army Signals did yeoman service, as did the Indian Army Signals, but there were too few wireless sets, too few trained men to operate them. Reliance had to be placed on the civil Post & Telegraph system, hopelessly insecure and liable to sabotage. On the wide fronts we were expected to hold, sometimes in dense jungle, wireless was unreliable, field telephone cable was liable to be cut and 'runners' were easily ambushed. The only reliable 'nets' were those operated by the Gunners, and later, when they arrived in Burma, the tanks of 7th Armoured Brigade. For much of the time we were no better off for the passage of information than Raglan in the Crimea, or Wellington in Spain.

Communications from Burma Army to New Delhi were of course much better. However messages were liable to delay owing to the need to decode, and then encode again, Hutton's cables to Wavell in Java. This added considerably to the transmission time. During the decoding process, copies were made for the Viceroy, the Commander-in-Chief and the principal staff officers in New Delhi. In London copies were made for the Prime Minister, the Chiefs of Staff etc. None of this seems to have been realized by Hutton who was reporting to Wavell, his superior commander, often expressing views and mentioning hopes and fears which he would only have done to someone he knew well, and whom he might expect to understand him without reading too much between the lines. In the end this frankness was to be his undoing, although he might have been expected to take warning from a friendly signal from the CIGS, advising him to use the word 'withdrawal' instead of 'retreat', the latter not being a word included in the Prime Minister's dictionary.*

To add to this state of general confusion or uncertainty, there was virtually no information regarding the enemy, known to be concentrating across the border in Thailand. Owing to lack of funds, no attempt had been made to set up agents in Thailand. On 6 January a flight of six aircraft of the Indian Air Force landed in Moulmein, intended for reconnaissance, I imagine. They were Wapitis, biplanes with long years of service on the North-West Frontier, and of course obsolete. On 7 January the Japanese strafed the airfield and damaged most of them. The rest took off for Mingalodon and we never saw them again.

* Nor for that matter was it used by the Japanese, who always referred to retreating as advancing in the opposite direction.

They were unlikely to have been of much use. Colonel Pelly, the Commissioner, who had told me proudly some months earlier that hardly a leaf could drop in Tenasserim without his hearing of its fall, expressed himself astonished that so little was being reported by the village headmen. The most likely explanation is that they were being intimidated by the considerable number of Thakins who had infiltrated the area ahead of the Japanese.

This almost total lack of information greatly contributed to the state of unreality which I shall always associate with those weeks and months in Burma, before and immediately after the Japanese invasion. European civilians seemed to find it hard to believe that their comfortable existence was about to be rudely disrupted. When Mrs Pelly at last yielded to persuasion and consented to remove herself from Moulmein – 'for the time being', as she put it – she asked me to provide several trucks to convey her household belongings to the quayside; one, I believe, was for her cats. When I refused, she complained to Brigadier Bourke. Not long after her departure the Commissioner's bungalow received a direct hit in an air raid and was razed to the ground. When I went to inspect the damage soon afterwards I found a silver-framed photograph of Colonel Pelly lying in a flower bed, and took it away with me intending to restore it to its owner, but left it behind in the general confusion of our departure from Moulmein.

It was surprising how rapidly the town began to empty once the Japanese Air Force began to make its presence felt. First the well-to-do Indians set off for Rangoon, followed by those Burmans and Karens who had relatives they had to visit 'in the country'. The British and Anglo-Burman wives tended to hang on, hoping against hope that it was all a 'bad dream'. Moulmein had been a 'non-family' station when we moved there from Mandalay, but a few days after Pearl Harbor three or four British women arrived from Army Headquarters to work as cipher operators. One of them happened to be my wife, who brought with her our car, two dachshunds, her Burmese servant, and a pair of hunting prints, for no good reason that I could see.* She went to work in the headquarters and we met at irregular

* The two hunting prints still hang today in my hall.

intervals, usually in the one and only local hotel, where I acquired the dysentery that nearly led to my being invalided out of the army.

The dysentery caused me to be admitted to hospital. On my release I was horrified to find that my wife, together with Mrs Pelly and her daughter, were still to be evacuated. By that date the Japanese had crossed the frontier and had made mincemeat of the brigade intended to turn them back. Fortunately there were still trains running from Martaban to Rangoon, although the ferries were uncooperative. Accordingly I hired two *sampans* at about 4 pm on 22 January, paid an exorbitant price to two unwilling boatmen, and set out across the three-mile-wide river. My wife, I and the two dachshunds occupied one *sampan*; Maung Shwe, our servant, with two suitcases, the other. The journey seemed to take hours. On one occasion we ran aground on a sandbank, the other half occupied by a dead elephant, twice the size of a captive balloon and stinking. On another, a couple of Japanese naval 'Zeros' came sweeping down the river, shooting up whatever came into their sights. It made sense to me to take to the water while the planes howled overhead, but I climbed back aboard, wet and dripping, to see my wife sitting calmly in the prow, the two dachshunds still attached to her by their leads.

The 'Rangoon Mail' was still running. She left at 7 pm for Rangoon, the dachshunds still firmly attached. I gave her my pistol, for which action I believe I am still liable for court martial, kissed her warmly, and wished her the best of British luck. She needed it. Her train was halted several times by enemy air attacks and I did not hear of her again for weeks and weeks. She beat the Japanese out of Moulmein by rather less than a week!

CHAPTER SEVEN

We Abandon Moulmein

> 'Regular soldiering and discipline make no appeal to them' [i.e. the Burma Rifles].
> *Wavell's Dispatch on the 1942 Burma Campaign*

While I was in hospital in Moulmein, I was visited by a young Karen *havildar* (sergeant) who had served under me when I was Adjutant of the 4th Burma Rifles. His name was Saw Lone and we were of much the same age and great friends. He was a Christian and came from a village not far from Tavoy, where his people worked in the tin mines.

He told me that the Japanese were massing in great strength across the border at Raheng and were collecting large numbers of elephants, ponies and bullocks, the Thai authorities being very cooperative. Then he told me something which interested me greatly. He said his village had been recently visited by a party of Thakins, all wearing a kind of khaki uniform, led by a young Burman who had made a very favourable impression on the villagers. He had told them that the Japanese would be coming as liberators, not conquerors, and that the British would be swept away like logs in the monsoon spates. He strongly advised them to cooperate with the Japanese when they came, and to hinder the British in every way possible. From the description Saw Lone gave me of the young Burman, and from what I learnt later, I have little doubt that this was Aung San, who led the Burmese National Army against us and who was to be assassinated shortly before Britain recognized Burma as an independent sovereign state on 17 October 1947.

Saw Lone then told me that were the Japanese to defeat us at Kawkareik, which at the time he seemed to think unlikely, he would have little option but to return to his village to look after his family and property. The Karens' relations with the Burmans, who predominated in Tavoy, were uneasy, and he had no doubt there would be trouble if the British departed. His duty then must be to look after his aged parents, wife and children.

I asked him if he had reported this information and he said he had told the Intelligence officer in his battalion. I wanted to pass this on to Merton but he had left with brigade tactical headquarters for Ye, together with 4/12 FFR. In my diary on 16 January I had written: 'Brigadier and Appleby [the Brigade Major*] came in to see me before they go. Brigadier very pessimistic . . . "Mert" gets it in the neck from the Brigadier – he forgets to take the "thunder-box"!'

I did pass the information on later to Lieutenant-Colonel Tommy Thompson, Assistant Adjutant and Quartermaster General at Headquarters 17 Division, when he looked in to see me. He told me then that Jacky Smyth had little faith in the Burma Rifles and had asked for the 2 KOYLI to stiffen the Moulmein garrison. Saw Lone had given me considerable food for thought, and I wondered how I would react in a similar situation to his.

At 0400 hours on Tuesday, 20 January 1942, the advanced guard of 55th Japanese Division crossed the border into Burma at Myawaddy and Palu. The first troops they encountered were 'D' Company of 1/7 Gurkha Rifles, dug in at milestone 51 on the road from Kawkareik over the Dawnas to Myawaddy. Tavoy had been taken by III/112 Infantry Regiment of the 55th Division the previous day. So far as we were concerned, at brigade headquarters in Moulmein, the fog of war now surrounded us completely – accurate information seemed to be unobtainable, rumour was rife.

When it was decided at Imperial Japanese Headquarters in November 1941 that war was unavoidable, all plans for the southern drive were based on the capture of Singapore. Burma was essentially a secondary objective, and regarded to some extent as a sideshow. The much vaunted Japanese Intelligence accurately estimated the Burma garrison to be 27,000, 15,000 of

* Senior staff officer in a British brigade headquarters.

which were Burmese troops whom they regarded as being of poor quality.

Headquarters XVth Army had originally been based in Osaka in Japan. Of its two Divisions, the 55th (under Lieutenant-General Yutaka Takeuchi) had been involved in the occupation of French Indo-China; it was 14,000 strong. The 33rd (under Lieutenant-General Shozo Sakurai), 16,000 strong, had been in Central China. They were both battle hardened formations. 55th Division was moved up to the frontier first, while 33rd Division was moving into Thailand from China. At the outset of the campaign General Iida's headquarters were in Bangkok. His command was eventually to be increased to four divisions, one of them being the *élite* 18th Imperial Guards Division, but that was some way in the future.

The encounter battle on the Dawnas was a grim foretaste of the campaign to come. It contained the ingredients of all that made the Japanese such formidable opponents. The speed with which they seized the fleeting chance; the exploitation of every weakness; the ruthlessness with which they drove forward across terrain considered impassable; the skilful handling of their mortars; their stamina and, let it be said, their courage.

All was confusion inside the thick bamboo jungle but, as always when fighting against the Japanese, it was the danger of being out-flanked and cut off that worried Brigadier Jones of 16th Brigade and his subordinate commanders. In less than forty-eight hours he had been driven off the Dawna positions and was falling back on Kawkareik, having blown the already prepared demolitions east of Sukli. Orders for withdrawal had been issued, but in many cases communications had failed. For reasons still to be explained, brigade headquarters disintegrated (around 1800 hours on 21 January) despite every attempt by the Brigadier and his Brigade Major to stop the rot. Panic set in. The 1/9 Jats, given the task of holding a bridgehead at Kyondo, which was a ferry station, set fire to their trucks and ammunition and fled. With them went most of the brigade staff and the other hangers-on.

Meanwhile the 1/7 Gurkha Rifles, less a detached company watching the Three Pagodas Pass to the south, together with

4 BURIF, were withdrawing on Kyondo in more or less good order. However, there were no ferries nor transport waiting for them. They crossed the river by local craft, after destroying transport and the ammunition they could not carry, then marched through the jungle until they reached a steamer station from where they could be ferried down to Martaban. Some of them had not eaten for three days, all were exhausted. 'D' Company of 4 BURIF, under Major Thackeray, was cut off near Mepale. They conducted a fighting retreat to Pa-an on the Salween, crossing two unbridged rivers, killing thirty Japanese without loss and bringing back all weapons and equipment. The men were all Kachins. It was a gallant effort and there was talk of giving Thackeray a decoration, but it came to nothing. Instead, Hutton was determined to sack Brigadier Jones, who had been away from his headquarters when the panic first started; only Smyth's determined support saved him.[1]

The Japanese were astonished by the ease of their victory. All reports 'at this time agreed that the enemy was in confusion and panicky, and hastily withdrawing to Moulmein'.[2] General Iida's reaction was predictable. On 26 January he ordered General Takeuchi to press on forthwith and take Moulmein, for which operation 55th Division could muster only four infantry battalions, five batteries of field artillery, two squadrons of cavalry and two companies of engineers, at most 8000 men. Their lines of communication over the Dawna Range were still interrupted by demolitions; the track (it was hardly a road) from the border to Raheng, the base in Thailand, was still barely usable by motor transport. They would have to carry on men and animals all they would need for the battle ahead. They did – but it was a bold decision.

Accurate reports of what had happened took some time to reach us in Moulmein. On 22 January I was fully occupied getting my wife away. On 23 January I noted: 'News very bad. Japs have broken through at Kawkareik. 16 Brigade burnt all their equipment . . . 17 Div are clearing out their HQ. BM very trying. Food ghastly. Merton virtually doing no Intelligence work – only messing and damned bad at that. New Brigade HQ at Duguid's house . . . Burnt all our documents &c . . . State of chaos in Moulmein. Higher command still deciding whether to hang on to the place or not. They still say it is to be a "second Tobruk"!'

Rumour fed on rumour. One straggler from 4 BURIF whom I met across the river in Martaban told me the entire battalion had been taken prisoner. Another, an officer in the 1/9 Jats, said at least three Japanese divisions were pouring across the frontier. Every Burman with any sense had left Moulmein for the jungle. The streets were deserted, apart from a constant procession of trucks moving down to the jetties, as Headquarters 17 Division was backloaded across the Salween. Japanese aircraft were overhead for most of the daylight hours, their targets the airfield and the marshalling yards at Martaban. At night the howling of packs of pi-dogs, roaming the streets in search of food, made the air hideous. The few people remaining flitted from place to place, arousing suspicion as fifth columnists, while out in the countryside villages burnt, mostly the work of dacoits or evidence of the settling of old grudges. Law and order had broken down completely.

At this eleventh hour we in 2nd Burma Brigade were working flat out to put Moulmein into a state of defence, although the means with which to do so were lamentably lacking. My time was spent trying to find and then issue barbed wire, sandbags and the like. Most of our previous stocks had been given to 16th Brigade and lost at Kawkareik. We had no mines, and precious little artillery ammunition and mortar bombs. However, we did have the contents of Leon Chye's liquor store at our disposal, and drank our "Dimple Haig" as if it were water. It was the expectation of what lay in store for us that dominated our minds, when we had time to think about it. I was reminded of that feeling many years later, when flying over the mountains of the Western Aden Protectorate in an army light aircraft. Suddenly the noise from the engine ceased and the pilot said to me over the intercom, 'Brigadier, I am going to force land. Watch out for the bump.' Looking back over the years, it was the waiting for it rather than the bump itself that has lingered longest in my memory.

Wavell had visited Hutton on 24/25 January, reporting to the

Chiefs of Staff that he did not regard Rangoon as being in any immediate danger. He ordered Hutton to forestall any Japanese attack on Moulmein by taking vigorous *offensive* action, Wavell's touch with reality appearing to have vanished altogether. Hutton therefore ordered Smyth to hold Moulmein at all costs, 2 KOYLI being told to move to Moulmein from the Shan States. Smyth, who had all along argued that Moulmein was indefensible with the troops at his disposal, at once countermanded the order for 2nd Burma Brigade to move west of the Salween. There was a conference in Moulmein on 28 January, attended by Hutton, Smyth and the brigade commander. No doubt it was at this conference that Brigadier Bourke expressed his views on the defensibility of Moulmein in clear military tones. This could not have pleased Hutton since, before leaving for Rangoon, he and Smyth agreed to replace Bourke by Brigadier Roger Ekin, commander of 46th Infantry Brigade, who had only just arrived with his brigade headquarters at Hninpale, near Bilin. Ekin knew nothing of the situation in Moulmein, where Bourke had been stationed for nearly a year. Smyth did not tell Ekin until 30 January, nor Bourke for that matter; as for the brigade staff we were left completely in the dark.

'Those whom the Gods seek to destroy, they first drive mad,' we are told. This had a peculiar application to Moulmein during those last few days in January. Our first contact with the advancing Japanese occurred on 26 January when a company from 4/12 FFR was attacked at Mudon, fifteen miles south of Moulmein. Another company of the same regiment, sent out to assist a company of the 1/7 Gurkha Rifles, withdrawing from the Three Pagodas Pass[3] on the Thai frontier, was attacked near Mudon on the night 29/30 January, and cut off from Moulmein. They crossed the Salween later in country boats and rejoined their battalion at Kyaikto. To add to all the confusion, Merton and I were in trouble with Appleby.

We had been discussing our prospects, agreeing we would not put our shirts on our chances of getting out of Moulmein alive, when Appleby, who had overheard our conversation, accused us of being defeatist: he was almost beside himself with rage, refused any further discussion and placed us both under arrest.

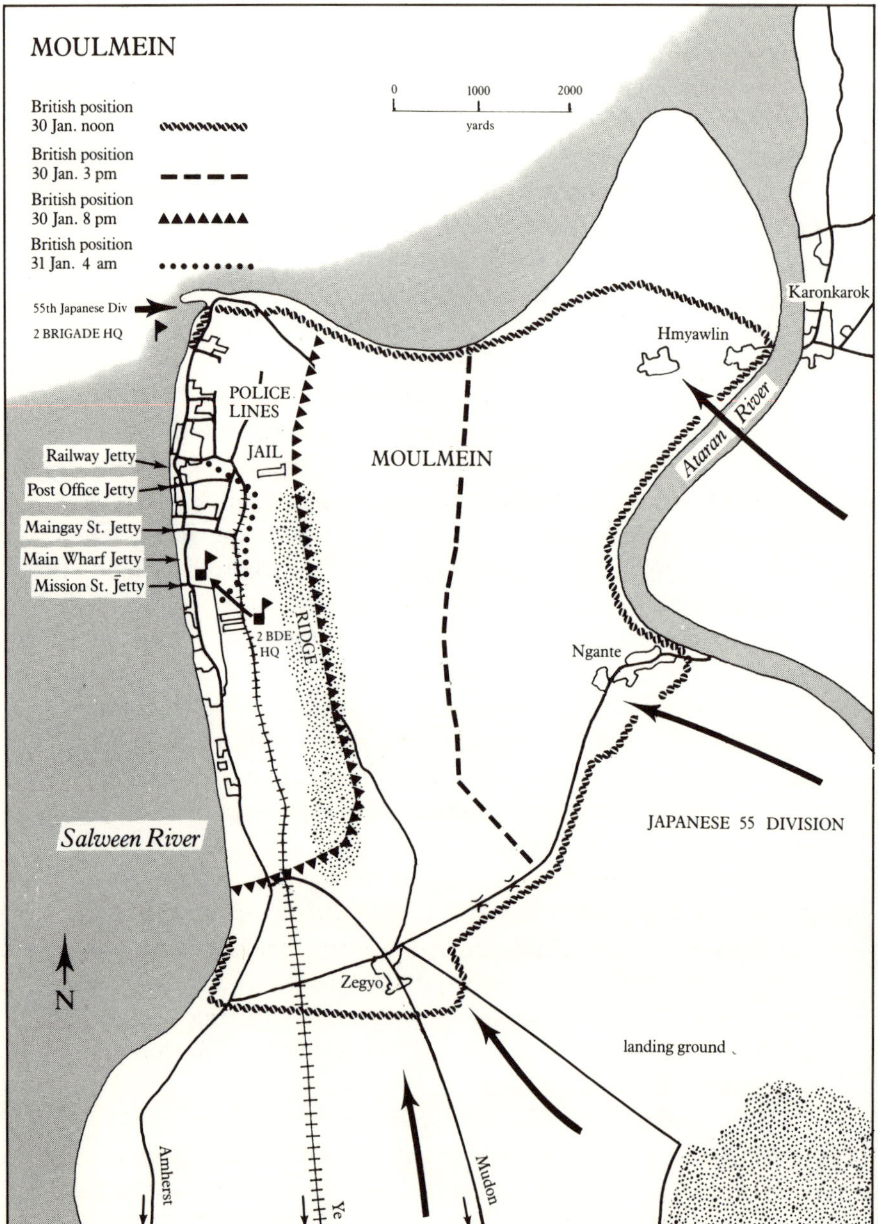

MOULMEIN
British position
30 Jan. noon
British position
30 Jan. 3 pm
British position
30 Jan. 8 pm
British position
31 Jan. 4 am
55th Japanese Div
2 BRIGADE HQ
0
1000
2000
yards
Karonkarok
Hmyawlin
POLICE
LINES
JAIL
MOULMEIN
Ataran River
Railway Jetty
Post Office Jetty
Maingay St. Jetty
Main Wharf Jetty
Mission St. Jetty
2 BDE
HQ
RIDGE
Ngante
JAPANESE 55 DIVISION
Salween River
N
Zegyo
landing ground
Amherst
Ye
Mudon

Then he stormed out of the room. I had work to do, as had Merton, but technically we had to remain where we were until an escort was produced. Some time passed, and then we agreed to go across to brigade headquarters where we found the Brigadier in a towering rage. He had been looking for us everywhere, he stormed. Appleby had collapsed (from a nervous breakdown, as it transpired), and he wanted me to fill in as Brigade Major until Major L. G. Wheeler, 3 BURIF, arrived. He would later be relieved by an officer who was being sent from Headquarters 17 Division to take over as Brigade Major. All this was being explained as messages came pouring in, by telephone, signals and via orderlies.

The defensive perimeter of Moulmein was about eleven and a half miles in extent, forming a rough rectangle. The eastern side was the ridge, wooded and dominated by several pagodas; houses belonging to Moulmein's more prosperous residents were dotted along it. The western side was the Salween, with its wharves and jetties. The Salween also marked the northern side, just below its junction with the Ataran; while the southern boundary extended from the suburb of Zegyo to the Railway Jetty, a distance of about 2000 yards. This was considered to be the most likely Japanese line of advance. Enclosed within this perimeter were a maze of streets and lanes, most of the houses being of wood. There were extensive timber yards where elephants were employed to shift the logs, and an attractive park, Salween Park, where brigade headquarters had been established in the PWD Bungalow.

8 BURIF under Lieutenant-Colonel Bowers defended the southern sector, extending up onto the ridge where they joined hands with 7 BURIF (Lieutenant-Colonel McCarthy) who were responsible for most of the ridge. In the north, watching the crossings across the Ataran, were 3 BURIF (less two companies) commanded by Lieutenant-Colonel Taylor. 4/12 FFR (Lieutenant-Colonel Edward), less the company cut off in Mudon, were in brigade reserve; they usually referred to themselves as the 4th Sikhs and were an exceptionally good unit. So were 12 Mountain Battery, under Major John Hume, whose 3.7″ pack-howitzers delivered a surprisingly lethal shell. We

also had a section of 60 Field Company, Madras Sappers & Miners, who could fight as well as any infantryman. The force was far too small to defend such an extended area, much of it built-up with excellent covered lines of approach for an enemy exceptionally skilled in field craft. Despite everyone's opinion to the contrary, Hutton, after the hastiest of reconnaissance on 28 January, calculated we had a fair chance of holding Moulmein with a brigade. It was an extremely foolish decision.

On Friday 30 January my diary records:

> Merton wakes me about 0100 hours. Says he thinks he can hear firing. Most extraordinary 'whooping' noise, which we can't place. Also the continuous howling of starving pi-dogs. We get dressed and lie down clothed. About 0700 hours heavy firing from Zegyo; Japs had tried to rush through 8 BURIF LMG post in some of our own 30 cwt lorries which they presumably captured at Kawkareik. No time for breakfast so hurry over to Brigade HQ. Everyone very worried and L. G. Wheeler tells me there is Jap attack on aerodrome. 12 Mountain Battery are firing; main attack seems around Zegyo. Watts who is commanding Kokine detachment on aerodrome is directing fire.[4] Japs have surrounded him by midday. Heavy firing all the morning; 8 BURIF are steady but 3 BURIF are shaky. At 1200 hours Brigadier Ekin from 46 Brigade arrives to take over command from Bourke; no one knows why, and Bourke very unhappy but stays to help out Ekin . . . Also Major Green 6/13 FF Rifles arrives as BM. He was GSO III HQ 17 Div . . .

Ekin was later to write: 'Early on 30 January I was told of the Army Commander's order that I was to take over Moulmein. On arrival there at 12 noon (after a sixty-mile journey) the Jap attack had already begun, and I had to assume command of troops I had never seen, on ground I did not know, with the BM out of action, later replaced by one who was also a stranger to Moulmein.'[5]

He had been placed in an impossible situation and it was fortunate that Bourke, with great generosity of spirit, agreed to remain to give Ekin the benefit of his experience. He says that

Ekin told him, 'You and I will fight this battle together' – which they did.

During the afternoon I went up onto the ridge where 8 BURIF were under some pressure. Dick Lewin, of 2 BURIF, who would later succeed me as staff captain, accompanied me. Mortar bombs were bursting all round us as the Japs tried to work their way up the wooded slopes. It seemed more incongruous than frightening. I can recall feeling very hungry. We visited the Forward Observation Post of 12 Battery, established in the ruins of the Commissioner's house. We were given some tea by Myles Elton, one of the battery subalterns, as I surveyed the battle-scarred lawns where not long before I had attended one of Mrs Pelly's garden parties. As we left, 8 BURIF, or it may have been 7 BURIF, carried out a bayonet charge to shift some Japs digging in at the far end of the garden.

On our return to brigade headquarters, the BM told me to wire in the headquarters. 'If it doesn't keep the Japs out, it will keep our chaps in,' he said. By now, about 1600 hours, 3 BURIF had virtually disintegrated, causing 7 BURIF to extend their line. 4/12 FFR now became responsible for the ridge, Lieutenant-Colonel Ivor Edwards-Stuart later recording: 'The battle raged all day and as night fell the advantage was still with us, although the Jap forces were increasing and, without reinforcements, holding Moulmein was militarily quite out of the question. During the day Brigadier Ekin had arrived to take over command of the defence – a most unjustifiable slur on Brigadier Bourke, who had previously conducted the defence most capably.'[6]

Earlier in the afternoon Smyth had told Hutton he would either have to reinforce us by at least two battalions, or withdraw us. Hutton agreed to a withdrawal, but insisted that the west bank of the Salween and Martaban must be held. Since we were having difficulty in getting reports from our units, I was sent to 4/12 FFR just before darkness fell. There the Adjutant, Atiq Rehman,[7] told me that everything was under control, but the troops were very tired. I went back to report this to Wheeler, who had remained with us after handing over to Green as BM, whereupon he collapsed at my feet, muttering, 'This can't be true! It can't be true!' But it was. I did not see Wheeler again for several days, but the collapse of two brigade majors in the space of a few hours was more than anyone could bargain for.[8]

As night fell, the Japs increased the pressure. They overran the troop of four Bofors anti-aircraft guns in the northern sector; there was a fierce fight before they were abandoned, all but one being put out of action. Around midnight Ekin told Smyth he doubted whether Moulmein could be held during daylight; Smyth authorized him to withdraw at his discretion. The steamers waiting at Martaban were moved into midstream, Ekin at the same time reducing the defensive perimeter. 7 BURIF were shaky (they had had many desertions) and 8 BURIF were exhausted. Only 4/12 FFR and the battery gave us much confidence. The Japs were now on the ridge and our headquarters was under fire. We were to move to the old telephone exchange, a brick building near Mission Street Jetty.

When this was decided, I was in another room destroying documents, and my Gurkha orderly, a reservist of the 7th Gurkhas who was plainly subnormal, omitted to pass on the information that we were about to move. Some two hours later I found myself alone in the building, the house under heavy machine gun fire, and the Japs yelling their heads off from the far side of the park, about 800 yards away. My car had fortunately not been hit but the starter motor was inclined to be temperamental. We beat a hasty retreat down the drive, Rifleman Amrit Bahadur pushing like hell while I manipulated the choke. With luck we made it. Shortly after 0200 hours I located brigade headquarters in the old telephone exchange, surrounded by blazing buildings. All Moulmein seemed to be burning.

Inside the headquarters I ran into Brigadier Bourke and the Brigade Major, Jimmy Green, who did not seem to have noticed my absence. We were to cross the Salween at dawn, they said, and in the meantime I had better find someting to eat. Bourke told me with a wry smile that he had not expected to begin this war in the same fashion as the last; apparently he had been staying with his mother in Bruges in Belgium until a few hours before the German Uhlans cantered into the town in August 1914.

Outside in the street I sat on the running board of my car while our estimable field cashier, 'Pinkie' Bodeker, handed me a mug of piping hot, sweet and milky tea. As I raised it to my mouth there was a colossal explosion, hurling me across the road until I came to rest on the pavement opposite. En route I had removed most of the skin from my left arm and leg (I was wearing a shirt and shorts at the time). I must have been mildly concussed because I can remember coming to with Bodeker bending anxiously over me, with yet another mug of tea in his hand. I was lucky to get away with no more than an extremely sore and septic side.

We began to withdraw from Moulmein at 0800 hours on 31 January. By then the Japs were on the ridge and controlled most of the north of the town. There were several counter-attacks to drive the enemy back but the situation was so confused that no one knew what was happening. When 12th Battery joined us, John Hume, the battery commander, discovered that one of his sections (two guns) was missing. Collecting some of his own men and some of 4/12 FFR, he fought his way back into the town and recovered his guns. At the Post Office Jetty 2nd Lieutenant Mehar Dass, whose Bofors anti-aircraft troop had been overrun the previous evening, learnt that the guns were not being guarded. Taking a party of men with him, he returned to the guns, dragging back the only gun that had not been disabled. Unfortunately they failed to load it onto the ferry and Mehar Dass returned to the shore to round up the rest of his party. He was later reported to have been taken prisoner.

Brigade headquarters, 4/12 FFR, 12 Mountain Battery and part of 8 BURIF were the last to cast off – at 0830 hours according to my diary:

> Decision taken at 0400 hours to evacuate at daylight . . . Terrific fires in the bazaar. Evacuation at daylight from Kaladan, North and Mission Street Jetties. Bayonet charge at daylight in Salween Park, led by 'Bonzo' Bowers [OC 8 Burma Rifles]. Evacuation completed by 0830 hours. Brigade headquarters leaves last. Large force of bombers passed over while we waited on jetty. No bombs fortunately. Japs already on South Jetty before we

> leave. Crossing very slow. Shelled the whole way over by Jap guns from Battery Point. Most uncomfortable. Crossing took about fifty minutes. On arrival in Martaban there was chaos. The Japs were shelling trains and causing casualties . . . eventually got away in train about 1200 hours. Meet Brigadier in Thaton who sends me to Kyaikto . . . Dog tired.

It was a miracle that we brought away so large a part of the garrison with relatively few casualties. Only outstandingly poor Japanese marksmanship can account for it. 'Most uncomfortable' must be the understatement of my life. Shells landed all round us but only one small ferry was hit, and that late in the afternoon. I believe the injuries I received when blown up earlier in the morning had to some extent anaesthetized me, at least mentally. I remember Brigadiers Ekin and Bourke, together with the CO of 4/12 FFR (Lieutenant-Colonel 'Donny' Edward), standing on the upper deck and admiring the view as if on a pleasure trip down the Thames to Tower Bridge.

We left behind in Moulmein 617 men, most of them missing. Many came straggling in during the course of the next few days. We lost four Bofors guns but brought away all our mortars, mountain and machine guns. Two British officers were killed. Brigadier Ekin was later to write to the Official Historian: '. . . Moulmein would have been a severe task for the best trained and most experienced staff and units, and we were not in that category! I regard this action as a very considerable achievement by the fighting troops and services, and one of the best things they did in this phase of the Burma campaign.'[9]

Ekin might have added that the mistakes that were made were largely owing to Hutton himself. It was Hutton, admittedly with Smyth's concurrence, who had insisted on replacing Brigadier Bourke by Brigadier Ekin after battle had been joined. The collapse of the Brigade Major just before battle began, followed by the collapse of his temporary replacement, was of a piece with the whole business. It merely made the muddle worse. The failure to determine until the very last moment whether or not to hold Moulmein was planning at its very worst, due entirely to Wavell's and Hutton's refusal to permit Smyth to fight the battle as he thought best. It was also inexcusable that the decision to bring the KOYLI down to Moulmein to strengthen the garrison was delayed so long that they arrived to detrain at Thaton at the moment we were disembarking from the ferries at Martaban.

It seemed to me at the time, and the succeeding years have not caused me to change my mind in any way, that the man who came out of it with the most credit was my Brigadier who, for no good reason explained to him at the time, was superseded by another in the middle of the battle. No signal was sent, no telephone explanation was given; merely the hope expressed, by General Smyth, that he would remain in a position of the greatest danger to give his replacement the benefit of his advice. There can be few instances in British military history of such a situation occurring. Nor was there any attempt made then or later, either by Generals Hutton or Smyth, to provide an explanation for their action. After disembarking at Martaban and marching part of the way thereafter towards Thaton until the trucks sent to meet them had arrived, Brigadier Ekin returned to take over command of his original brigade, the 46th, while Bourke and his staff were conveyed to Kyaikto to re-form 2nd Burma Brigade.

The most unfortunate consequence of the Moulmein affair was its damaging effect on the morale of the Burma Rifles. The 8th, almost entirely Indian, fought excellently. The 3rd in Moulmein, the 4th at Kawkareik (with the exception of the Kachin company) and the 6th in Tavoy had not done well. 'The Burma Rifles are unreliable,' Brigadier Bourke said to me as we watched a company of 3 BURIF streaming back at one stage in the battle. He said it to me forty-eight hours later when we were back in Kyaikto. I doubt if he ever changed his mind. It boded ill for the future since something like 50 per cent of the Burma Army was composed of locally-enlisted troops.

CHAPTER EIGHT

We Move to Nyaunglebin

'If you lose the initiative against a good enemy you will very soon be made to react to his thrusts; once this happens you may well lose the battle.'

High Command in War
by Field Marshal Montgomery[1]

Although Montgomery was doing no more in the above than stating the obvious, General Wavell in distant Java held identical views. He could not understand why the Japanese were making such rapid progress in Malaya and he was determined it would not be repeated in Burma. He flew to Rangoon on 23 January to have a pep-talk with Hutton, whose problems he never seems to have appreciated, although he did agree that the Burma Rifles were proving to be unreliable:

'Japanese advance in Tenasserim should not have had results it did,' he signalled the Chief of the Imperial General Staff. 'Trouble started at Tavoy where indifferent battalion Burmese Rifles . . . apparently allowed itself to be surprised and then gave in without putting up fight. Troops at Mergui were never attacked but were withdrawn rather hastily for fear they might be cut off.'[2]

Wavell's views might have been changed by something more than a cursory glance at a large-scale map but the problems provided by the topography, and the appalling state of the land communications, did not seem to dawn on him. And, it could be argued, why should they have done? If the Japanese were able to get across the country with such comparative ease, why couldn't we? Therefore, in Wavell's opinion, there was absolutely no reason why a strong brigade should not hold Moulmein indefinitely against anything Wavell thought the Japanese could deploy against them. He thought they were attacking in small parties, infiltrating round the flanks, 'jitter parties' as they came to be called later; he might have thought differently had he known that the 55th Division was about to deploy two complete *infantry regiments* in its attack on Moulmein. But he did not know this and was furious to learn on his return to Java that Moulmein had been evacuated on 31 January.

Hutton's explanation for Moulmein's evacuation included: 'Intelligence still practically nil. No air support for troops possible as total air force available about eight fighters and six Blenheims in addition to AVG who threaten to leave at any moment.'[3] We had counted fourteen Japanese bombers cruising leisurely overhead as we waited to board the ferry on 31 January. Presumably it was only the fact that they did not know the dispositions of their own forward troops which prevented them from blowing us all apart.

For those of us who had served with them, and who therefore felt to some extent responsible for the criticisms levelled against the Burma Rifles, much of it seemed to be unjust. The expansion policy had been disastrous (as indeed it proved to be in the Indian Army during 1942 and 1943). It was not our soldiers' fault that their natural skills in the jungle had been ignored, their training instead concentrated on open warfare. As was later to be demonstrated, when employed in their natural element they could make rings round the Japanese. Nor was it surprising that there should have been so many desertions when there was a retreat on their own home ground. Most of those who deserted in the early days were Karens with long memories of ill-treatment at the hands of the Burmans. It was asking a great deal of them to leave behind their womenfolk and families. Nevertheless, and there is no point in dodging the issue, from January 1942 onwards few of the British and Indian soldiers fighting in Burma felt much confidence in the Burma Rifles – apart from the 8th Battalion, which was wholly Indian in composition.[4]

During those first two weeks in February, when the campaign in Malaya was galloping to disaster and that in Burma lurching from one narrow escape to the next, it was unfortunate that our three generals were in poor physical shape. Smyth's anal fistula had reopened and was causing him a great deal of pain. His chief doctor, Mackenzie, kept him going with strychnine injections, but left him in no doubt that he was a sick man. On Mackenzie's advice Smyth wrote to Hutton on 8 February requesting some days' sick leave as soon as the situation had stabilized.

Meanwhile Hutton, anxious to finalize with Chiang Kai-shek arrangements for the introduction of Chinese troops into the campaign, left for Lashio in north Burma to meet the Generalissimo. He flew in a Lysander, piloted by Flight-Lieutenant Tate; Hutton's ADC, Lieutenant Nigel Chancellor, flew in a second Lysander, piloted by Flight-Lieutenant Mann. Lysanders did not have the range to fly from Mingalodon to Lashio in one hop; taking off at 3 pm on 2 February, they landed first at Toungoo (an AVG base) to refuel, and again at Heho in the Southern Shan States. By then it was dusk and Hutton would have preferred to stay the night there. But his pilot wanted to press on to Lashio so they took off in the gathering gloom. As Mann followed suit in the other Lysander, he suddenly realized that his ground landing lights had ceased to function.

Hutton's pilot had his problems too. Soon after leaving Heho, his intercom with Hutton failed and there was no way the two men could communicate with each other. About 8.30 pm, in total darkness, Hutton suddenly realized his pilot had changed direction – almost 180 degrees. He had lost the Mandalay–Lashio railway line he had been following and was fast running out of petrol. Spotting a cleared area of jungle, south-east of the railway, Tate attempted a crash-landing. Unfortunately one of the wings hit a tree stump, swinging the plane round and smashing the cockpit where the pilot was pinned to his seat and unconscious. Hutton, badly shaken, managed to scramble out to find the plane was on fire. For the next thirty minutes, which he was later to describe as 'the worst in my life', he endeavoured to beat out the flames with his uniform jacket.

Meanwhile the pilot of the accompanying plane, seeing the scene below but knowing he had no landing lights, decided to give the ADC the chance to parachute down. Accordingly he climbed to 2400 feet before ordering the wretched Chancellor to scramble up onto the wing and launch himself into space.

Chancellor had only flown once before, let alone ever parachuted, but he did as he was told, ending up suspended in a tree by his harness, but otherwise only cut and bruised. Mann then landed his plane alongside Tate's, concussing himself in the process and completely writing off his plane.

By then a party of villagers had arrived and they worked heroically to free the injured Tate, who died some days later from his injuries. The other pilot recovered. The shaken Hutton, accompanied by his equally shaken ADC, was taken to Lashio by rail-car where he had his meeting with Chiang Kai-shek. From all accounts it was a satisfactory one but hardly ideal; Hutton, naturally, was badly shocked, and really in no condition to conduct negotiations with the Chinese head of state.

There was, in any case, little enough time to discuss matters in detail. On arrival in Lashio, still presumably tunicless, Hutton was handed a signal ordering him to return to Rangoon next day. Wavell was expected on 4 February and wanted to confer with Hutton. At least Hutton had twenty-four hours in the train to recover from what must have been a most unpleasant experience.

Wavell's turn was yet to come. Returning from Singapore on 10 February, five days before the city's surrender, Wavell fell five or six feet over a sea wall, breaking a rib and severely bruising himself. With great difficulty he was got back to his plane and flown next day to hospital in Batavia. A difficult patient, he insisted on returning to duty long before he was fit to do so. It must be remembered that Wavell was nearly sixty, and Hutton only eight years younger, when they both survived such narrow escapes from death.

For those of us serving at the time in 17th Indian Division, it was General Smyth's state of health which concerned us the most. He was furious with Hutton for being forced to defend positions – at Kawkareik and at Moulmein – which seemed to him to be military nonsense. Nor was he hesitant in saying so. When Hutton had agreed to our withdrawal from Moulmein, he insisted that Martaban and the west bank of the River Salween should be held 'to the last man and to the last round', a catch-phrase which soon lost all kind of meaning in Burma at that time. Smyth preferred to fall back to the line of the River

Bilin, purely as an intermediary position, while he proceeded to turn the River Sittang into a really formidable defensive position. Hutton would have none of it; nor would Wavell have done, had it ever been referred to him.

Putting Ekin back in command of 46th Brigade, Smyth reinforced him with the KOYLI, just arrived from the Southern Shan States. They were still wearing their *topis* and a shortage of picks and shovels compelled them to use bayonets to dig slit trenches. They were a good battalion, in fine heart, but there were only about 250 of them. The 3/7 Gurkha Rifles with a company of KOYLI were to defend Martaban, which was being bombed and shelled daily by the Japanese. There were some sixteen miles of river line to defend, but with much of it swampy or covered in thick jungle the result was hardly in any doubt. On 7 February the enemy infiltrated across the river, established a road block which cut the defenders off from 46th Brigade headquarters at Thaton, and then proceeded to mortar the Gurkhas into submission. But the KOYLI cleared the road block with a bayonet charge and the 3/7 Gurkhas withdrew after dark on 9 February, having first destroyed their transport. They then marched for fifty miles through the jungle before arriving at Thaton. It later transpired that a message had been sent from Headquarters 17 Division ordering the withdrawal from Martaban but that the messenger had been killed at the Japanese road block. As Ekin was to comment many years later: 'The unreliability of our W/T sets within brigade groups was a constant trouble and made the passing of orders over wide areas in the jungle a hazardous business.'[5]

The immediate effect of the loss of Martaban was that the Japanese were now in control of the Salween estuary, with the ability to land troops wherever it suited them. Seaborne landings between Moulmein and Rangoon were to be added to the host of other difficulties with which Generals Hutton and Smyth had to contend.

In 2nd Burma Brigade we were engaged in that not infrequent military activity of reorganizing. Since we had left behind in Moulmein more or less everything we possessed (including the Brigadier's Dunhill pipes to which he attached a quite extraordinary sentimental value), there was not a great deal we could do to render ourselves battleworthy. Several of us had not shaved for days, others were shirtless. We had been summarily dumped in a collection of buildings on the outskirts of Kyaikto and told to get on with it. Headquarters 17 Division had moved into Kyaikto a day or two ahead of us and not surprisingly had taken over every building worth the name. Not that Kyaikto was much of a metropolis at the best of times.

Apart from the usual Medical, Supplies and Ordnance detachments, all we had been left with were the two companies of 3 BURIF who had run faster than anyone else to the jetties at Moulmein. Jacky Smyth seemed to think they would recover their *élan* if sent to defend the Sittang bridgehead, which seemed to us to be about the most important task in the entire Division. Brigadier Bourke made the point forcefully when the General came to see us that same night, but nothing seemed to come of it.

On the following day, Friday 6 February, we were formed up on the platform of Kyaikto station to greet General Wavell, no less. He arrived in some kind of rail-car, accompanied by Hutton. Wavell looked very tough and the reverse of welcoming. After casting a glance of near-loathing at the lot of us, it seemed to me that he fixed me with his one good eye (he lost the other in the First World War), and then barked out, 'Take back all you have lost!' I did not dare open my mouth but I hope my expression showed that I would certainly do my best. Then he passed on to speak to someone he obviously recognized, leaving me to my thoughts, and to the Brigade Major's rebuke ringing in my ear, 'For God's sake, Jimmy, next time you intend to chat with the Commander-in-Chief, make sure you shave first!'

Wavell, Hutton and Smyth then departed, presumably to visit the forward troops. 'I bet he gives Jacky Smyth a rocket,' the Brigadier told me. 'Neither he nor Hutton are in favour of the Divisional Commander's plan to fall back behind the Sittang.' Surprisingly, however, according to Smyth, Wavell hardly uttered a word, inquired about no plans, and offered no advice. Smyth had asked him to say a few words to the senior members of his staff and brigadiers but was sadly disappointed by Wavell's response. He told them the Japanese were overrated, their fighting ability was exaggerated, and that he was pleased that General Smyth was planning an offensive to drive them out of Burma.[6]

Our Intelligence (or lack of it) was such that on the very day Wavell was day-dreaming aloud, the Japanese 33rd Division, well-seasoned after several years' campaigning in China, crossed the Burma–Thai border in the vicinity of Pa-an, on the east bank of the Salween about twenty miles upstream from Moulmein. Its Commander, Lieutenant-General Shozo Sakurai, had orders to cover the northern flank of the 55th Division as it advanced along the road/railway axis Martaban–Thaton–Kyaikto, the objective being the destruction of 17th Indian Division and the seizure intact of the bridge over the Sittang. Sakurai was to make use of the jungle tracks running east to west for his advance. General Iida moved his advanced headquarters of XVth Army to Moulmein in order to coordinate the operation.

During the night of 10 February II/215 Infantry Regiment crossed the Salween at Kunzeik and soon became involved in a fierce battle with the 7 Baluchis of 46th Brigade. The Baluchis were a young and unseasoned battalion but they fought like veterans. Although they were overrun by the morning of 12 February, the Japanese had been forced to deploy the whole of 215 Infantry Regiment (i.e. a complete brigade) before the Baluchis were defeated. One of their officers, Captain Siri Kanth Korla, who later became a general in the Indian Army, was awarded an immediate DSO for gallantry. Only five officers, three VCOs and sixty-five soldiers managed to get back to brigade headquarters at Thaton; their CO, Lieutenant-Colonel Dyer was killed in action.

Smyth was now confronted by *two* Japanese divisions. Although he had been reinforced by 48th Gurkha Brigade (Brigadier Noël Hugh-Jones), and now had in addition 46th Brigade (under Ekin), 16th Brigade (under Jones), and 2nd Burma Brigade (ourselves), both 16th Brigade and ourselves had been badly mauled – in fact *we* hardly existed as a fighting formation. On 5 February the Brigadier had sent me to see how what remained of 3 BURIF were getting on at the Sittang. In my diary I wrote: 'The road to Sittang still in very rudimentary state – just a dusty track. God help us if we have to withdraw along it. Why, oh why, didn't we start building strategic roads two years ago?' I went on to say that I did not think much of 3 BURIF, although I was glad to see that L. G. Wheeler was back with them.

We had settled down to our task of preparing Kyaikto for defence, although picks, shovels and barbed wire were in short supply, when on 12 February we were told to move to Nyaunglebin, on the railway between Pegu and Toungoo, where we were to come under the command of the GOC lines of communication (Major-General Wakeley). We were to be responsible for some fifty miles of river line, from just above the Sittang bridge to Shwegyin, on the east bank of the river about fifteen miles from Nyaunglebin. There were local ferries at Shwegyin and Kunzeik, the latter ten miles north of the bridge. 'All we get to look after some fifty miles,' I wrote, 'are 3 and 7 BURIF both about 350 strong. No artillery, no sappers, no medical. Scrape together 7 lorries and one jeep by begging, borrowing and stealing. Most of us glad to be leaving 17 Div but sorry to be out of the fray.'

Brigadier Bourke took me with him on his first visit to the Sittang bridge after receiving his orders. There he told the GOC that he could not accept responsibility for defending such a wide front without at least one more infantry battalion, preferably British or the 4/12 FFR. His protest was noted – he delivered it very forcefully as I recall – and later he put it in writing, pointing out that the ferry site at Kunzeik was absolutely vital and must be strongly defended. He was to be proved right within a few weeks, since it was by this route that 33rd Japanese Division crossed the Sittang in its encircling movement on Rangoon, but we were not given another battalion.

We arrived in Nyaunglebin by train on 15 February. In view of the fact that within three days 17th Division was to be involved in fierce fighting along the Bilin River, the comments in my diary are interesting: 'Nyaunglebin not much of a town – about 10,000 inhabitants . . . All very pleasant and quiet. War seems a long way away . . . Life still normal here – trains running, bazaar open . . . Trains pour through from Rangoon loaded with refugees. Hear on wireless of heavy fighting on Bilin. That is no obstacle for the Japs.'

Headquarters 2 Burma Brigade. *Left to right:* Lieutenant W. Cruikshank, Major S. J. H. Green, Brigadier A. J. H. Bourke, Captain C. G. Merton, 2nd-Lieutenant W. Smith.

General Iida, GOC XVth Japanese Army.

Japanese assault at the Sittang.

Japanese advancing into Yenangyaung.

Major-General D. T. Cowan.

Lieutenant-General 'Vinegar Joe' Stilwell.

Lieutenant-General T. J. Hutton.

Major-General J. G. Smyth, VC.

The Governor of Burma and General Alexander (*above*).

Generals Alexander and Bruce Scott at Nyaunglebin, March 1942 (*right*).

Below left to right:
General Bruce Scott, Sir John Wise, Generals Alexander, Wavell and Slim, and Brigadier Davis.

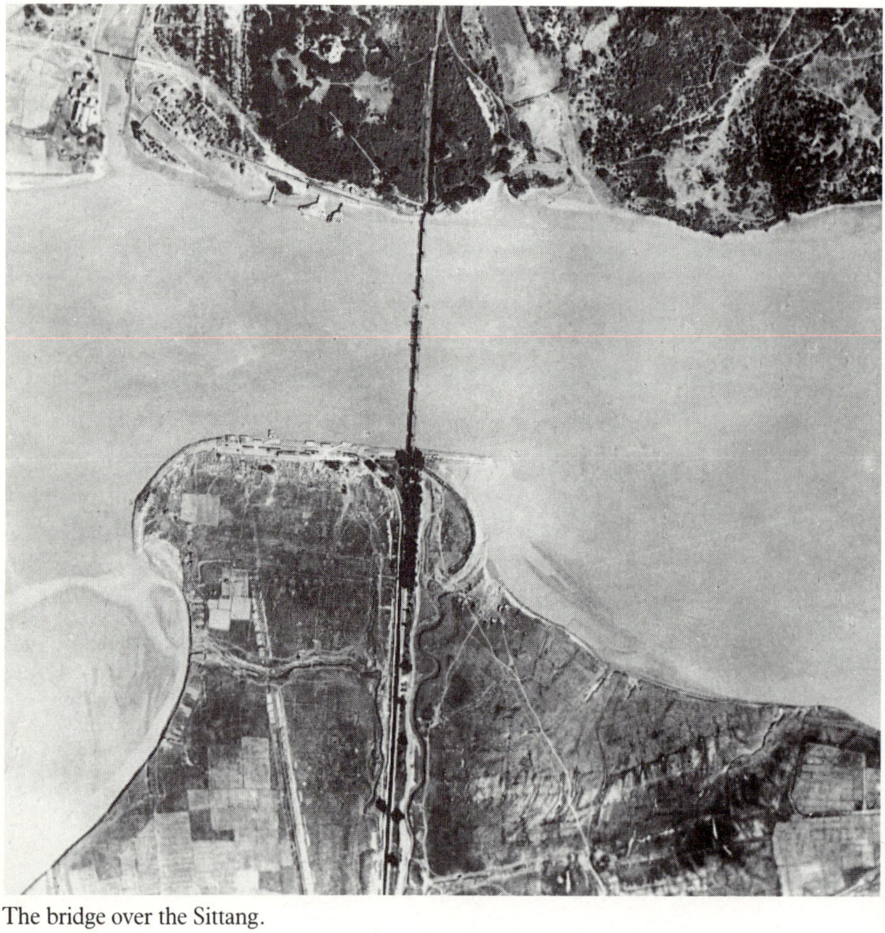

The bridge over the Sittang.

Japanese troops firing on the bridge.

Japanese soldier crossing the bridge after its capture.

Lieutenant-Colonel G. T. Chadwick, CO 2 KOYLI, before the Retreat, in Maymo (*above*), and three months later, during the Retreat, collecting firewood near Kalewa.

CHAPTER NINE

The Sittang Disaster

'Never fight with your backs to a broad river. It is an invitation to disaster.'

Sir Harry Smith on Aliwal, 28 January 1846[1]

If the battle fought on the River Sittang on 23 February 1942 did not lose us Burma, it certainly lost us Rangoon – which in the end came to the same thing. It must therefore rank as being one of the most decisive battles fought during the decline and fall of the British Empire, although at the time it was the surrender at Singapore eight days previously that filled the headlines of the world's newspapers.

I first saw the Sittang bridge on the morning of 6 March 1941 when the train carrying 4 BURIF from Mandalay to Moulmein passed over the river. I remember it clearly because many of our Karens came from Tenasserim and there were loud cheers as we drew up beside the platform of Mokpalin station for our morning meal. Later I walked back with *Subedar* Aung Bwint, our senior Karen GCO, to inspect the bridge. It was an impressive piece of engineering, more than 500 yards long from shore to shore, below which the river swirled at an impressive rate, although March was the dry season and the river was low. Upstream of the bridge there was an antiquated ferry, adequate to carry the occasional vehicle or bullock cart from shore to shore, but no more than that.

We had travelled thirty miles from Pegu before we arrived at the bridge, for most of the time along an embankment raised high above the rice fields. Divided one from the other by low banks, they were set hard as concrete at that time of the year; by the July monsoon they would turn into a swamp stretching as far as the eye could see. Only a cart track ran alongside the railway, between the watering stop at Waw, sixteen miles east of Pegu, and the bridge itself; but along the track there also ran the telephone line linking Rangoon with Moulmein and areas farther south. Eight miles short of the western end of the bridge was a small village, Abya. The countryside was flat with very little cover, apart from the orchards round the scattered villages.

The east bank was different. A collection of three low hills overlooked the railway line; they were covered with thick scrub jungle. The line itself turned sharply south before entering quite a deep cutting, beyond which was the railway station. Immediately overlooking the bridge was a hill crowned by a pagoda, and 500 yards further on was a large statue of the Buddha. From there, looking east, there seemed to be nothing but jungle. Aung Bwint explained there was a track of sorts running through the jungle to Kyaikto, where the road to Thaton and Martaban began, but it was only usable in the dry weather, and then solely by the occasional bus, truck or cart. He came himself from Thaton and was familiar with the countryside. During the building of the bridge, he said, a great deal of stone had to be quarried out of the hills south of Mokpalin, Aung Bwint's father acting as contractor for some of the labour employed. The quarries were still in use, a two-mile spur of line connecting them with Mokpalin railway station.

The bridge became of much more interest to me after Headquarters 2 Burma Brigade was established at Kyaikto on our arrival there from Moulmein. They were working hard to plank it for the passage of trucks; Merton and I spent a morning watching the Sappers toiling away to cut the timber required. 'Rather like building the pyramids,' Merton commented, adding, 'and we've left it too late as usual.' We walked up to Pagoda Hill where a platoon or two of 3 BURIF were digging slit trenches, not very enthusiastically, and then across the bridge to the far side where some anti-aircraft gunners (I think they were Burma Auxiliary Force) were building up sandbag emplacements. The trains seemed to be running normally although everything stopped the moment the noise of a plane was heard;

even at this very early stage in the campaign we were becoming acutely air-conscious.

The journey back to Kyaikto in the back of a badly-sprung Chevrolet truck along a track thick with dust had little to commend it, but we were rescued by the stationmaster at Mokpalin who was proposing to visit his opposite number at Kyaikto in one of those curious contraptions propelled by a crew of four men working a kind of up-and-down balance which I remembered having seen in American films. We bowled along, about eight feet above the paddy fields that stretched down to the river bank. On the other side of the line there was almost continuous scrub jungle, intersected by numerous dry *chaungs* draining down from the high ground to the coast.

Arriving back at Kyaikto, I set off for divisional headquarters on my daily mission to scrounge a few more essential bits of military equipment. There I was introduced to a new Brigadier, just arrived from Rangoon, it appeared. He was smoking an enormous cheroot and in some curious fashion gave one a feeling of great confidence. His name was Cowan, until a few days previously Director of Military Training at Army Headquarters in India. Hutton had sent him to Smyth as a spare brigadier, just in case Hutton wanted to sack one – *pour encourager les autres* – but Smyth chose instead to keep Cowan, whose worth he greatly valued, as his right-hand man. He proposed to employ him as his Brigadier General Staff, an appointment usually reserved for Corps and higher headquarters. On 12 February he sent Cowan to Rangoon to ask Hutton for permission to do this, at the same time entrusting him with an extremely important message for the army commander. Cowan was to make clear Smyth's fear of being outflanked on his left by what now appeared to be another Japanese Division (33rd) which had virtually destroyed 7/10 Baluch at Kunzeik, and done the same to 5/17 Dogras at Duyinzeik. 17th Division was becoming dangerously dispersed as Smyth endeavoured to cover all likely enemy approaches, including seaborne landings on the Gulf of Martaban. In Smyth's judgement there was a very real danger that he might be cut off from the Sittang crossing. He wanted therefore to concentrate on the line of the River Bilin, with permission to withdraw to the Sittang *in sufficient time* to make it a strong defensive position.

Cowan returned with his mission only half accomplished. Hutton agreed that he should act as Smyth's BGS (could it have been because he had more faith in Cowan than in Smyth?), but he refused to give permission for any withdrawal from the Bilin without his (Hutton's) express sanction. On the next day, 13 February, Hutton informed Wavell (and New Delhi) that although he had every intention of fighting it out east of the Sittang, it might become necessary to withdraw behind that river. This came as a great shock to the Governor of Burma and his Council, increasing the alarm and despondency among those who still remained in Rangoon.

It probably infuriated Wavell, recovering from his injuries received in Singapore, which was about to capitulate. When it was followed by the news that Smyth had already withdrawn to the Bilin (on 15 February), to which Hutton also took exception, Wavell sent Hutton one of his angriest signals. But the fact remains that Smyth got back behind the Bilin just in time, the 33rd Japanese Division launching its first attacks against Smyth on 16 February. The battle that followed, involving a reinforced 16th Brigade (under Jones), and the newly arrived 48th Gurkha Brigade (under Hugh-Jones), was the only battle fought by 17th Division *as a division* while under Smyth's command. Although the Japanese affected to make light of it later, they were in fact brought to a halt in very tough fighting of a kind they had not hitherto experienced in Burma.

The Bilin was no real obstacle, Smyth's real fear being that his left flank, which was in jungle, might be turned, and his right, where the river entered the Gulf of Martaban, might also be turned by seaborne landings. It was extremely hot, acute thirst adding yet another dimension to the normal exhaustion of battle. 2 KOYLI suffered particularly from the heat, but fought very well. Smyth sent Hutton a situation report on the afternoon of 18 February informing him that 16th Brigade had been 'fought to a standstill', and another later: '. . . I have put in my last battalion which is really capable of active operations, i.e. 4/12th. Having done so I hear of a party of enemy approaching along the coast, which we shall try and deal with as best we can.'[2]

At this stage of the battle we in 2nd Burma Brigade, nearly 100 miles away from the Sittang bridge at Nyaunglebin, were responsible for the bridge defences. We had extremely unreliable communications with 3 BURIF, defending the bridge, and hardly any transport; I think we had succeeded in misappropriating a staff car for the Brigadier. Back in Rangoon the 2nd Duke of Wellington's Regiment, just disembarked from Calcutta with all their transport still to follow from India, were ordered by Hutton personally to send a company by rail to strengthen the bridge garrison. This was soon countermanded; the 7 Baluchis, still recovering from their hard fight at Kunzeik, were sent to Kyaikto. This chopping and changing, a great deal of which was countermanded almost as soon as it was ordered, had in many instances to be conducted through the medium of the Burma Post & Telegraph which continued to operate with quite remarkable efficiency, if with a considerable degree of insecurity where the enemy was concerned.

On 19 February, Brigadier Bourke took Merton and me with him to see exactly what was happening on the Sittang. Dropping me off in Pegu, with instructions to collect as much transport as I could lay my hands on, he and Merton went on to Sittang by rail-car. There, as it happened, he met the divisional commander, telling him that he could not possibly hold the line of the Sittang from opposite Nyaunglebin to the bridge without more troops. Merton, reporting the conversation to me later, said Bourke could hardly have made his point more plain. He also put it in writing.

In the meantime I visited every transport pound in Pegu, stuffed full of American Lease-Lend vehicles like jeeps (worth their weight in gold to us), and succeeded in laying hands on several of them. I also ran into Lieutenant-Colonel Basil Owen, commanding the 'Dukes', who had just arrived in Pegu ahead of the rest of his battalion. 'God alone knows where we go from here, Jimmy,' he said. 'Have you any idea?' I told him that my Brigadier was at that very moment attempting to discover the answer to that question, and we parted, neither of us any the wiser.

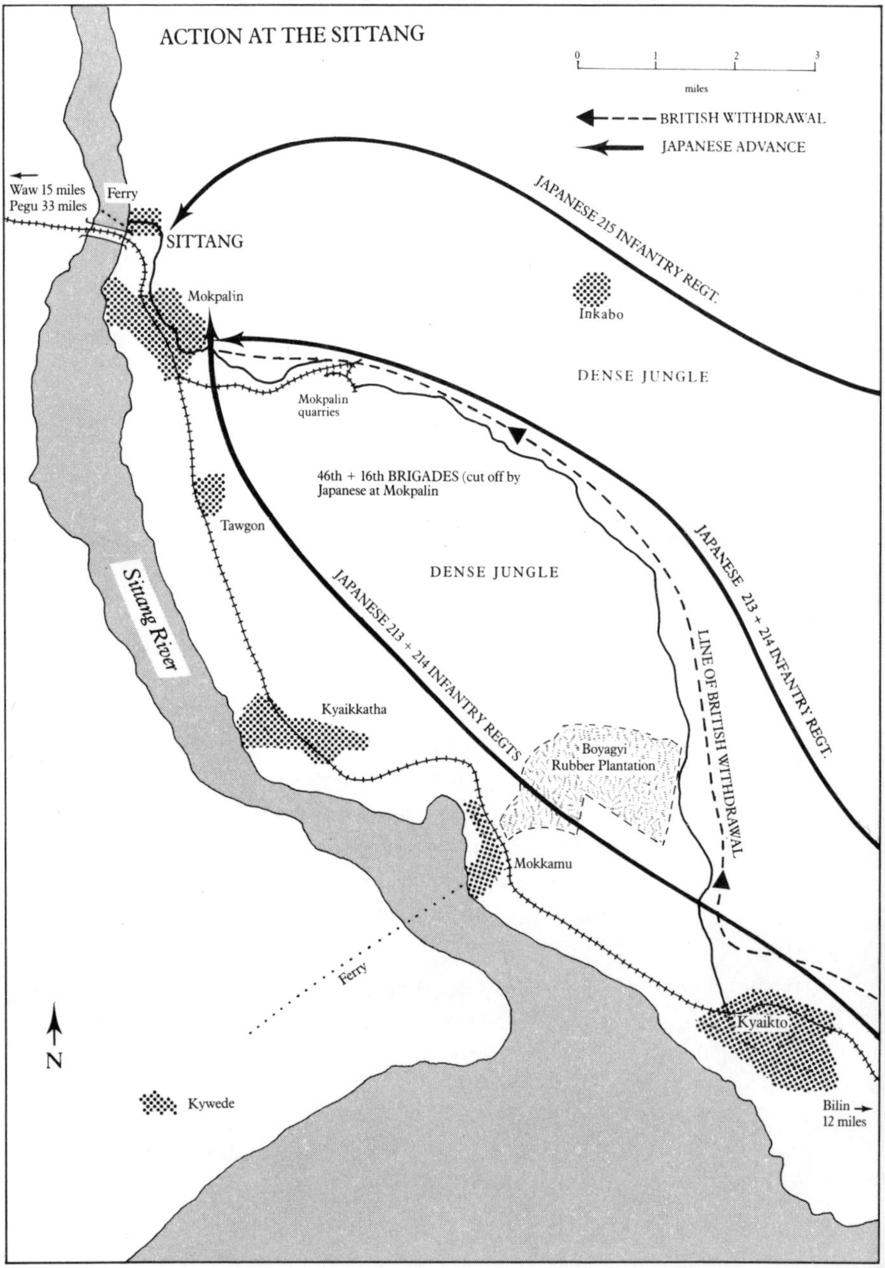
ACTION AT THE SITTANG
0 1 2 3
miles
BRITISH WITHDRAWAL
JAPANESE ADVANCE
Waw 15 miles
Pegu 33 miles
Ferry
SITTANG
JAPANESE 215 INFANTRY REGT.
Mokpalin
Inkabo
DENSE JUNGLE
Mokpalin
quarries
46th + 16th BRIGADES (cut off by
Japanese at Mokpalin
Tawgon
DENSE JUNGLE
JAPANESE 213 + 214 INFANTRY REGT.
JAPANESE 213 + 214 INFANTRY REGTS
LINE OF BRITISH WITHDRAWAL
Sittang River
Kyaikkatha
Boyagyi
Rubber Plantation
Mokkamu
Ferry
Kyaikto
N
Kywede
Bilin
12 miles

Hutton visited Smyth that same day and reluctantly gave him permission to withdraw from the Bilin line to the Sittang as soon as he thought it necessary. Hutton confirmed this by signal on his return to Rangoon. Headquarters 17 Division acted immediately to issue orders for the withdrawal, the Bilin being a good thirty-five miles east of the Sittang, with enemy air activity making day movement difficult. Moreover, since both 16th and 48th Brigades were in close contact with the enemy, breaking off action during daylight would probably be impossible. However 46th Brigade under Ekin was moved to the Boyagyi Rubber Estate outside Kyaikto to be available for counter-attack if required. Smyth's plan was that 48th Brigade (all Gurkha and probably the freshest) would cover 16th Brigade's withdrawal after dark on 19 February, thereafter breaking contact itself and moving straight back to the Sittang bridge to act as the close bridge garrison. This would mean a march of more than thirty miles across country, most of it at night, much of it in scrub jungle, with the frequent bunds between paddy fields impeding both men and mules.

16th Brigade, once back in Kyaikto, would join forces with 46th Brigade, acting as rearguard. Divisional headquarters and all available transport would be sent back to Mokpalin after last light on 19 February. Unfortunately, however, the planking of the bridge to take vehicles had yet to be completed, as had its preparation for demolition. It was therefore vital that the enemy should not be permitted to follow up immediately.

Ekin, commanding 46th Brigade, was not happy with this plan. Since his brigade was nearest to the bridge, he considered he should move back there at once, together with as much transport as could be collected, and prepare a strong bridgehead. He was also convinced that the Japanese would carry out their usual outflanking tactics, working round through the jungle north of the Kyaikto–Sittang track, establishing road blocks, and, if possible, rushing the eastern end of the bridge. He therefore begged Smyth to let him take 46th Brigade back to the bridge at once.

Smyth, concerned to break contact with his 16th and 48th Brigades, uncertain even if this could be done successfully, would not agree. He said he must hold Kyaikto as a firm base until both the other brigades were through. He agreed with Ekin that the enemy might well try to outflank him on the north but he had sent out reconnaissance troops to provide him with prior warning of any such attempt. They were to let him down badly.

It is very easy to be wise after the event, particularly when writing of war when everyone is tired, strained, short of sleep, operating mostly on guesswork, not always confident either of one's troops or their commanders. Smyth, additionally, was in great physical pain, not helped by his determination to visit as many of his soldiers as possible. The fact remains that had he taken Ekin's advice, the disaster at the Sittang might never have occurred.[3]

The Japanese had been disagreeably surprised by the strength of the resistance they had encountered along the Bilin. General Sakurai concluded that the best way to dislodge 17th Division would be to use his complete 215th Regiment to outflank the British line from the north, at the same time landing part of the 55th Division from the sea in order to turn the British southern flank. This plan, with the admittedly limited objective of clearing the main Bilin–Kyaikto highway, was to take place during the night of 19/20 February. All preparations for it were being made when the Japanese Signals intercepted a message in clear from a unit or formation in 17th Division giving orders for the withdrawal to Kyaikto. It was a gift from the gods. Sakurai at once ordered 215th Regiment, less one battalion, to march instead directly for the Sittang, using only jungle paths and avoiding Smyth's northern flank. The bridge was to be taken by *coup de main*. The remainder of 33rd Division was to follow up the retreating British, and 214th Regiment was to capture the station at Mokpalin, thus completing the British encirclement. The race for the bridge was on, but the Japanese, by intelligent anticipation and a good deal of luck, gave themselves a head start.

16th Brigade managed to break contact, helped by the morning mists, and after a long, thirsty and exhausting march, much interrupted by air attacks, reached Kyaikto by the evening of 20 February. 48th Brigade found it harder to disengage, one of its battalions, the 9 Jats, only getting away after support from the RAF, some of whose bombs caused them casualties. But by 2230 hours on 20 February Brigadier Hugh-Jones had his brigade back at Kyaikto, resting their weary limbs under the rubber trees of the Boyagyi Estate. Most of Headquarters 17 Division was back at Mokpalin, apart from Smyth himself and a small tactical headquarters.

During that day, when the tired but by no means despondent 16th and 48th Brigades were trudging back to Kyaikto, there arrived at Kyaikto station the best part of 600 officers and men of the 2nd Duke of Wellington's Regiment, still minus much of their transport but otherwise the freshest troops to have been seen in those parts for several weeks. The way this battalion was mishandled still beggars belief, forty-two years after the event.

Sent up from Rangoon the previous day, the most obvious task for them would have been to dig themselves in round the Sittang bridgehead. Instead they were bundled on to Kyaikto, detrained on 20 February, and ordered to withdraw to the Sittang forty-eight hours later. Within that time they had lost most of their weapons, all their transport, all their kit and upwards of 300 well-trained and well-officered troops. God alone knows what the 'Old Duke' would have said about it, had he been still alive!

Whoever was controlling the situation at the bridgehead, it certainly was not Headquarters 2 Burma Infantry Brigade. On 21 February, according to my diary, an American who appeared to have gone off his head was driving up the Pegu–Toungoo road stopping every Lease-Lend truck he met and setting it on fire. We managed in the end to persuade him to let us have several trucks (I cannot remember how many but certainly a dozen or more), and an even more valuable consignment of jeeps. For some weeks at least Headquarters 2 Burma Brigade was mobile again.

The first troops to move back from Kyaikto were 4/12 FFR early on 21 February, accompanied by the Malerkotla Sappers & Miners who were to prepare the bridge for demolition. The bridge was not yet ready for traffic but some vehicles had been transported across the river by the power ferries that had been placed there. Then the Japanese Air Force came into prominence, causing endless delays as truck after truck, negotiating the narrow, dusty track through the jungle from Kyaikto, went up in flames.

It has been claimed that twenty-four hours were lost in organizing the withdrawal. Wavell's Dispatch says it was 'badly mismanaged by HQ 17 Div'. Davies, Hutton's BGS, described it as 'disgracefully mismanaged'. The grounds for such severe criticism are not easy to establish. Smyth had wanted to get away behind the Sittang *days* before either Wavell or Hutton would agree he could do so. As it was, Hutton's written permission did not arrive until the evening of 19 February, after which orders had to be issued and brigade commanders briefed. By then it was dark, several units were in close contact with the enemy, communications were appalling and everyone was tired, hungry and thirsty. Kyaikto, the first stage of the withdrawal, was fifteen miles away, with wounded to be carried and transport to be negotiated over *chaungs* and the bunds between paddy fields. Many of the troops had been engaged in battle for as long as seventy-two hours.

After Kyaikto, it became incomparably more difficult. The single track, unsurfaced, pock-marked with bomb craters, barely wide enough for one vehicle to pass another, with those carrying wounded to be given priority, was hedged in by jungle so thick that men easily became lost if they wandered far from the track. Control over any sub-unit much larger than a platoon was virtually impossible. There were no 'walkie-talkies' and communications depended mostly on 'runners', many of whom lost their way. It was blazingly hot and water bottles were soon emptied. No one knew anything about the enemy, but rumours abounded. Last night he had been howling round the flanks, making the night hideous with his yells and mortar bombs; today he had simply vanished into thin air. A 'jitter party' had attacked Smyth's tactical headquarters at 0500 hours on 21 February, achieving little but adding to the general feeling of alarm and despondency. Complete rifle companies became cut off from the rest of their battalions (Captain Dennis Simmonds of the 'Dukes' was a case in point), and went wandering round in circles until they either regained the track, or found some other route towards the river.

Breakdown in communications, a general feature of the campaign at the time, meant that for several crucial hours Headquarters 17 Division was out of touch with the Burma Army and its brigades.

The situation at the Sittang on the morning of 21 February was that the bridgehead was held by 3 BURIF, only about 200 strong, and one company of 2nd Duke of Wellington's Regiment which had arrived at the bridge in the early hours of 20 February. The 'Dukes' company was in reserve on the west bank, with orders to counter-attack across the bridge if required. Just before dark on 21 February 4/12 FFR arrived to strengthen the bridge defences; they had had a hellish march from Kyaikto, attacked from the air by both the Japanese and the RAF. Lieutenant-Colonel Donny Edward, the splendid CO of 4/12 FFR, was dismayed to find so little had been done to build up the defences, but decided to wait until first light on 22 February to remedy this deficiency. There was a mass of administrative transport jammed bumper to bumper between the river and Mokpalin, where the 7 Baluchis, greatly reduced in numbers, were guarding the supply dumps. Only one span of the bridge had been prepared for demolition, the Malerkotla Sappers (Major Orgill) setting to work as soon as they arrived from Kyaikto to improve on this.

The modern British Army carries its house on its back. This means a great number of vehicles of all shapes and sizes. It also means many small units involved with supplies, ammunition, casualties, etc. All these and more were lined up, waiting to cross the bridge, in an area about the equivalent in extent of Green Park, with only dirt tracks intersecting it and overlooked by a steep-sided and jungle-covered ridge. There were no military police for traffic control, a problem that was to remain almost throughout the retreat from Burma. Communication was restricted to word of mouth, mostly from the overworked staff officers of Headquarters 17 Division, the larger part of which had arrived at Mokpalin by 21 February. No one knew precisely what was happening.

As if the gods were truly lined up on this occasion with the Japanese, it seems that someone got the bomb-line wrong when briefing the few remaining RAF and VAG crew's at Mingalodon. Extensive inquiries by Air Vice-Marshal D. F. Stevenson, Air Officer Commanding in Burma, failed to identify the culprit, but the fact remains that throughout 21 February the soldiers wearily withdrawing along the congested Kyaikto to Mokpalin track were persistently attacked by their own aircraft, as well as by the Japanese. It required several hours to sort this out, given the appalling communications with Rangoon, by which time the withdrawal had been considerably delayed.

1/4 Gurkha Rifles of 48th Brigade reached the Mokpalin quarries in the evening of 21 February having been machine-gunned and bombed from the air during their march. One of their companies was missing, and everyone was exhausted. They had lost touch with 48th Brigade headquarters. At 0100 hours on 22 February the CO was told to take his battalion across the bridge immediately to deal with a possible 'drop' by Japanese parachute troops to seize the *western* approaches to the bridge. There Lieutenant-Colonel Joe Lentaigne, commanding 1/4 Gurkha Rifles, was to take under command the company of 'Dukes' already alerted to deal with such an attack.

Smyth had by now arrived at the Sittang, followed shortly afterwards by Brigadier Hugh-Jones and Headquarters 48 Brigade. The transport was beginning to cross the bridge. Smyth ordered Hugh-Jones to take charge of the bridge defences, establishing his headquarters on the west bank. Meanwhile, the staff officer from Headquarters Burma Army, who had brought the information about the possible parachute attack, also told Smyth that 7th Armoured Brigade had arrived in Rangoon, and were unloading their own tanks. It would be two or three days before they could arrive in the battle zone.

There was no news of the Japanese. Smyth, worried lest his division was being outflanked, had positioned FF2 about five miles north-east of the Kyaikto–Mokpalin track, to provide warning of any Japanese advance. FF2, almost entirely Indian in composition (with one or two British officers), was mounted on Burma ponies, lightly armed and intended for reconnaissance duties only. The officer commanding FF2 divided his force in two, the better to watch the most likely enemy lines of approach.

At 1430 hours on 21 February both parts of FF2 found themselves heavily engaged by the Japanese advance guards of 215th Regiment making for the Sittang, and withdrew north-west to the river. Crossing by country boats some seven miles above the bridge, they then retreated across country to Pegu. *No report of this engagement by FF2 with the enemy, rapidly closing on the bridge, ever reached Smyth.**

At this time 16th and 46th Brigades were still in Kyaikto, sheltering in the Boyagyi rubber estate where they had been attacked on several occasions by the RAF and AVG, as well as by Japanese aircraft. The two brigade commanders, Jones and Ekin, had agreed that 16th Brigade was to start its march to the Sittang at 0515 on 22 February, to be followed immediately by 46th Brigade.

There had been another disaster during the night of 21 February when a truck overturned while crossing the Sittang bridge. It took two hours to remove the obstruction but by dawn the 1/4 Gurkha Rifles were digging in on the west bank. Headquarters 48 Brigade with Brigadier Hugh-Jones was doing likewise, and Headquarters 17 Division was on its way to Abya, from where signal communications with Headquarters Burma Army could be assured. So far, it seemed, so good.

At 0830 hours on that Sunday morning, 22 February, a detachment of the Baluchis, moving along the railway line from Mokpalin to take up positions west of the bridge, came under heavy mortar fire. The Japanese had arrived and were within an ace of cutting off Smyth's retreat. Smyth at the time was east of the bridge, inspecting 1/4 Gurkha Rifles' defences. On his way there he had stopped to talk with Colonel Mackenzie, his senior doctor, who had spent the night with one of the field ambulances waiting to cross the bridge. Smyth was only half way back across the bridge when firing broke out as the Japanese attacked from the north-east, taking Mackenzie and many others prisoner. It was to be a long three years before Mackenzie was released from captivity in Rangoon Jail.

* Author's italics.

There then followed a state of total confusion that continued for the next forty-eight hours. No one knew what was happening, other than in his immediate vicinity. The Japanese, who had been driven forward by forced marches along jungle tracks, were in little better position. Men acted on the spur of the moment, not always wisely. Some 300 *sampans* had been collected on the west bank of the river to help in the withdrawal; all were destroyed, as were the three power-driven ferries, lest they fell into enemy hands. Transport was set on fire, mule drivers panicked, abandoning their animals, and many made a mad rush for the bridge. The jampacked mass of transport at Mokpalin would have been there for the Japanese to seize had it not been for the 2/5 Gurkha Rifles, newly arrived from Kyaikto, who cleared the railway station and fought their way through scrub jungle almost to the summit of Buddha Hill. They were shortly joined by 1/3 Gurkha Rifles, also newly arrived after an exhausting night march.

4/12 FFR added to their laurels at the Sittang. They were moving up to take over the key position of Pagoda Hill when the Japanese launched their attack. The Burma Rifles broke almost immediately, although the remainder of this weak battalion subsequently did well that day. 4/12 FFR had to fight hard to retake Pagoda Hill, where Captain S. H. J. F. Maneckshaw[4] was severely wounded, receiving the immediate award of the Military Cross. 7/10 Baluch were then brought up to strengthen the bridgehead, as was 'D' Company of the 'Dukes', once more ordered back to the east bank. That afternoon 1/4 Gurkha Rifles were also brought back across the Sittang to strengthen the bridgehead.

Three weeks later, Lieutenant-Colonel Abraham was to report, 'In the jungle the Japs had complete moral ascendancy.'[5] He was not far wrong. It required two long, hard years of training before the British and Indian armies were able to wrest it from them. Perhaps it was the feeling of isolation which was so frightening. Where were the enemy? What would happen if one were wounded? Who would know? Panic was never far from the surface. The slightest rustle led to prickles all over. Trigger fingers became itchy, although ammunition was in short supply.

Back in Kyaikto, on the morning of 22 February, Brigadier Jones's 16th Brigade had marched at dawn for the Sittang. Progress was slow along the dusty track and attack from the air led to frequent dispersal into the jungle. Both Jones and Ekin (46th Brigade) had been warned by Smyth at 0100 hours that the Japanese were moving round the northern flank, Smyth emphasizing the need 'to get a move on'. But with only one track (and that inadequate) with vehicles, wounded and all the other paraphernalia of war to be moved along it under constant threat from air attack and ambush, the pace was certain to be slow. It was late afternoon before 16th Brigade reached Mokpalin to find fighting in progress, preventing any farther movement towards the bridge.

46th Brigade, following behind, had become separated from 16th Brigade by as much as one mile; this delay was caused by the need to wait for a company which had been out on patrol. The Japanese, following up on the flanks, rapidly established a road block. Fierce fighting failed to dislodge the enemy. Eventually Brigadier Ekin decided to sweep the jungle west of the track, taking with him about 400 men. They made slow progress and eventually lost contact with each other, as well as with the main body, the remnants under Ekin eventually reaching the railway south of Mokpalin after dark. The 'Dukes', together with 3/7 Gurkha Rifles and what was left of 5/17 Dogras, eventually cleared the block, joining up with 16th Brigade around 1700 hours, tired and thirsty after marching fourteen miles and fighting a hard battle. 4 BURIF, part of 46th Brigade, had marched along the railway from Kyaikto, encountering no opposition; a company of the 'Dukes', cut off from the main body, also followed the railway line, at one stage having to take to the jungle to avoid about 1000 Japanese who were advancing on the Sittang by this route. It is hard to understand why Brigadiers Jones and Ekin did not select the railway, rather than the track through the jungle, for their marching troops. Vehicles, of course, were another matter.

The scene that Sunday night was one of indescribable confusion, with Brigadier Hugh-Jones fighting hard to retain the bridgehead against repeated Japanese attacks. 16th and 46th

Brigades, or what was left of them, were cut off at Mokpalin one mile away. Communications had failed, trucks were burning, stragglers were trying to work their way through the thick scrub to the bridge, officers were searching for their soldiers, soldiers were looking for their units. No one had eaten since dawn. 17th Division's artillery (5 Field Battery, Burma Auxiliary Force and 5, 12 (one section), 15 and 28 Mountain Batteries), grouped at Mokpalin Railway Station, were in almost continuous action, sometimes firing over open sights, in an attempt to blast a way through to the bridge.

Smyth had moved back to his advance headquarters at Abya, seven or eight miles from the bridge, after nightfall. He was due to meet Hutton the following morning near Pegu, highly inconvenient though this would be. Smyth had placed Hugh-Jones in command of the bridgehead, impressing on him that the Japanese must not be allowed to capture the bridge.

The battle raged throughout the night. Enemy pressure on the bridge increased, at one stage causing 3 BURIF to break and run for safety across the bridge, but the rest of the line held firm. At 0330 hours on 23 February, however, the Japanese infiltrated onto the railway line, resisting all attempts by 1/4 Gurkha Rifles to dislodge them; from this position they could bring fire to bear on the entire length of bridge. Hugh-Jones, who had no means of knowing what had happened to the other two battalions in his Brigade, 1/3 and 2/5 Gurkha Rifles, tried desperately to make contact with the other two brigades but without success. Meanwhile Jones and Ekin, equally in the dark, were planning a joint attack towards the bridge as soon as it was light.

As dawn approached, Japanese pressure on the bridgehead increased. There was almost continuous firing by mortars, machine guns and light artillery. Major Orgill, commanding the Malerkotla Sappers who were responsible for blowing the bridge, wondered how it could be done in daylight under such heavy fire. Hugh-Jones, responsibility weighing heavily upon him, wondered the same. What then transpired is best told in the words of Cowan, Smyth's BGS:

> Hugh-Jones had a conference with Lentaigne [OC 1/4 Gurkha Rifles] and Edward [OC 4/12 FFR], and it was

> their considered opinion that the bridge should be blown because they did not consider the troops would 'stand up' to a Jap attack of any intensity. Furthermore, they considered that all officers and other ranks who could get over the river had already done so. All this information was given to me on the telephone by an officer deputed by Hugh-Jones, as the latter had gone forward to arrange for evacuation of the bridgehead troops. Who the officer was, I have never been able to find out. You will remember I woke you up and told you all this and asked for your formal permission for Hugh-Jones to blow the bridge.[6]

'A terrible decision had to be made by Smyth,' wrote General Davies. 'If he blew the bridge he sacrificed the bulk of his division. If he failed to blow the bridge and it was secured intact by the enemy, the way to Rangoon lay open with nothing interposing. General Smyth blew the bridge. In my opinion a heroic and inevitable decision.'[7]

It was a brave decision, that is certain. There can be no more difficult decision for a general to take in war than to blow a bridge with most of his troops on the far side of the obstacle. Whether it was inevitable is less certain; clearly Hutton did not regard it so, nor, in all likelihood, did Wavell. Hutton considered the Japanese would have had great difficulty in capturing the bridge in daylight, but he probably failed to take into account the exhaustion of the troops holding the bridgehead, only one British company, one Indian and one Gurkha battalion, all exhausted, hungry and thirsty, with very little fire support and fast running out of ammunition. Almost certainly, Hutton over-estimated their chances.

At 0530 hours on Monday, 23 February, Major Orgill and his Sappers blew the bridge over the River Sittang.[8] There was a colossal explosion as one span collapsed into the river. The Officer Commanding 1/3 Gurkha Rifles and one Gurkha rifleman with a light machine gun covered the Sappers as they blew the bridge. There followed a stunning silence, 'and for a brief period a deadly hush reigned over the battlefield.'[9]

Half an hour after the destruction of the bridge, Brigadier Jones at Mokpalin received a wireless message from Headquarters 17 Division, communications having been at last restored at that late hour. It was from 'Punch' to 'Jonah' and was in clear – 'Friends waiting to welcome you at the east gate.'[10] It had obviously been sent before the bridge was blown, but was heartening nevertheless. Jones decided to hold the position round Mokpalin until night, withdrawal to take place across the river, by raft and swimming, under cover of darkness. This plan had, however, to be modified, as the Japanese shelling and mortaring increased. At 1115 hours twenty-seven Japanese bombers bombed the massed transport, gun lines and defensive positions, causing great damage and setting the jungle on fire. 4 BURIF broke, leaving a gap in the perimeter. 2 KOYLI, much reduced in strength and particularly exposed to enemy fire, were greatly heartened by their Commanding Officer, Lieutenant-Colonel Keegan, who strolled from position to position, talking to and encouraging his men. But he, too, was seriously wounded. At 1430 hours Brigadier Jones decided that withdrawal must take place at once, issuing orders to fall back to the river.

Those who got away by boat, by raft or by swimming across the river swollen to 1½ miles by the incoming tide, owed a great deal to the covering force which held off the Japanese throughout that long, hot and thirsty day. It was composed of 2 KOYLI, 3/7 Gurkhas, 5/17 Dogras and 8 BURIF, none of them more than 200 in strength. They held out until nightfall, some escaping across the river after dark, others going into captivity.

One who escaped was a Mr Bill Crowther, then serving as Medical Sergeant with the 'Dukes'.

> On the morning of February 23, 1942, I found myself behind a machine gun and Bandsman Les Williams feeding the belt through. While our ammunition lasted I suppose we were enjoying ourselves . . . When our ammunition ran out I started to dismantle the gun, throwing the breech block into the river. I said: 'Follow it, Les.' To which he replied: 'Not me. I've to take my chances with the Japs. I can't swim.' I offered to take him but he wouldn't have it. So I shook hands with him, wished him the best, and dived in. I was born on the side of the Tyne (Newcastle) and spent my childhood days swimming in it, so the Sittang held no terror for me. Mind you, there

were still snipers and aircraft. How long I spent in that river I don't know – helping chaps to anything that floated. Some time during it a bullet, practically spent, entered my right leg. I bled a lot, but it didn't hurt. I was put in hospital (later) . . .'[11]

'All through the night of February 23,' wrote Tim Carew, 'and throughout the 24th, 25th and 26th, men of the 17th Division staggered into Waw,* single, in twos and threes, in parties of twenty or thirty . . . when it seemed that all who could come in had done so, it was found that of twelve original battalions of infantry there now remained only 80 British officers, 69 Indian and Gurkha officers and 3335 other ranks; this represented a deficiency of approximately 5000. Their armament totalled 1420 rifles, 56 light machine guns and 62 tommy guns – a loss of about 6000 weapons.'[12] 17th Division had lost many of its men, nearly all its guns and most of its transport. It had virtually ceased to exist as a fighting formation.

We did not hear of the disaster at Headquarters 2 Burma Brigade until visited on 25 February by a liaison officer from 17th Division. He told me 'he was handed two identity disks by an Indian soldier who had taken them off a dead British officer who had been murdered while apparently resting in a Burmese village on this side of the Sittang. His head had been almost severed by a *dah* cut. I asked what name was on the disk and he replied, H. B. Owen. I was terribly sorry because it must have been Basil . . .'[13]

It took some time for the magnitude of the disaster to sink in; and if we were in the dark for twenty-four hours or more regarding events taking place within fifty miles (as the crow flies) from us, Major-General Bruce Scott, GOC 1 BURDIV, was even less well-informed. He had been involved in moving his troops out of the Southern Shan States and came down to visit us at Nyaunglebin on 1 March. For some reason both the Brigadier and Brigade Major were away temporarily – probably visiting units – and it fell to me to brief him. After I had finished there was a long, long pause. 'Good God!' he said. 'Good God!'

* Smyth moved his headquarters on 23 February from Abya to Waw, from where there was a motorable track to Pegu.

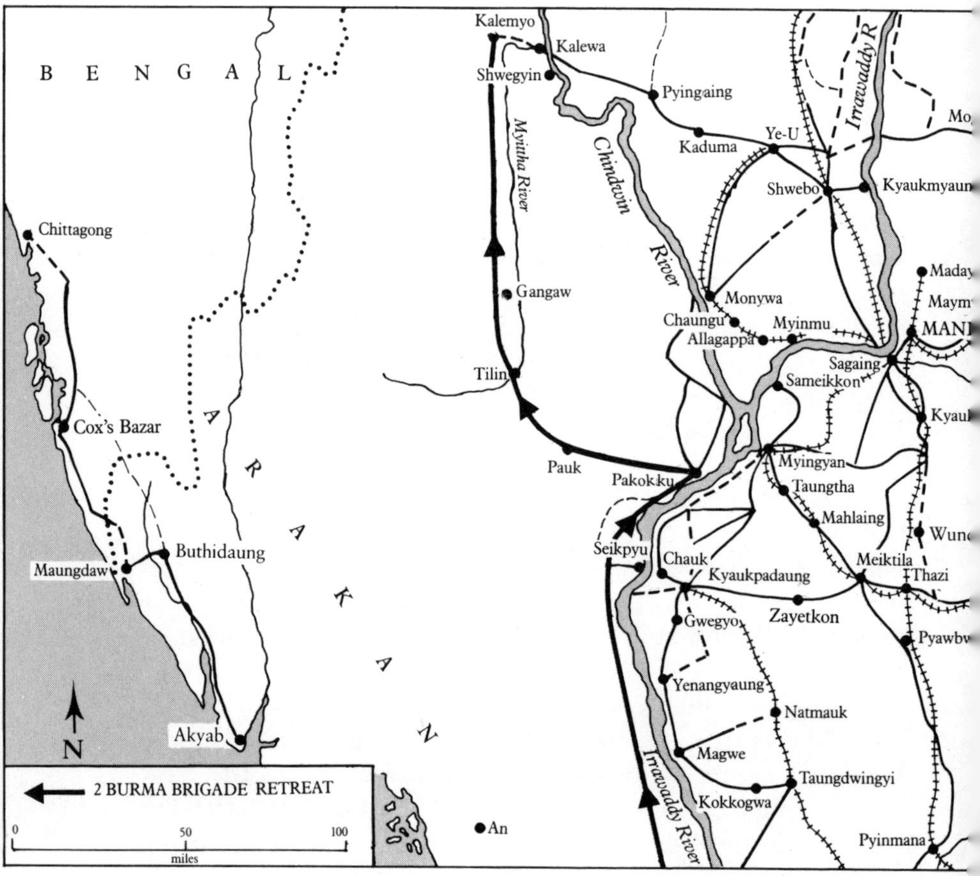

B E N G A L
A R A K A N
Chittagong
Cox's Bazar
Maungdaw
Buthidaung
Akyab
N
2 BURMA BRIGADE RETREAT
0
50
100
miles
An
Kalemyo
Kalewa
Shwegyin
Myittha River
Gangaw
Tilin
Pauk
Pakokku
Seikpyu
Chindwin
River
Pyingaing
Kaduma
Ye-U
Shwebo
Irrawaddy R
Kyaukmyaun
Monywa
Chaungu
Allagappa
Myinmu
Sagaing
Sameikkon
Myingyan
Taungtha
Mahlaing
Meiktila
Thazi
Chauk
Kyaukpadaung
Zayetkon
Gwegyo
Yenangyaung
Natmauk
Magwe
Taungdwingyi
Kokkogwa
Irrawaddy River
Pyinmana
Pyawbw
Wun
Kyau
MAN
Mayn
Maday
Mo

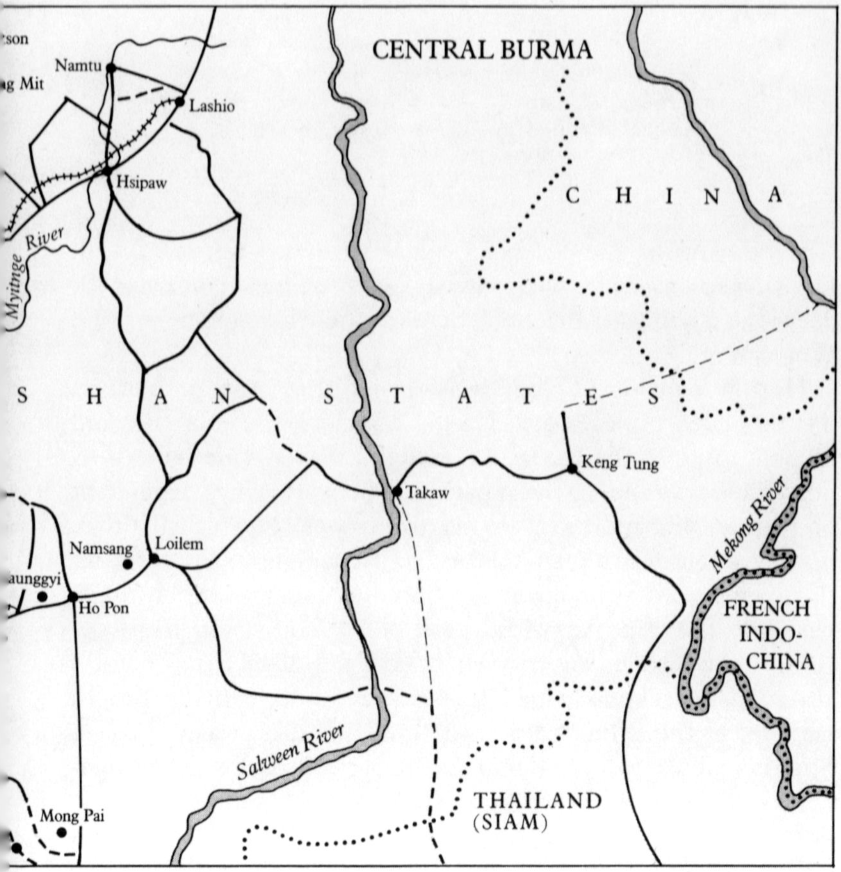
CENTRAL BURMA
Namtu
Lashio
Hsipaw
Myitnge River
CHINA
SHAN STATES
Keng Tung
Takaw
Namsang
Loilem
Ho Pon
Mekong River
FRENCH INDO-CHINA
Salween River
Mong Pai
THAILAND (SIAM)

CHAPTER TEN

Wavell Shuffles the Pack

> 'He possessed above all generals of his time that calmness of courage in the midst of tumult, that serenity of mind in time of danger, which the English call cool-headiness . . .'
>
> *Voltaire on Marlborough*[1]

The blowing of the Sittang bridge, with two-thirds of 17th Division still to cross, will long be one of the most controversial decisions taken by a British general in the whole of the Second World War.

Hutton considered the decision to blow was premature, possibly even unnecessary. He did not think the enemy would be able to cross the bridge in daylight. Nor did he believe its possession was vital to the Japanese, who were not as dependent on wheeled transport as were his own troops. The fact that they did not attempt to repair the bridge immediately may bear out this contention, although it can only be hindsight on Hutton's part. He thought the withdrawal of 17th Division from the Bilin to the Sittang was mismanaged, if not downright dilatory, although he acknowledged that he might have made Smyth hang on to the Bilin position too long.[2] Hutton was critical of Smyth's failure to provide an adequate garrison for the bridgehead sufficiently early for proper defences to be prepared, just as he was critical of Smyth's positioning his headquarters eight miles west of the bridge, where the only communication with the officer responsible for blowing the bridge was a very indistinct civil telephone line. Surely Smyth, or his senior staff officer (Cowan), should have remained on the bridge until the whole of the Division were safely across?

Cowan did not agree, writing many years later to Smyth: 'As a result of the Bilin delay we were doomed. We withdrew much too late, over a ghastly dirt track. We were bombed to hell by our own aircraft. We were already surrounded by the Japs. Much is made of the fact that the transport was not sent back earlier. I am under the impression that it could *not* move across the Sittang any earlier as the bridge decking had not been completed . . . I think it would have been wise to have sent Ekin's brigade back to the bridge the day before we commenced our withdrawal. You will remember Ekin pressed for this?'[3]

Smyth attributed the delay in starting the withdrawal to the order he had been given by Hutton. There was to be no withdrawal from the Bilin without Hutton's express permission. Hutton has already admitted that this permission was perhaps unduly delayed. Smyth's decision not to send back Ekin's 46th Brigade ahead of the other two brigades in order to form a strong bridgehead on the Sittang is understandable, if in the circumstances unfortunate. Both 16th and 48th Brigades were in close contact with the enemy and Smyth did not know whether he would require 46th Brigade to counter-attack in order to permit one or both of them to break clear.

Hutton is critical of Smyth's positioning himself at Abya, eight miles to the west of the river, before the bridge was blown. Smyth has made it quite clear that his reason for doing so was in order to maintain communications with Headquarters Burma Army in Rangoon. His wireless set, although the most powerful available in Burma at that time, could not *guarantee* to reach Rangoon if climatic conditions were adverse, whereas at Abya there was a civil telephone system that could be used as an alternative means for communication. Moreover he was under orders to meet with Hutton the following day, midway between Rangoon and the Sittang, presumably to discuss the imminent arrival of 7th Armoured Brigade, and by locating himself at Abya he was virtually halving the distance he would have to travel. There was of course telephone as well as wireless communication between the bridge and Abya, but wireless was notoriously difficult at night with the sets as they were at that time.

For both these reasons Smyth moved back from the river after darkness had fallen, the firing across the river having died down for a time. He took with him Cowan, leaving his GSO I (Simpson) and a small Operations staff to assist Hugh-Jones at Headquarters 48 Brigade. Smyth had impressed on Hugh-Jones, in whom he had implicit confidence, that in no circumstances was the bridge to be allowed to fall intact into enemy hands. He reserved for himself the final decision 'to blow', unless for some unforeseen reason Hugh-Jones could not get in contact with him.

It is of course arguable that given the circumstances at the time, Smyth ought to have remained at the bridge. He had placed an appalling load of responsibility on the shoulders of Hugh-Jones; so much so that after agonizing over it for many years to come, Hugh-Jones one day walked out into the sea and was drowned. 'He was a Sittang casualty if ever there was one,' Smyth was later to write.[4]

Smyth was truly on the horns of a dilemma, due entirely to his wretched communications. He had to keep his army commander informed while at the same time he was full of anxiety concerning his troops still east of the river. From hindsight he might have been better advised to have remained himself at the bridge, sending Cowan back to Abya to deal with Hutton, or *vice versa*. But war is not an exact science, a general often having to make up his mind with insufficient information, and when he himself is desperately fatigued. Napoleon's decisions during the afternoon of 18 June at Waterloo are an excellent example of this. I do not believe it would have made any difference to the final outcome wherever Smyth was situated, and it is only right to add that he ever afterwards accepted full responsibility for the decision to blow.

He certainly cannot be blamed for the delay in preparing the bridge to take wheeled transport. This was the responsibility of Burma Army, i.e. Hutton's. On 4 February Smyth wrote to him: 'I went with my officiating CRE [Commander Royal Engineers] yesterday to the Sittang Bridge and we were rather horrified by the bad state of the road and the poor arrangements to get lorries over the river.'[5] Hutton in his turn was critical of 'the withdrawal of the Field Company attached to the Division which meant no guard rails on the bridge, and also meant that the lorry which broke down on the bridge could not be moved more quickly'.[6] Presumably Hutton is referring here to the removal of the Burma Sappers & Miners Field Company which had been taken away, despite Smyth's objections, to help prepare demolitions in Rangoon.

It is less easy to defend Smyth's failure to provide a strong bridge garrison sufficiently far ahead. '3 BURIF reorganizing and resting at the Sittang bridge,' he wrote to Hutton on 4 February; 'they have had two bad shows and want reorganizing and retraining.'[7] Brigadier Bourke, who was at the time responsible for the bridge defences, protested forcibly both verbally and in writing against the use of 3 BURIF for this purpose. We had little faith in them as a fighting unit. It was only on the morning of the day when withdrawal from the Bilin line began that Smyth sent 4/12 FFR back to strengthen the bridge defences; they arrived so exhausted after a trying day's march that their CO decided to rest them overnight before taking over the bridge defence from the CO of 3 BURIF. It was certainly a tragedy that the 2nd Duke of Wellington's Regiment, a completely fresh British battalion from India, was not utilized to strengthen the bridge garrison instead of being sent to Kyaikto where they detrained only to begin withdrawing two days later. It has to be assumed that this was with the agreement of Headquarters 17 Division – a most unfortunate decision if this was so.

The battle of the Sittang was from beginning to end a succession of blunders. There can be no doubt that Hutton's refusal to permit Smyth to withdraw behind the river at his own pace and time was the principal cause for what followed; backseat driving seldom works in war, and it is far better to replace the driver. Nor was Wavell free from blame, attempting to control operations from faraway Java. Hutton was of course subject to pressure from both the Governor and from Air Vice-Marshal Stevenson to keep the Japanese as far away from Rangoon as possible, but his insistence on retaining a hold on Tenasserim should have resulted in an all-out effort to improve communications with that province from the moment he became Army Commander. Such an effort was wanting.

On Smyth's part, it was a serious error in judgement not to

have made certain that the bridgehead was securely held days before he withdrew from the Bilin. There was plenty of time in which to do this. He also made a mistake in refusing to send 46th Brigade back to the Sittang when Ekin pleaded to be allowed to do so; this was, probably, Smyth's cardinal error.

The shockwaves following the blowing of the Sittang bridge had a catastrophic effect in Burma. Hutton had prepared Wavell, India Command and the War Cabinet for the consequences of a withdrawal behind the Sittang in an appreciation dated 18 February. He made it clear that if the Sittang defences were penetrated, the evacuation of Rangoon would be inevitable. Such plain speaking astounded the Governor, Dorman-Smith, and his Council who set in train two days later the first stage of the Evacuation Plan for Rangoon. It astonished Wavell, still reeling under the blow of Singapore's surrender, and came as a thunderclap in Whitehall and New Delhi. It was the Viceroy, Linlithgow, who reacted the most violently.

'Our troops are not fighting with proper spirit,' he cabled the Secretary of State, Leo Amery. 'I have not the least doubt that this is in great part due to lack of drive and inspiration from the top.'[8] Amery at once got in touch with the Governor: 'Have heard doubts cast on Hutton's quality as fighting leader. Have you any misgivings as to his being the right man? Your telegrams so far have been appreciative.'[9]

Dorman-Smith and Hutton enjoyed a good working relationship, although it was not until some time later, when both men were smarting under their Burma wounds, that the two became friends. But Dorman-Smith was a politician, and it is common in British politics when things go wrong to change the politician rather than the policy; therefore, the Governor's reply was cautious, only specifying that if Hutton were to be changed, his successor should be from the British rather than the Indian Army. Meanwhile Churchill had repeated Linlithgow's telegram to Wavell, requesting his views and adding: 'If you concur with the Viceroy, we will send [General] Alexander at once.'[10]

Like Dorman-Smith, Wavell was non-committal. He said he would prefer to defer a decision until he knew whether or not the 7th Australian Division would be landed in Rangoon, adding that he had always thought Hutton would be 'a resolute and skilful commander', although Alexander's more forceful personality might encourage the troops. On balance, though, he preferred to leave things as they were.

But Wavell had lost confidence in Hutton. He told him later that he 'kept blowing hot and cold'.[11] Hutton's accurate, but pessimistic, appreciation of 18 February angered Wavell; as did Hutton's action on 21 February when only part of a convoy was allowed to land in Rangoon, the balance carrying administrative units being turned back to Calcutta. Wavell made this perfectly clear to Hutton when he met him, in company with the Governor, at Magwe on 1 March: 'Wavell's feelings were manifest when I met him at Magwe on 1st March. He stormed at me in front of the Governor, the AOC and a number of officers and civilians in a most excited way and I felt the only dignified thing to do was to make no reply. I certainly felt then, and still feel, that if he had had his way the whole Army and a large number of civilians would have been captured in Rangoon by the Japanese.'[12] It was on that occasion that Wavell countermanded Hutton's order for the immediate evacuation from Rangoon.

By 1 March, however, the die had been cast. Hutton had been informed on 22 February that Alexander was to relieve him, the reason given being the proposed increase in strength of Burma Army. But this deceived no one, for Hutton and Alexander were both of the same rank. To make matters worse, Hutton was to remain in Burma as Alexander's Chief of Staff. This led him to quote many years later from Arthur Bryant's *Wellington*: 'Of all the awkward situations in the world that which is most so is to serve in a subordinate capacity in an Army which one has commanded.'[13] It was a situation he had to endure, increasingly sceptical of Alexander's tactics, until he was relieved at his own request by Major-General J. J. W. Winterton early in April. Alexander asked him to remain in Burma, presumably in an advisory capacity, but Hutton, finding his situation intolerably irksome, returned to India finally on 26 April 1942. He was not given another active command.

Although Hutton was probably more sinned against than

sinning, it cannot be denied that his relief by Alexander (Alex) did provide a boost to morale. Alex had a charisma wholly lacking in Hutton's case. Wavell, in his characteristically taciturn fashion, did nothing to soften the blow. Indeed, in his correspondence with Hutton six months later when both men were writing their Dispatches of the 1942 Campaign, Wavell never gave an inch. He may have underestimated the Japanese, he said, but the real reason for our defeat by them was poor fighting spirit and bad leadership. He was even less forthcoming when it came to the case of Major-General J. G. Smyth, VC.

After Wavell visited 17th Division at Kyaikto on 6 February, he said nothing to Hutton that might have implied some lack of confidence in Smyth as a commander. Indeed, in a signal on 17 February 1942 Wavell told Hutton: 'I have every confidence in judgment and fighting spirit of you and Smyth . . .'[14] As already explained, Wavell said virtually nothing to Smyth, either by way of praise or blame, but merely commented that in the course of the rail journey from Pegu to the Sittang he had noticed the open nature of the country. He had concluded that tanks could operate over it and had therefore decided to ask for an armoured brigade to be sent to Burma. The 7th Armoured Brigade, less one regiment, was dispatched forthwith from the Middle East, for which everyone who served in Burma in 1942 had cause to be grateful to Wavell.

Two days after Wavell's visit, Smyth was visited by Major-General Treffry Thompson, an old friend who was Hutton's Deputy Director of Medical Services at Burma Army. Thompson was disturbed by Smyth's physical condition, especially when told of the recurrence of Smyth's fistula problem. Thompson insisted that Smyth should attend a medical board. One was duly convened, its president Colonel Mackenzie, the senior doctor in 17 Division. Doubtless under some pressure from Smyth himself, the board found Smyth fit to carry on, but recommended he was given two months' sick leave at the first opportunity. This must be one of the most absurd recommendations ever made by a medical board, given the strain under which Smyth was labouring, but Jacky Smyth could be very persuasive when he put his mind to it. The board proceedings were sent to

Rangoon where only Hutton and Thompson saw them. No copies were sent to Army Headquarters in New Delhi and the actual board proceedings were lost in the upheaval of the move of Burma Army Headquarters from Rangoon to Maymyo a few days later. Mackenzie, the only man who could have vouched for them, was taken prisoner at the Sittang.

General Ekin was convinced that Smyth's physical condition was the cause of some of the mistakes he found otherwise hard to explain. 'The trouble with Jacky,' he said, 'was that he always looked so damned cheerful, however bloody he might be feeling. The night I saw him after swimming the Sittang, he seemed to be his same old cheerful self.'[15]

The fighting on the Bilin and the Sittang were hardly calculated to make things easier for an already sick man. Ekin, who saw Smyth shortly after he, Ekin, had swum the river, thought him a very sick man indeed, although he was outwardly in good spirits. On 25 February, Smyth wrote confidentially to Hutton requesting the two months' sick leave recommended by the medical board. He said 17th Division would require several weeks to reorganize and reequip, all of which could be overseen by Cowan while Smyth recovered his health. Smyth received no reply to this letter although Treffry Thompson told him later that he had strongly advised Hutton to send Smyth on sick leave.

In his *Personal Record* Hutton has stated that he had no part in Smyth's removal from command, although it was 'in every sense justified'. He adds that he was not consulted. However, among Hutton's papers there is a copy of a signal from Burma Army to New Delhi dated 26 February (i.e. three days *before* Wavell replaced Smyth by Cowan) and signed by Goddard, Hutton's chief administrative staff officer. The signal, which was marked 'Personal to Military Secretary from Hutton', was unequivocal: 'Ref my DO re Smyth; he now asks in writing for two months' leave as soon as he can be spared. Medical authorities report him fit. I visited him yesterday and he appeared well and cheerful. I made no suggestion he was to blame for recent reverses. This is not the moment to spare people to proceed on leave and I must assume that he has lost confidence in his ability to command and should be relieved. Propose to appoint Cowan and dispatch Smyth to India forthwith. Wire approval.'[16]

Hutton was, of course, aware at this time that he was shortly to be replaced by Alexander, but it is difficult to understand why he should deny taking any part in Smyth's replacement. It is equally hard to understand why Smyth should have requested sick leave instead of allowing himself to be evacuated to hospital, from where he would almost certainly have been sent to India. He appears to have been curiously blind to the fact that for the General to ask for sick leave immediately after a disaster like the Sittang was almost certain to be misconstrued, not only by his superiors, but also by the officers and soldiers of his Division. It must indeed be assumed that his poor physical condition had impaired his judgement.

Smyth handed over to Cowan on Wavell's orders on 1 March, leaving Mingalodon on 2 March in the RAF Blenheim which was taking Wavell to Lashio to meet Chiang Kai-shek. The two men sat at opposite ends of the aircraft without exchanging a word. At Lashio, Wavell left Smyth to kick his heels while he conferred with the Generalissimo. The following day they flew to Calcutta, finding that Alexander's plane had just landed. Alex and Wavell had a short meeting without any attempt on Wavell's part to include Smyth in the discussion. Instead, Smyth was informed that Wavell wished to fly on to New Delhi alone, Smyth's baggage being dumped on the tarmac. 'Wavell strode past me without any sign of recognition,' wrote Smyth.[17]

The first plane provided for Smyth's onward journey to New Delhi crashed on take-off. Smyth and the pilot, a Sikh, had a narrow escape. Another plane was produced, and with the same pilot Smyth flew on to New Delhi where he was reunited with his wife. On the following day he received an official message that on the orders of the Commander-in-Chief he was deprived of his Major-General's rank (which was still only temporary), and had been immediately retired from the Service. He was to inform the Commander-in-Chief of the country in which he intended to reside.

Smyth spent the next six months, when he was not in hospital being treated for his serious condition, struggling to rehabilitate his reputation as a soldier. In this he received strong support from Treffry Thompson and from General Hartley, the Deputy Commander-in-Chief, but Wavell was obdurate. Smyth was even refused the honorary rank of Major-General on the grounds that he should have had himself medically examined before proceeding overseas. Eventually Smyth returned to Britain, an embittered and disappointed man, to make a new and successful career for himself. He made a reputation as a writer and journalist, became an MP, was created a Baronet, and founded the Victoria Cross/George Cross Association, dying in 1983 when nearly ninety. He never ceased explaining how the disaster at the Sittang came about, nor squabbling with Hutton as to where the blame really lay. It was a sad end to what had at one stage been an outstanding military career.

He was not, of course, the only disappointed general to come out of Burma in 1942. Hutton was another, and so in a sense was Wavell, who was never to get the measure of the Japanese. On the day the Sittang bridge was blown, Wavell was closing his headquarters at Lembang in Java. ABDACOM had been wound up, Wavell's instructions being to reassume his appointment as Commander-in-Chief in India. He was completely out of touch with the situation in Burma, to the extent that his Chief of Staff, General Pownall, makes no mention of the Sittang disaster in his diary.[18] On 21 February, two days *after* Hutton had authorized 17th Division's withdrawal from the Bilin to the Sittang, Wavell sent him no less than three signals, demonstrating clearly how far removed Wavell was from the real situation.

In the first he asked, 'Why on earth should resistance on the Sittang cease? Are you not still successfully holding Bilin River?'[19] In the next, 'There seems on surface no reason whatever for decision practically to abandon fight for Rangoon and continue retrograde movement. You have checked enemy and he must be tired and have suffered heavy casualties. No sign that he is in superior strength.'[20] And finally, 'You should draw up at once plans for counter-offensive with Armoured Brigade and all available troops. If at all possible Sittang River must be crossed and counter-offensive be made east of river.'[21]

At the time these messages were being drafted, the exhausted, thirsty, bewildered soldiers of 17th Division were struggling back to Kyaikto and to the Sittang, hammered by their own, as well as by the enemy's, Air Force and followed closely by no less than two strong Japanese divisions; without much information, or much direction from above, and, if the truth be told, not much confidence in their high command.

Wavell followed up the above messages with another to General Hartley in New Delhi on 23 February. He believed different tactics should be adopted to stop the Japanese. Mobile groups should be formed to operate between the Rangoon–Mandalay highway and the River Sittang, using the railway as a base. Armoured trains might be improvised. 'Close cooperation with Air Force essential and there must be arrangements to distinguish our troops from enemy from air. *Coloured umbrellas of local type might be useful.*'[22] He failed to make clear how those carrying the umbrellas could differentiate between their own and enemy planes until it was too late to do so!

Wavell left Java on 25 February, but with his usual ill-luck when travelling by air, his plane caught fire and had to divert to Colombo. He was back at his desk in New Delhi on 27 February, having experienced nothing but disaster since leaving for Java at the end of December. Titan though he may have been, few generals in British history have undergone such a succession of hammer blows yet still remained 'bloody but unbowed'. And there were more to come.

On 1 March he was at Magwe in Central Burma, conferring with the Governor and Hutton, beside himself with rage at the news that Hutton had given orders for the evacuation of Rangoon and had turned back the convoy bringing the 1st Indian Field Regiment* and 63rd Indian Infantry Brigade, due on 3 and 5 March respectively. Wavell at once countermanded those orders, ordering Rangoon to be held. And at his meeting with General Alexander at Dum-Dum airport on his way back from Burma, Wavell emphasized yet again the vital importance of hanging on to Rangoon. By so doing, he only narrowly escaped losing the greater part of the Burma Army.

* Artillery with 25 pdrs.

There could hardly have been a greater contrast than Alexander and Hutton. Alex looked, and was, every inch a soldier, although not all those who served under him rated him all that highly. General Tuker, who commanded a division under him in Italy, considered that Alex was 'quite the least intelligent commander I have ever met in a high position',[23] but then Tuker could be caustic on occasions. By and large, however, Alex radiated confidence as well as the ability to get the best out of a host of conflicting and self-opinionated allies. It was a genius he shared with Marlborough. Voltaire's description of Marlborough, which heads this chapter, fits Alexander more exactly than any other British general since Marlborough's time – that 'serenity of mind in time of danger which the English call cool-headiness'.

Above all, perhaps, as the next few months would certainly show, Alexander was lucky. 'It was Napoleon who said he preferred lucky generals,' wrote Hutton. 'He would have liked Alex but would have had little use for Wavell whose luck was abysmal.'[24]

CHAPTER ELEVEN

Retreat to Toungoo

'That was a remarkably poor show.'
Field Marshal Montgomery
to the author, 1946

When Field Marshal Montgomery visited the British troops in Trieste in 1946, he made it plain to me that he did not think highly of those of us who had taken part in the Retreat from Burma. I felt I owed him an apology. His attitude differed markedly from Alexander's, whom I met by chance when we were withdrawing to Toungoo. Alex was as spick and span as if about to arrive at the Horse Guards, making me feel lamentably scruffy in the ill-fitting shirt and slacks issued to me after Moulmein. He offered me a mug of tea before inviting me to sit down beside him, then he proceeded to cross-examine me about the Burma Rifles. What did I think of them? Were they likely to stand up to the Japs? There was nothing patronizing about him. He was genuinely seeking information. Then he told me 2nd Burma Brigade would soon be going across to the Irrawaddy front where he expected we would be able to take part in the offensive he was planning. It did my morale a lot of good.

It is, of course, part of a general's job to put a good face on things when all around there seems to be chaos. Alex was a past master in the art. His Chief of Staff, General Winterton, has correctly said that when the situation appears to be hopeless, to be realistic may well be regarded as defeatist.[1] Alexander believed that a commander should always be optimistic, however bad the situation. He was therefore sometimes critical of our Corps Commander's[2] down-to-earth comments, preferring himself to give the impression that victory was just round the corner. I have to admit that he profoundly impressed me, if not Brigadier Bourke. 'I don't believe it,' he said.

If a general is not to lose the confidence of his soldiers, he must be careful not to advocate the impossible. The mobile tactics proposed by Wavell after the Sittang battle, to some extent supported by Alexander when he first arrived in Burma, came into this category. The Burma Army lacked the means to make itself mobile in a terrain like Burma's. Our dependence on mechanical transport tied us to the roads, making us vulnerable to air attack. Few British armies have been so hopelessly road-bound as we were.

Neither the Japanese nor the Chinese were similarly afflicted. They impressed porters in large numbers, used bullocks and elephants, often carrying ammunition and several days' supplies on the soldiers themselves. Their diet was simple: rice, and dried fish when they could get it. Officers and soldiers lived hard, far harder than we had been accustomed to do in peace-time training.

Nyaunglebin was a quiet little market town when we arrived there on 15 February. The trains were running normally and there was little evidence of any anxiety. It was so peaceful that Merton decided to bring his wife down from Maymyo, although I, mindful of my experience in Moulmein, advised strongly against it. So did the Brigade Major, but Merton was adamant. We implored him not to tell the Brigadier, who would be furious. Mrs Merton arrived five days later, by which time the situation had altered dramatically.

On 20 February, acting on a very pessimistic review by Hutton, the Governor set in motion Stage Two of the Rangoon Evacuation Scheme. There was an immediate panic. The police virtually collapsed. People fought to get on trains, roads were jammed by cars, bullock carts, bicycles, tricycles and anything else that would move. Men, women and children sat on carriage roofs, clung on to buffers and outside carriage windows, sat on top of each other inside carriages, and fought with knives to gain a footing. Lunatics were turned loose from the asylum, wild animals escaped from the zoo, criminals were released from the jails, and chaos reigned for days on end. Looting, usually accompanied by arson, was rife. The army had to take over, shooting looters on sight, imposing curfews. Almost overnight a great city was reduced to a shambles.[3]

The first we knew of it in Nyaunglebin was when hordes of refugees began to pass through the town. 'Enormous refugee traffic along roads,' I noted in my diary on 21 February. 'Streams of lorries and cars pass through all day. Also large numbers of Indians and Chinese on foot. People are getting anxious here.' It was like a visitation by locusts. The bazaar was stripped clean, houses were broken into and looted, the roads were strewn with human ordure, and a large part of the town was set on fire. I happened to see Lady Dorman-Smith passing through in the Governor's Rolls, staring straight ahead, quite expressionless. Her world, too, was crashing around her. Much of my time was spent at the railway station, helping to control the clamouring mob. It must have been about this time that the Burmese sub-divisional officer thought it wise to make a bolt, first handing over to us several lakhs of rupees from the government treasury. It was to come in useful later.

Around this time 2 BURIF joined us from Papun on the Salween, where they had been since early February. Withdrawn from Mergui by sea on 20 January, 2 BURIF, possibly the best of the original 20 BURIF battalions, had as yet seen very little action. Their lot seemed to consist of being posted hither and thither, marching for countless miles across terrible country. They did finally end up in 2nd Burma Brigade, where indeed they had started, but by then they consisted mostly of Chins and Kachins. The CO, Dennis O'Callaghan, was difficult to handle, I found, but he certainly kept his battalion together.

Everything went from bad to worse after the Sittang disaster. 'Tremendously long trains pass through daily going north,' I noted on 27 February. 'One ordnance special must have been more than a quarter of a mile long. Thousands of refugees in cars, buses, on bullock carts and on foot are streaming through. Chaos reigns supreme. The entire town is evacuating. Pathetic scenes at station where people struggle to board trains.' To add to our troubles were the stragglers from the Sittang battle.

Singly, in twos and threes, sometimes more, soldiers came through Nyaunglebin, some by road but most by train. 'I pulled a complete platoon of 4/12 FFR off one train,' I wrote. 'They were in good heart but totally lost.'

On 28 February 2nd Burma Brigade was transferred from 17th Division to 1 BURDIV, which was moving down from the Shan States to close the gap with 17th Division, then at Pegu. We were also to cover the concentration of the Vth Chinese Army at Toungoo. A Chinese colonel who visited us briefly said the VIth Chinese Army was taking over in the Shan States, but it was a pity we had not permitted them to move earlier. It would take them a long time to concentrate at Toungoo and we wondered how much time the Japanese would give us.

When General Bruce Scott visited us on 1 March, to learn for the first time of the Sittang disaster, he was almost equally appalled by the sight of the procession of bullock carts, moving nose to tail, that choked the roads for as far as the eye could see. 'How am I to move my Division through that lot?' he asked. He told us that 1st Burma Brigade would be moving down to join us, after which the Division would attack south to link up with 17th Division. In the meantime we were to concentrate our brigade in and around Nyaunglebin, which meant pulling back 1 BURIF from Daik-u, fifteen miles south, and 7 BURIF from Shwegyin, on the far side of the Sittang.

Blowing the bridge at the Sittang did check the Japs, but not for long. They virtually broke off the battle after dark on 23 February, thereby enabling far more of our troops to cross the river than at one time seemed possible. Most of them were without weapons, of course. The Japanese needed time to regroup and plan their next move, but General Iida had set up advanced headquarters of XVth Army in Kyaikto only forty-eight hours after Smyth's headquarters had left the place. He decided to waste no time trying to repair the bridge but instead moved upstream to ferry his troops across the river at Kunzeik and other suitable places. On 27 February Iida ordered 55th Japanese Division to cross the Sittang on 3 March, take Daik-u (which 1 BURIF had left only the previous day), and then turn south in order to encircle and destroy 17th Division which was reported to be reforming at Pegu. 33rd Division, which had had a very exhausting battle at the Sittang, was to reorganize and then follow 55th Division across the Sittang to Daik-u. It was not, however, to get involved in the fighting round Pegu; instead it was to march due west through the Pegu Yomas, a densely forested range of hills, until it met the main Rangoon–Prome highway. It was then to turn south, its objective Rangoon; the sooner this could be accomplished, obviously the less time the British would have to bring in reinforcements. Time was therefore of the essence, as Iida made abundantly clear to General Sakurai, commanding 33rd Division.

In my diary on 2 March I noted that 'the Japs are now infiltrating into Daik-u', and on the following day, 'Japs are now in Daik-u in force. They are infiltrating across the Yomas and are obviously trying to cut off 17 Div.' But the administrative miracle that was taking place around me left me with little or no time to reflect on the operational significance of such diary entries.

It was in fact little short of a miracle that the Burma Army was provided with the wherewithal to conduct a campaign for a further three months, at the same time supplying the locust-like Chinese armies with much that they needed. The man who deserves the credit was Major-General (now Lieutenant-General) E. N. Goddard, whose thankless task it was to be Major-General-in-charge-of-Administration at Headquarters Burma Army. It was due largely to Goddard's drive, administrative skills and willingness to ride roughshod over all bureaucratic opposition that Burma Army was able to retreat as far as the Chindwin and still have the petrol to propel its vehicles, the ammunition to fire from its guns, the medical stores to attend to its wounded and the food to keep both men and animals on their feet. He had the greatest trouble trying to persuade the railways and Irrawaddy Flotilla Company to adjust themselves to the harsh realities of war, but by one means or another he succeeded in shifting the main base of Burma Army from Rangoon to Mandalay-Meiktila-Shwebo between the end of December 1941 and the beginning of March 1942. It was a colossal effort.

Logistics is not a branch of the military art that appeals to most ambitious soldiers. The fact that it is something the military are particularly good at escapes the notice of most people; only the former Imperial German Army gave the Quartermaster-General the importance he merits in the military hierarchy. Generals may receive knighthoods for winning battles, but precious few receive them for providing them with the necessaries without which battles cannot be won – and for the lack of which they are likely to be lost. It might be mentioned, in passing, that Goddard was no exception to the general rule.

If we knew on 4 March that the Japanese were already heading west towards the Pegu Yomas, presumably this information must have been relayed to Headquarters Burma Army. There was obviously a chance that the road from Rangoon to Prome would be blocked, jeopardizing the withdrawal of the Rangoon garrison, as well as that of 17th Division, now fighting hard at Pegu. But Alexander had on arrival cancelled Hutton's order for a withdrawal, at least until 1st Indian Field Regiment and 63rd Indian Infantry Brigade could be disembarked in the now deserted docks. Only on 6 March, late in the afternoon, with 17th Division hard pressed in Pegu, did Alex change his mind, giving orders for the demolition plan to be carried out immediately and for the withdrawal from Rangoon to Prome to begin early on 7 March.

At 0400 hours that same morning, shortly after Alexander's advance guard had passed up the Prome road towards Tharawaddy, Major Takonubu, commanding III/214 Infantry Regiment, part of the 33rd Japanese Division, halted two kilometres east of the road, a little beyond the village of Taukkyan where the road from Rangoon forks to the right for Hlegu and Pegu, and to the left for Tharawaddy and Prome. When Takonubu's patrol reported the road clear, he at once set up a road-block designed to protect the Japanese columns as they crossed the Rangoon–Prome road prior to turning south towards Rangoon.

Meanwhile the main British column had set off from Rangoon, leaving the city under a dense pall of smoke as the demolition squads did their work with remarkable efficiency. It was seventeen miles to Taukkyan where the leading troops ran head-on into Takonubu's road-block. It was attacked by 1st Glosters, supported by tanks of 7th Armoured Brigade, but they were repulsed. Takonubu, fearing lest the Japanese movement across the road would be delayed, reinforced the block with more troops, machine guns and mountain artillery.

Alexander's advance guard had just arrived in Tharawaddy when the news of the road-block reached them. It was at once decided to attack the block from the north. This too failed. So did successive attacks by 2/13 FFRif and 1/11 Sikhs, both battalions newly disembarked in Rangoon, inexperienced and still recovering their 'shore legs'. 1/10 Gurkha Rifles, a more seasoned battalion, fared no better, despite gallant support from 7th Queen's Own Hussars with their 'Honey' tanks. By nightfall the situation seemed to be desperate. 'Alexander actually got to the point of suggesting that the troops might disperse and try to make their way north through the jungle,' wrote Hutton,[4] for whom it must have been doubly grim, knowing that had it not been for Wavell's intervention and Alexander's postponement of the withdrawal from Rangoon, none of it need have happened.*

There was just as much confusion on the Japanese side. It had never occurred to them that the British would abandon Rangoon without a fight; General Sakurai had reasoned that the sooner he attacked the city, the less chance the British would have of bringing in reinforcements by sea. Speed was vital. Therefore when Colonel Sakuma, Commander of 214th Infantry Regiment, received news of the fighting at Taukkyan, he ordered Major Takonubu not to become too deeply involved. He then reported the situation to General Sakurai and his Chief of Staff. Both men agreed that a battle at Taukkyan would delay 33rd

* Maj-Gen. Ian Lyall-Grant, who landed at Rangoon on 7 March in command of a Field Company of the Bengal Sappers & Miners, has written: 'An attack to clear the block [at Taukkyan] that evening failed. We dossed down in a rubber plantation and late that night received our first message of the campaign . . . It said briefly that a further attack on the block would be made the next morning; if it failed we were to break the unit up into small parties of a dozen men or so who were to make their way out independently to India! A charming prospect! India was 700 miles away, we had one paper road map of Burma and the locals were none too friendly!'

Division's task of capturing Rangoon as quickly as possible. Takonubu, who had by then been wounded, was ordered to break off the battle as soon as it was dark, continuing the advance to Rangoon by moving across country *west* of the main road. Takonubu did this at 2030 hours, 1/10 Gurkha Rifles reporting later that large numbers of the enemy had been seen crossing the main road, some of them within 200 yards of the Gurkhas' outposts. This, when first reported, was discounted at Alexander's headquarters near Taukkyan. When, however, at first light on 8 March, a final attempt was made to dislodge the road-block, tanks from 7th Hussars found the enemy had gone; the road was open.

The Japanese undoubtedly lost a wonderful opportunity to finish the campaign in early March, rather than in May. Commenting on this, General Davies has written, 'Surely this was one of the most remarkable instances of a missed opportunity ever recorded.'[5] The truth was that the Japanese, by the speed of their advance, had outrun their supplies. Neither the 33rd nor 55th Divisions had been re-supplied since crossing into Burma six weeks previously; ammunition in particular was dangerously low. On 26 February Headquarters Southern Army had proposed to General Iida that he should temporarily postpone the aim of capturing Rangoon, concentrating instead on dealing with the Chinese, reported to be moving down from the north. Iida, however, insisted that Rangoon must be captured first in order that the port could be opened and his dangerous logistical situation eased thereby. 33rd Division was therefore ordered to press on to Rangoon, although both Generals Iida and Sakurai anticipated having to fight hard for the city.

Sakurai was astonished to find Rangoon empty, his 215th Infantry Regiment entering the city around midday on 8 March. The singlemindedness of the Japanese may account for the story of the British civilian whose departure from Rangoon was for some reason delayed.* Hastening in his car along the road to catch up with the retreating British, he was halted by engine trouble. He was endeavouring to rectify this when he saw approaching a long column of Japanese, headed by an

* Possibly apocryphal, but it went the rounds in Burma at that time!

officer on a white horse. As the officer approached the civilian removed his hat and bowed, and the officer saluted in return. After an interminable time the column passed, the engine successfully started, and the civilian sped on up the empty road to catch up eventually with Alexander's column.

Although the war was coming steadily nearer to us, there was remarkably little information about what was happening in Rangoon, and around Pegu. Most of my time was spent at the railway station, marshalling trains and trying to get people away. We were visited by seven Japanese bombers on 2 March, the gruesome remains lying around the place for days. Fortunately this inspired Brigadier Bourke to move his headquarters out of the town, already a charred ruin. We set ourselves up in a mango grove at Milestone 102. On 4 March we heard that 5/1 Punjabis were coming to join us from 13th Indian Brigade. 'Thank God,' I wrote in my diary. 'These Burmese troops are not reliable. Very many desertions. Complete Burman platoon of 1 BURIF deserted with all their weapons. I took two lorry loads with me to Toungoo to go into jail. HQ BURDIV is now in Toungoo. 1 Burma Brigade are coming down here soon. 5 BURIF are in Kyauktaga (about 20 miles north of us) with 2 Battery.'

Merton had by now bowed to the inevitable and sent his wife back to Maymyo; she had been with him little more than a week. Patrols of 1 BURIF reported Japanese in Pyuntaza, between Daik-u and Nyaunglebin, a road-block having been established on the bridge across the Yenwe Chaung, just south of Pyuntaza. 'A' Company of 1 BURIF, under Captain Moir, were ordered to clear it. Moir put up a splendid show, I recorded in my diary, actually breaking up the block himself, but he was killed whereupon his troops, all of them Chins, withdrew. 'I hear they have cut off Moir's head and stuck it on a spike on the bridge – the swine!' I wrote. It is hard to believe that anything useful had been achieved, the gap between us and 17th Division being effectively sealed as more and more Japanese crossed the Sittang.

Brigadier Bourke was increasingly convinced that no reliance could be placed on the Burma Rifles. He never missed an opportunity to make this clear to any senior officer visiting his brigade headquarters. Although he has since been criticized for downgrading his Burmese troops, the truth was that at the time most of us agreed with him. It is easy to make excuses for the failure of the Burma Rifles battalions to stand firm, but the fact remains that in far too many instances they proved to be the weak link in the chain. When 1 BURIF left us for 1st Burma Brigade in exchange for 5/1 Punjabis, I was delighted, although the Karen companies of 1 BURIF were later to do sterling work fighting against the Japanese in the jungles and hills of their native Karenni, east of the Sittang. They were indeed delightful people and as brave as the bravest, but were ill-suited for the kind of positional warfare we were expecting them to fight. Moreover, always at the back of their minds was the fate of their families, at the mercy not only of the Japanese but of the Burmese, whom they feared and distrusted even more.

Throughout the campaign the passage of information was bad, leaving most of us in the dark about what was happening elsewhere than in our own immediate vicinity. In 2nd Burma Brigade during those first two weeks in March, we knew virtually nothing about what was happening in Pegu, fifty miles to the south, where 17th Division was supposedly reconstituting itself after the Sittang *débâcle*. This was in fact accomplished with remarkable speed and success, although two or three separate battalions had had to be amalgamated to make one effective fighting unit. 2 KOYLI, only about 200 strong, were amalgamated with 2 'Dukes', about 400 strong, to form the 'King's Own Dukes' under Major R. M. H. Tynte of the Cameronians, who was soon to be killed. 46th Brigade, which had suffered the worst at the Sittang, was broken up; 17th Division then consisted of 16th and 48th Brigades, with 7th Armoured Brigade in support. 7th Armoured Brigade (7th Hussars and 2nd Royal Tanks) had arrived in Rangoon from the Middle East on 21 February, as had 1st Cameronians from India. They had moved up to Pegu immediately after the Sittang battle, effectively covering the reorganization of 17th Division and its re-equipment, but were unable to prevent the Japanese infiltration across the Sittang towards the Pegu Yomas.

There were now five British infantry battalions in Burma.* Two, the Glosters and KOYLI had been part of the original garrison; the 'Dukes', West Yorkshires and Cameronians had been in India for several years, employed mostly in internal security duties, before being sent to Burma. All were regular units, their regular content much reduced by the requirement to help form new units in India Command, and with the exception of the 'Dukes', who had served on the North-West Frontier from 1935–7, hardly any of their junior officers and NCOs had ever been in action before. They had, however, the remarkable resilience of the British soldier, as well as the ability to see the humorous side of situations that were in fact very, very far from being funny. I remember asking a soldier in the 2nd Royal Tanks how the fighting in Burma compared with his experiences in the Western Desert in Egypt. 'Much the same amount of shit flying around,' he replied, 'but the trouble with these Japanese bastards is that they don't run away like the Italians!'

We never had a British battalion in 2nd Burma Brigade, although in the early stages we expected to have 2 KOYLI. The best combination would probably have been a British, an Indian and a Gurkha battalion, with a reconnaissance unit of Burma Rifles, but there was never the time for such a reorganization. I have to admit a certain weakness for the 4/12 FFR and the 12th (Poonch) Mountain Battery; they were both first-class fighting units.

During those early days of March, my time was spent either marshalling trains in the station yard, where I became quite an expert in shunting wagons, or driving the 200 miles to Toungoo and back, begging, borrowing or stealing supplies for 2nd Burma Brigade. We had managed to acquire several jeeps and, accompanied usually only by my orderly, I drove many weary hours along the dusty road, high above the sunbaked paddy fields that stretched eastward to the Sittang and westward to the Pegu Yomas, both hidden from view in the heat haze. It was blazingly hot from soon after sunrise until nightfall, and we rode

* A sixth, 1st Royal Inniskilling Fusiliers, was flown in to Magwe early in March, the last reinforcements to reach Burma Army. They too came straight from Internal Security duties in India.

wide open to the elements as a precaution against air attack. Japanese fighters seemed to find anything a target, sometimes even a solitary individual dashing desperately for cover. There was something malign about them. As for our own planes, we hardly ever saw one.

Meanwhile, there was hard fighting at Pegu, where the 55th Japanese Division was fighting to finish off 17th Division. General Smyth had advocated the withdrawal from Pegu on 28 February, having already moved his headquarters to Hlegu, 20 miles south-west of Pegu on the road to Rangoon; but Wavell countermanded this on 1 March when he visited Headquarters 17 Division, deciding to appoint Cowan to relieve Smyth, whom he considered to be 'a sick man'. There followed some of the fiercest fighting of the entire campaign as 7th Armoured Brigade and 48th Brigade fought to hold Pegu. Meanwhile, as were standard Japanese tactics, a road-block was established, effectively cutting off the Pegu garrison from Hlegu, where Headquarters 17 Division, together with a sadly reduced 16th Brigade, had been actively preparing for a Japanese onslaught.

None of this was known to us, or at least to me, until one day I picked up a British soldier thumbing a lift by the roadside. He was a 'Jock' from the Cameronians, cut off in some Japanese attack. Travelling always by night, lying up by day, he had walked the best part of fifty miles. He told me of the incident at Payagye where several of his comrades, stripped and tied to trees, had been used for bayonet practice by the Japanese; he did not go on to explain that a platoon of his regiment, after finding the bodies, had killed every Japanese and Burmese they had found in Payagye, and would have killed more had there been any more to kill. The bestial behaviour of the Japanese, as also of their Burmese allies, was an eye-opener to me. There was to be much more of it later.

The extent of Burmese collaboration with the Japanese will long continue to be a matter for debate. It is probably true that the vast majority of Burmese wished only to be left alone to get on with their lives. They saw no reason why they should die, either for us or the Japanese. It would have been stupid to have expected otherwise. Nevertheless, there was a very strong pro-independence movement, particularly among the intelligentsia, priesthood and students. Tagging along with them was the criminal element, to be found in any country.

At the outset of the campaign I cannot recall feeling any unease whenever I found myself by chance on my own in a Burmese village. Speaking Burmese as I did, there was no obvious change in relationships. But shortly after the Sittang disaster an incident occurred that led me to take precautions. I had stopped in a village between Pegu and Nyaunglebin to buy cigarettes. The headman invited me to his hut to drink tea. We had no sooner entered than we were joined by five or six men, all armed with *dahs* (knives). They squatted down, listening, while I talked with the headman, a surly fellow with a pronounced squint. My orderly, carrying a tommy gun he had never fired (we were desperately short of ammunition), stood by the door, looking on uneasily. One of the company suggested that the Japs would soon be in Nyaunglebin. When I said that we should eventually return, although we might temporarily be compelled to retreat, they laughed sarcastically. Someone took out his *dah* and began to sharpen it on a stone. Clearly it was time to go.

We went out to the jeep, two or three of the men slipping away as we did so, possibly to set up an ambush. I motioned to the headman to get in beside me, and when he declined I stuck my pistol into his side. As we drove off he cowered into his seat, obviously terrified of being shot, either by his own men or by me. I could see men running between the houses as I put my foot down and headed for the main road. Two miles farther on I tipped the headman out, warning him to keep a civil tongue in his head in future. I don't know which of us had been the most scared. It taught me a lesson. I never dared tell Brigadier Bourke who would undoubtedly have reprimanded me for being so foolhardy.

Undoubtedly, many Burmese actively supported the Japanese, fighting sometimes far more fanatically on their side than they ever did on ours. The spirit of Independence is a heady wine. They were, however, at their worst with the Indians, who suffered much worse from Burmese brutality than the British ever did. One particular incident has lived in my memory for nearly half a century.

I was standing one February morning beside the railway line, watching the columns of Indian coolies pouring through Nyaunglebin, when my eye was caught by a beautiful Indian woman, striding along like a Rajput princess, her child clasped to her left hip. She was tall and well-built, her black hair fastened in a bun, her pleated dark red skirt swinging like a kilt at every stride. Bangles at her wrists and ankles tinkled as she passed, her kohl-rimmed eyes meeting mine for a brief moment. She might have been a Gujar, or Brinjari, or from some other shepherd tribe that favours the dress of Rajasthan.

I was to see her again – twice. First, a few days later, and many miles farther on. She was still striding along the railway line, child on hip, head held high. I offered her my water bottle but she marched on regardless, disdaining any kind of help. When next I saw her, she was beyond it.

We were driving back from Toungoo, towards the evening. Road and railway, both on embankments, were only a few hundred yards apart. The endless procession of refugees, interspersed with bullock carts, came on and on. Those who died, or who fell by the way – the sick, the very old, the very young – were thrown down the embankment by those who followed behind. They lay there, stinking, for days on end. Suddenly there was a break in the refugee traffic, for perhaps a mile or so, until, rounding a bend, we came across some bodies lying in the road. A bright red skirt caught my eye and we stopped the jeep.

She lay there, her long black hair streaming out into a pool of fast congealing blood, her throat cut from ear to ear. One arm was raised across her face, warding off the blows. Her bodice had been ripped off, the haft of a knife protruding between her breasts. The bright red skirt had been pulled up above her waist in a final obscene gesture. The child, a little way apart, lay with its brains spilling out onto the tarmac. The bodies were still warm, the attack obviously having taken place only minutes previously.

A shot from my orderly distracted me. Some men were

running across the paddy fields beyond, Burmese with their *lungyis* pulled up above their knees so as to run faster. Guilty or not guilty? I never stopped to think but at that distance, with only a tommy gun, it was virtually impossible to hit, and they soon disappeared in the heat haze.

War is a nasty business, however it is fought. There are those who seem to believe that it is better to be killed by bullet, bayonet or grenade than by atomic bomb, but death is death whichever way it arrives. Kill or be killed is a meaningless expression for those who have never been called upon to face such a stark alternative. The killing of twenty-seven Burmese villagers by the KOYLI in April 1942,[6] because they suspected them of giving away their position to the advancing Japanese, was, if true, a nasty business, but none of us who fought in that campaign will cast a single stone. For there were similar incidents, without any doubt. The cold hard fury of the Cameronians when they found their bayoneted comrades; the 'Dukes' who found their popular commanding officer with his throat cut, after accepting Burmese hospitality. The Marines bayoneted to death after the raid on Henzada; the Indians maimed, raped, slaughtered in their thousands by gangs of bloodthirsty Burmese ruffians. In such circumstances, sadly, an eye for an eye, a tooth for a tooth, becomes the watchword – and it is a total delusion to believe otherwise.

It is only the anonymity of war that makes it bearable. The newspaper seller from Osaka and the bus conductor from Glasgow are faceless men when dressed in khaki, firing at each other with intent to kill. It is only when war becomes personalized, as in the case of the Indian woman so brutally murdered, that its full horror dawns on one. I sometimes wonder what would have happened had Hitler not stayed his hand for a time after Dunkirk; if the German hordes had poured across the Channel and subjecting us to Nazi rule. What would we have done? Acquiesced? I doubt it.

We were talking one night, the Brigadier, Merton and I, about the so-called 'Traitor Burmans' who were beginning to figure prominently in Situation Reports in March 1942. 'I bet they are all members of the Thakin Party,' said Merton. 'The

Thakins are disloyal to a man.' 'Disloyal to whom?' asked the Brigadier. 'To us? Or to Burma?' He went on to wonder aloud at the gullibility of such ardent nationalists. 'With us, they will get their independence sooner or later,' he said. 'With the Japanese, never!'

I was to be reminded of this conversation after our battle at Shwegyin. Among the prisoners was a Burmese aged about thirty-five, wearing a khaki shirt and a *lungyi*. He was one of the leaders, Merton said. I never discovered what happened to him. I was only in the room for a short time while Merton questioned him, speaking in Burmese, although the man spoke good English. I was greatly impressed. Speaking directly to me, in answer to one of Merton's questions, he said: 'What right have you got to ravage my country, to turn it into a waste, burning the houses, forcing the people to take refuge in the jungle? Burma isn't yours – it is ours!'

We did not have much trouble with 'Traitor Burmese' on our side of the Pegu Yomas, although no doubt there were some of them about. But on the western side, right up the Irrawaddy valley, places like Tharawaddy, Henzada and Prome were nests of anti-British 'resistance' fighters. We were to come up against some of them when 2nd Burma Brigade attacked Shwegyin on the east bank of the Sittang on 11 March. This was the first occasion when 1 BURDIV went into action against the Japanese and their Burmese supporters.

The plan was for 1st Burma Brigade to attack south from Nyaunglebin to capture Pyuntaza, and then to exploit south to Daik-u. The original intention had been to link up with 17th Division in Pegu. But on 10 March, 17th Division had broken through the 55th Japanese Division at Pegu and Hlegu, and had withdrawn up the road to Prome, with a covering force on the Henzada–Tharawaddy line. This being so, it was hard to understand why 1 BURDIV should have continued with the attack. 2nd Burma Brigade was to protect 1st Brigade's left flank by capturing Shwegyin and Madauk, for which purpose we were given the 5/1 Punjabis in place of 1 BURIF. 'I think we make on the deal,' I wrote in my diary on 7 March. 'They are a good battalion.' They certainly were.

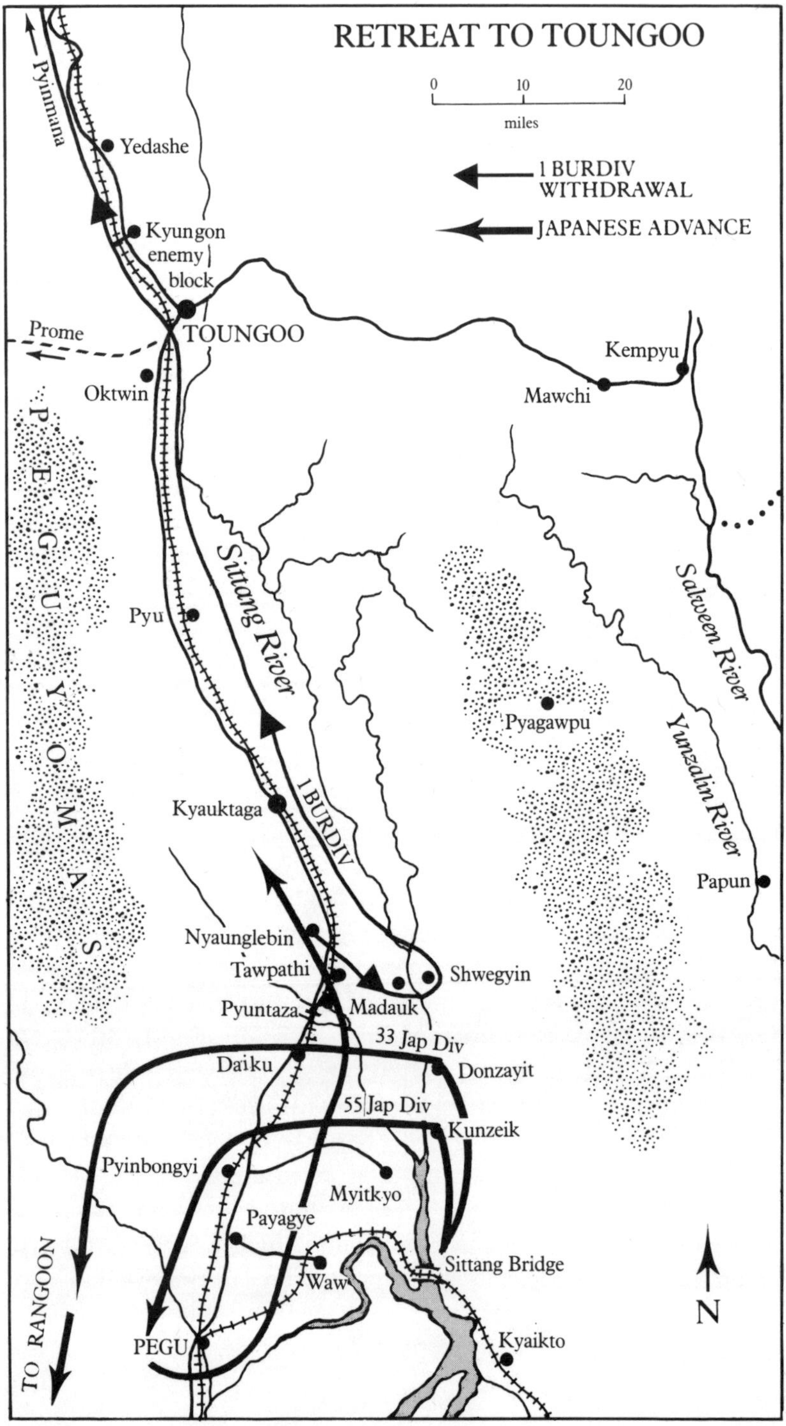
RETREAT TO TOUNGOO
0
10
20
miles
1 BURDIV WITHDRAWAL
JAPANESE ADVANCE
Pyinmana
Yedashe
Kyungon
enemy
block
TOUNGOO
Prome
Oktwin
Kempyu
Mawchi
PEGU YOMAS
Sittang River
Pyu
Salween River
Pyagawpu
Yunzalin River
1 BURDIV
Kyauktaga
Papun
Nyaunglebin
Tawpathi
Shwegyin
Pyuntaza
Madauk
33 Jap Div
Daiku
Donzayit
55 Jap Div
Kunzeik
Pyinbongyi
Myitkyo
Payagye
Sittang Bridge
Waw
TO RANGOON
N
PEGU
Kyaikto

We detrained 5/1 Punjabis at Kyauktaga because Nyaunglebin station was a shambles. This was fifteen miles north of us and we were desperately short of troop-carrying transport. There was much discussion until eventually it was agreed they should march, our few trucks being employed in ferrying them forward company by company – an interesting example of how road-bound we were becoming. All infantry should expect to march; indeed this same battalion a few weeks later was to cover thirty-nine miles in sixteen hours and still be fit to fight by the end of it.

1 BURDIV's baptism of fire was a case of mixed fortunes. On the right, 1st Burma Brigade got into Pyuntaza, 2/7 Rajputs advancing with some *élan* only to be held up at the road block just south of the town. The Japanese then counter-attacked in strength, a platoon of 5 BURIF detailed to protect a section (two guns) of 2nd Mountain Battery, deserting *en bloc*. The gunners had to get their guns away in a hurry, the resultant disorder being reflected in the rapidity of the Rajputs' initial withdrawal. Finally, the brigade reorganized about a mile north of Pyuntaza, 1 and 5 BURIF astride the main road and behind them 2/7 Rajputs, with 2nd and 23rd Mountain Batteries in support. For a casualty list of eleven killed, fourteen wounded and seventy-nine missing, we had accomplished virtually nothing. I happened to be at General Bruce Scott's advanced headquarters in Nyaunglebin when the final reports came in. His coolness surprised me, but, seeing me standing there, he took me by the arm and led me to one side. 'Do you think we shall ever get your Burma Rifles to stand and fight?' he asked. I am afraid to say I shook my head.

However, in 2nd Burma Brigade we were rather pleased with ourselves. 5/1 Punjabis, short of two rifle companies, had moved across country to Waing, on the Sittang, where 7 BURIF, no more than 250 strong, had established a bridgehead. At 0300 hours on 11 March the Punjabis crossed the river on rafts constructed by the Malerkotla Sappers. The Brigadier and Brigade Major watched the crossing. I remained at brigade headquarters, established in a pleasant little village, untouched by war. The attack on Shwegyin was due to begin at 0730, preceded by thirty minutes' bombing, but the RAF never appeared. Although we had no artillery support the Brigadier decided to continue with the attack, the Punjabis advancing down the road to the town supported only by their mortars. Driving the Japanese (and their Burmese and Thai allies) before them, the two companies on right and left kept touch by shouting their war cries, '*Sat Sri Akal*' by the Sikhs, '*Ya Ali*' by the Punjabi Mussalmans. By 1000 hours the town was ours. The Punjabis had four soldiers killed and one officer, two VCOs and fourteen soldiers wounded. They killed fifty enemy and took forty Burmese and Thais prisoner, but no Japanese.

On the other side of the river was Madauk, a town that straggled along both banks of the Sittang. 7 BURIF captured the west bank with little opposition, only to find that all boats had been taken across the river for safety. Major Kyadoe (a Karen)[7] then swam the river, returning with a boat which was used to ferry two platoons across the river. Joined by 'C' Company of the Punjabis, which had been following up the battalion, 7 BURIF then cleared Madauk on the east bank. We were all justifiably pleased by this success, Punjabis and Burma Rifles alike, and with good reason, since it turned out to be one of the few successful offensive actions in the entire campaign.

We were not left long in Shwegyin-Madauk. We were ordered to fall back across country to the Nyaunglebin–Toungoo road, twenty-five miles of extremely difficult 'going' across the dry paddy fields, most of it by night. We stopped eventually at Milestone 112, 1st Brigade having taken up a position south of us at Kyauktaga. 'This was a very pleasant little Indian village only a fortnight ago,' I wrote in my diary. 'Since then it has been evacuated and is now full of decomposing buffaloes and cattle. It stinks! Division used it as a transport park and it is very dusty. Nigel Loring and FF4 passed through . . . I go off on a recce, drive all day long, very tired . . .'

I had last seen Nigel Loring of Skinner's Horse, then serving with the BFF, playing polo in Mandalay in 1940. I recalled his gin consumption as being formidable; nevertheless he scored six goals. He was rather gloomy when we discussed the situation. He had been ordered to reconnoitre south towards the Pegu

Yomas, doubting whether all his mounted infantry *sowars* had their hearts in the game. 'I would give a lot for a squadron of Skinner's,' he told me. We heard later that he had been captured by the Japanese, many of his soldiers having galloped away to safety, and had been led by a rope tied round his neck to Daik-u. He survived the war in Rangoon Jail, dying some years later, doubtless as a result of his ordeal as a prisoner.

The Japanese certainly lost no time in following us up, 1st Brigade having a brisk little action at Kyauktaga on 16 and 17 March. 'It'll be our turn next,' said Merton gloomily after 1st Brigade had been ordered to withdraw through us. He was worried about his wife, from whom he had not heard since packing her off from Nyaunglebin. Neither had I heard from mine, for that matter, with possibly more reason for concern: someone had told me that the Japs were broadcasting lists of names on Saigon Radio of women taken by the Japanese off ships intercepted by them while sailing for Calcutta. My informant could not remember whether my wife's name had been among them, the inference being that it was. In fact she was safe in India. We were told later that the Japs had found the shipping lists on their capture of Rangoon, and had broadcast the names as part of their psychological warfare. I never did discover the truth of the rumour, but it added to my depression at the time when a recurrence of my dysentery was already making me feel miserable enough.

On 18 March we were holding a position just south of Gonde, 7 BURIF astride the main road, with 2 BURIF on the right and 5/1 Punjabis on the left. 1st Brigade had passed through us. Merton and I strolled down the road to gossip with McCarthy, CO of 7 BURIF. We stopped by a bridge, the road bending right and disappearing behind a field of sugar cane about 500 yards away. Merton was lighting one of his filthy cheroots while I swung my legs idly from the bridge parapet when suddenly a marching column appeared from behind the sugar cane. At first I thought it must be 1st Brigade's rear guard until Merton called out, 'Good God! They must be Japs!', at the same time vaulting over the parapet into the dry *chaung* below. I required no encouragement to follow suit, landing sprawling as 7 BURIF opened up with everything they had. A very shaken two officers made their way back to brigade headquarters where we were given a well-deserved rocket by the Brigade Major.

It was quite a brisk little battle while it lasted, but the Japs soon began to infiltrate round our flanks. I was told to go back to reconnoitre a new position for brigade headquarters, this time *behind* 1st Brigade. I remember so clearly being given these orders. The Brigadier was studying a map held by the Brigade Major, Jimmy Green, his pale face contrasting with his jet black hair, wearing the bush jacket, shorts, black hosetops and *chapplis* of the FFRif, was using his pipe as a pointer. Merton, four-square, a symbol of British ruggedness, was annoying the Brigadier by blowing cheroot smoke in his direction. Bill Smith, our young Signals subaltern, a man of great charm, completed the group. Suddenly, at tree-top level, a plane zoomed over us. Never have men fallen so flat on their faces so quickly, only to hear someone shouting, 'Don't shoot! Don't shoot! It's one of ours.' 'Impossible,' growled the Brigadier, picking himself up and dusting himself down, before giving me another well-deserved rocket for failing to post air sentries.

It was indeed one of ours, a Blenheim bomber operating from Magwe, the airfield now being used by the RAF and AVG, although not for much longer. 'Why do we see so little of the famous RAF?' I had grumbled into my diary the previous day. 'We haven't seen a fighter since Moulmein.' Nor would we. But we saw plenty of Japanese planes, fighters, bombers and reconnaissance. I don't know whether I disliked the bombers or fighters more, the former having the disconcerting habit of dropping their bombs all at once in one loud 'crump', the latter being quite capable of devoting their undivided attention to a single individual cowering behind a paddy bund, if no more worthwhile target presented itself.

The rest of our withdrawal, until we got behind the Chinese positions at Pyu, was a misery of moving by night, digging by day, and then moving off again after dark. 'It is difficult to believe men can fall asleep when marching,' writes Pat Carmichael, 'but it was quite common in the arduous conditions of the '42 campaign. A man would fight sleep for a long time while maintaining a fast pace, and then veer away for a few steps as he lost consciousness and collapsed. If he were lucky he might walk into a tree and bring himself back to life with a jolt . . . if not so lucky and no one at the rear of the column spotted him on the ground he would be lost.'[8] On at least two occasions I dozed off at the wheel of my jeep, to find myself at the foot of the embankment, fortunately still upright.

It was after passing through the Chinese lines that an incident occurred which has ever since convinced me that miracles do sometimes happen. I was driving back after a day spent reconnoitring yet another location for brigade headquarters, when my attention was drawn to what looked like a fire in some huts, about 600 yards away across the paddy fields. A column of smoke was usually the telltale sign of yet another Burmese attack on the refugees. Stopping the jeep my orderly and I, tommy guns at the ready, set off to investigate. A 30-cwt Chevrolet truck was drawn up behind the nearest hut. Beside it, adding to the flames and smoke, was an elderly Indian, surrounded by mail bags, the contents of which he was busily burning. He wore uniform of a kind, the badges of rank of a *subedar*. He was, he informed me, the sub-postmaster of such-and-such field post office. The mail he was burning, he said, was intended for 2nd Burma Brigade, now about to be overwhelmed by the enemy. He was endeavouring to ensure that none of our mail fell into enemy hands.

The mail bags were scattered around him, spilling out their contents. Heaven alone knows how many letters he had already consigned to the flames. I told him to stop. I would carry the mail back to brigade headquarters. He stood up, saluting, confident of a good job done. Idly, I put my hand into the nearest bag, drawing out a handful of letters. Two of them were from my wife, posted from Peshawar. It was the first time I had heard from her since Moulmein.

CHAPTER TWELVE

Vinegar Joe

'It's the hardest job I ever had handed to me.'
Lieutenant-General Joseph W. Stilwell, US Army[1]

'Enter the Chinese!' said the Punjabis' subaltern to me, as we drove through the sizeable township of Pyu on our way to Toungoo. 'Let's hope they are better at dealing with the Japs than we have been so far,' I replied, but without much conviction. The ill-equipped, shabbily uniformed soldiers straggling in single file past us looked in even worse shape than we did. Much of their equipment was slung on bamboo poles, carried between two men, and we saw them carrying a pig, tightly trussed and squealing. 'Tonight's rations,' said my companion. They were the advance guard of 200th Chinese Division (General Tai), part of Vth Army, which was taking over the Sittang front from 1 BURDIV. VIth Army was reported to be moving into the Shan States.

We were looking for Headquarters 1 BURDIV in Toungoo, only to find the town a smoking ruin. The Chinese had set part of it on fire in order to prepare their defences. Many of BURDIV's supplies had gone up in smoke, including all General Scott's kit and his household belongings. We drove on to Yedashe where we were told Divisional Rear Headquarters had been established. There we were mis-directed into a large compound, formerly a school, where a large number of Chinese, and a few American, officers were hanging about outside a building with a wide verandah and steps leading up to it. An American officer introduced himself to us; he was Colonel St John.

At that moment a violent row broke out, two men appearing

on the verandah. One was shouting at the other, his choice of expletives filling me with admiration since he never once repeated himself. The other stood strangely silent. He was wearing the rank badges of a colonel in the US Army. The angry man was wearing a cotton singlet, khaki slacks and campaign boots. His head was bare and almost shaved, his face was gaunt, his spectacles rimless. 'That's General Stilwell,' said St John. 'He's sure mad about something.' He certainly was for a few moments later he came bounding down the steps, two at a time and, ignoring our salutes, jumped into a jeep and vanished in a cloud of dust, still bare-headed. That was my one and only encounter with the famous 'Vinegar Joe', one of the most remarkable characters to take part in the Burma campaign.

It would have been difficult to credit, had we known it at the time, that this odd-looking man had been chosen by General Marshall to command the American invasion of North Africa ('Torch'), before being switched on Roosevelt's instructions to command the American forces in China, Burma and India, and – hopefully – to act as Chief of Staff to Chiang Kai-shek. His relations with Chiang, whom he nicknamed 'Peanut', as well as with his British allies are now common knowledge, although it must be said in his defence that Chiang was impossible to deal with. Stilwell's Anglophobia is less easy to understand. 'He had an inbred hatred of the English,' wrote Brigadier Field, who had served in Peking when Stilwell was US Military Attaché in China. 'He had developed hatred into a fine art, and seemed to dislike his own countrymen almost as much as the "Limeys".'[2]

Stilwell was, however, brave, and extraordinarily tough for his fifty-nine years. Like most American regular officers of that time, he had spent long years as a subaltern, promotion coming only late in his service; he may therefore be forgiven for being cynical.[3] Nor could he ever succeed in getting a straight answer out of Chiang, whose suspicion and dislike of the British was only matched by his determination to keep his armies intact. 'Chiang Kai-shek wasn't really interested in fighting Japanese, so long as they remained a respectful distance away from Chungking,' wrote Field. 'What he wanted was to build up an army copiously stocked with modern weapons with which he could eventually fight the Communist Chinese . . .'[4] Field claims that Stilwell never appreciated this.

General 'Pinky' Dorn, another Chinese 'expert' who served under Stilwell for most of the Burma campaign, and whose Anglophobia was probably a reflection of his General's, wrote of Stilwell that he was at times impatient, tough and caustic, but was basically understanding, humorous and kindly. He expected high standards, integrity and forceful action from both political and military leaders. For those who failed to 'measure up', or who tried to whitewash their mistakes and inaction, he had little patience.[5]

Unfortunately, Stilwell had little concept of the difficulties under which Alexander and his subordinate commanders were operating. Nor did he find Wavell, with his reserve, easy to understand – nor at a later date Mountbatten. Of the British generals, possibly only Slim had the personality to attract Stilwell. He was critical of the large British staffs, forgetting that the Americans were even worse in this regard. Field quotes Stilwell's own Chief of Staff as saying, 'The General, whenever we see him, which is not often, never tells us anything, and we might as well be back in the USA for all the good we are doing.'[6]

The only adjective to describe the Chinese was 'unreliable'. They had no logistics worth the name and time meant nothing to them. They travelled the country like the Tartar hordes, looting, stealing and burning. No Chinese general felt bound to carry out an order with which he disagreed; indeed, orders issued without the endorsement of Chiang Kai-shek's seal, which only he could confer on his subordinates, meant little or nothing. Their discipline was equally rough and ready. One of our liaison officers with the VIth Army told me of an incident when an elderly Shan woman complained that her blanket had been stolen. When reported to the local commander, he lined up his men by the roadside and asked the woman to identify the culprit. Although this was virtually impossible, she selected one at random, according to my informant. Immediately, the colonel shot him three times in the stomach, leaving him struggling in his death throes as the soldiers were marched away. When the British officer ventured to suggest that the crime scarcely merited such a punishment, the colonel replied, 'Why not? There are lots more where he came from.'

Very few Chinese spoke English, none of us Chinese. Interpreters were few and far between. Driving back to brigade headquarters after a long, hard day, I was stopped by a Chinese picket which at pistol point commandeered my jeep – and me – to drive back fifteen miles to collect their rations, a pig roasted whole. This inability to communicate, coupled with their disregard for human life and shortage of modern weapons, made co-operation with them almost impossible. How Stilwell and his staff bore with them is difficult to imagine.

Like the Japanese, they were skilful field engineers, erecting and camouflaging defences in half the time it would take our soldiers. They would also demolish bridges and construct road blocks in total disregard of the fact that we were still falling back through them. On 19 March I wrote in my diary: 'Spent entire night shepherding lorried column and 7 BURIF (in lorries) back to brigade rest area. We had to drive about 20 miles along roads packed with transport of 1 Brigade moving back, and Chinese moving up. Matters complicated by innumerable Chinese roadblocks, usually dozens of huge trees chopped down across roads. Met 23 Battery about 0100 hours and they saved my life by giving me tea . . . Dysentery has begun again and I don't feel fit. Very tired too. Been on the go for 48 hours and no sleep and have driven miles.'

Nevertheless, despite the difficulties, it was a thousand pities that Wavell had been so chary of accepting Chiang Kai-shek's offer to send his Vth and VIth Armies into Burma until so late. Wavell's reasons have already been explained, and were sound enough at the time, but it caused Chiang to lose 'face', so vital to the Chinese. He never really forgave us. When, later, both Wavell and Hutton were clamouring for Chinese support, Chiang was careful to keep his generals under tight control. Although he allowed 200th Division to move as far south as Toungoo, the remaining two divisions in Vth Army (22nd and 96th) were held back on Chiang's order south of Mandalay.

Meanwhile VIth Chinese Army was moving into the Shan States, thereby releasing 13th Indian Brigade from Karenni to rejoin 1 BURDIV. The Chinese put a detachment into Mawchi, an important mining centre, connected with Toungoo by a motorable road which crossed the Sittang about five miles east of that town. It was vitally important to control this road since it provided an excellent route into the Southern Shan States. In Karenni itself Karen levies had been raised, strengthened by the Karen company of 1 BURIF after 1st Brigade's arrival in Toungoo. They were to do excellent work under Captain Arthur Thompson, until compelled to withdraw under Japanese pressure.[7] The levies remained behind under Major Paul ('Stookey') Seagrim, originally of 20 BURIF, and a wonderful leader of men. Seagrim eventually gave himself up to the Japanese to prevent further harassment of the Karens. They executed him. A DSO was dropped to him by parachute in 1943, and he was posthumously awarded the George Cross. His brother, serving with the Green Howards in Tunisia, was posthumously awarded the Victoria Cross. A remarkable family record.

2nd Burma Brigade was to entrain at Kyungon, about four miles north of Toungoo. One mile away, on the far side of the road to Mandalay, was the airfield, until recently the AVG's main base in Burma. We could see the hangars quite plainly from the embankment, on which was drawn up our train, waiting for the engine which might or might not arrive today, tomorrow, or the day after. Beyond the airfield were patches of thick lantana bushes, dotting the plain as far as the Sittang, five or six miles away. Through field glasses we could just see the line of trees that marked the line of the river. The occasional figures we could see moving about on the airfield we took to be Chinese, digging like moles, as was their habit. We heard that the Chinese had been heavily engaged at Oktwin, ten miles to the south of us. 2 BURIF, 7 BURIF and 2nd Mountain Battery, which had just joined us, had been safely dispatched to Taungdwingyi on the Irrawaddy front; 5/1 Punjabis and brigade headquarters were bringing up the rear. We understood that 1st Brigade were entraining at Yedashe, the next station to the north, where I BURDIV rear headquarters were still established.

In my diary for 22 March I had recorded:

> Our train is sitting on an embankment at Kyungon, a few miles outside Toungoo, waiting for an engine to arrive to pull us away. We have been waiting for 24 hours now and one hasn't turned up yet. The whole of brigade headquarters and the 5/1st Punjabis are here, sitting about the embankment, and it is uncomfortably exposed with so much enemy 'air' about. Sandy Sandeman rode by with his troopers earlier this morning; they are carrying out a reconnaissance to the Sittang, he says. Rather him than me – it's too damned hot for a quiet ride in the country. Sandy reckons there must be a lot of pig in the *chaungs* between here and the Sittang and was moaning because he had left his hog-spears behind in Lashio. He also told me he was riding the best polo pony in Burma; probably true as she was a lovely little mare. He moved off with his column about nine o'clock – about sixty of them, and nearly all Sikhs.

"We watched them go," I was to write later,

> the curb chains jingling as they went, and the dust hanging over them in the still morning air. Behind them there lingered the smell of leather and sweating horses, and we were left with an unforgettable memory in a war which was waged mostly with machines. The Guides must have looked like that, I thought, as they scouted ahead of 'Bobs' on the way from Kabul to Kandahar. Then the dust cloud merged with the shimmering heat haze, and the sound of hoofs died away in the distance. Although we did not know it at the time, we had been present at a unique moment in all the long history of the British mounted arm.[8]

Sandeman, of the Central India Horse, was a great friend of mine, often staying with me during my bachelor days in Mandalay. He modelled himself on some character out of Surtees – Facey Romford, I fancy – and dressed the part, driving about in a gig and dispensing snuff to whoever was willing to partake. 'Financial pressure, dear boy,' he would explain, had driven him to Burma where he served with a battalion of the BFF, chasing polo balls with his spectacles tied on with a ribbon; without them he was as blind as a bat.

None of us knew that the Japanese were rapidly encircling Toungoo although, as we were sitting under some trees having lunch, a plane came over and machine-gunned us. 'We remained sitting – like BFs,' I recorded. However, after a series of fierce attacks against the Chinese at Oktwin, a strong Jap column swung west with the intention of outflanking Toungoo from that direction. A smaller column was moving on the east, between Toungoo and the Sittang. There had been hand-to-hand fighting during the night of 22/23 March, the Chinese holding firm and inflicting heavy casualties on the enemy. Fortunately at 1500 hours an engine arrived at last and we entrained and set off for Taungdwingyi via Pyinmana. We had left not a moment too soon.

On the following morning Tom Jones and Pat Carmichael of 23rd Mountain Battery, which was bivouacked near the airfield, rode over on their chargers to inspect the deserted hangars. Hardly had they reached them than 'there was gunfire from across the main road followed by shell bursts to the south . . . We looked at each other and dug in our heels.'[9] The Japanese were advancing from beyond the railway, more or less in a direct line from where our train had been sitting throughout the previous day. Within minutes 23rd Battery was in action, firing over open sights at one stage, the main problem being the difficulty of differentiating between Japanese and Chinese, many of the latter lining the road and railway embankment. It was by now imperative for the battery to withdraw, if it was ever to get away to rejoin 1 BURDIV; and this it did successfully, making for Pyinmana instead of Yedashe, where it was assumed the station might be under attack. It was a memorable march, fifty-three miles, of which the first forty-three had been covered in a little more than twelve hours, most of them in blazing heat and with hardly any water.

Sandeman, meanwhile, had made history, although he lost his life making it. After leaving us he had scouted eastwards across the paddy plain to the Sittang, returning early the next day when he bumped head on into the Japanese column making for the airfield. Presumably he mistook them for Chinese at first, only realizing his mistake at the very last moment, when he drew his sword and ordered his trumpeter to sound the 'Charge!' Some of his soldiers charged with him, others found discretion the better part of valour and galloped off to safety. It was the last mounted charge in the long history of British cavalry, but Sandy never lived to tell the tale.

While all this was happening we were trundling on to Taungdwingyi, across the parched, scrub country of what we knew in Burma as the 'Dry Zone'. The harsh laterite was broken and seamed by the monsoon rains, dense thickets of lantana breaking up the monotony. The Brigadier was worried about our mules, left with Dick Lewin, who was supposed to be following after us. He kept asking me where they were, delivering an imperial rocket when I said I did not know. Actually Dick had a very narrow escape getting the animals away in the dark, eventually entraining them miles up the line at Yedashe or Pyinmina – I am not quite sure which. He made light of it when he rejoined us at Taungdwingyi seventy-two hours later, but it was a brave effort.

We also heard later that BURDIV rear headquarters had been badly bombed, several friends of mine being wounded. One of them was George Cockburn, a member of the Burma Civil Service, whom I had known since we were both boys in Dunblane in Perthshire. Jack Lewis, another friend of mine, lost a leg, I was told. But information was almost impossible to obtain. 'What's the news?' was the usual greeting whenever anyone new visited headquarters. It was around this time, I think, that Brigadier Bourke was acting as GOC of 1 BURDIV, General Bruce Scott having gone to Prome to help form BURCORPS headquarters, prior to Bill Slim's arrival. It remains a complete jumble in my memory, the inevitable confusion of war made worse by the fresh onset of dysentery that seemed to dull the mind as well as weaken the body. I was beginning to think I was destined to leave my bones in Burma and, surprisingly, I didn't much care.

I remember that March as possibly the most depressing month in my life. We were continually retreating: reconnoitring, digging and occupying a position throughout the day, only to withdraw from it during the night. Tomorrow would be the same. It was blindingly hot, the few Burmese to be found in the villages and towns were palpably hostile, the constant danger of air attack made everyone jumpy, and there was a tension which affected each of us in different ways. The Brigadier was edgy, complaining about the food to Merton, objecting to wherever I had happened to house brigade headquarters. Jimmy Green found relief in 'being busy', constantly checking sentries, slit trenches for depth, etc. It drove us all mad. Merton was just plain gloomy, worried to death about his wife and children, hating the army and its idiotic ways. Dudley Lincoln of the Ulsters, who had stayed with us after 3 BURIF had totally disintegrated, only a platoon of Kachins remaining to defend brigade headquarters, told anyone prepared to listen how much he wanted to get away from the Burma Rifles and back to his British regiment. This irritated the Brigadier who pointed out quite reasonably that, however much he might happen to agree with Dudley's sentiments, his chances of achieving his ambition at that moment were nil; therefore, the less he talked about it, the better.

On the few occasions when we could sit round a table and relax (we still had whisky, although beer was as precious as rubies, and always warm), there was little discussion about retreating to India. The thought did not enter my head until weeks later. We were talking about counter-offensives; the sudden arrival on the scene of masses of our planes, not theirs; the possibility, now that the Chinese were involved, of the Japs being stopped, and then thrown back.

The most depressing aspect of the entire business was for me the evident hostility of so many Burmese, whose friendship previously I had taken for granted. Mr T. L. Hughes has put up a stout defence of the British administration, contending that 'the administration kept going until the end . . .'[10] Hughes, who did sterling work struggling to restore law and order in Rangoon after the panic evacuation in February, is to some extent supported by Hutton, who has written, 'Although the administration has been criticised my own opinion is that it stood up to the strain of war remarkably well.'[11]

From our point of view, that is the soldiers', we regarded the administration as patchy. Some officials did extremely well, others were no more or less than passengers. Hutton believed very strongly that the civil and military should have been put on a war footing before war actually broke out. This was probably unacceptable politically, but the objection hardly applies to Hutton's other criticism – 'The civil railways and inland water transport agencies could not be persuaded, until it was too late, that it was vital to have unified control and to form some military units.'[12]

It was in districts like Tharawaddy, Henzada and Magwe that the breakdown of civil administration had such disastrous effects. Magwe, in particular, had had a bad reputation for dacoity at the best of times; Tharawaddy and Henzada were Thakin strongholds. In Magwe district it was probably true to say that the majority of the population were against us, a *pongyi* in Taungdwingyi telling me that the sooner we left, the better for everyone concerned. Then he offered me his blessing – in English! That there was a fifth column is hard to deny.

Taungdwingyi, where we spent two or three days, was an odious place. 'No *bandobast* at all by Div, Corps or Army,' I wrote in my diary. 'The station compound is strewn with petrol – 75,000 gallons of high octane for the armoured brigade. Hope a bombing raid doesn't catch us out . . . I found a good spot for headquarters, near the station, but not too near – a small *pongyi kyaung* which is reasonably clean. Battalion commanders all helpful – even Dennis O'Callaghan!'*

The next day Brigadier Bourke set out for Prome to meet the Corps Commander. There he was told to form a defensive position round Allanmyo, on the east bank of the Irrawaddy, about fifty miles south-west of Taungdwingyi. He returned to tell us that we might be there for some time since it was the Corps Commander's intention to recapture Rangoon before the monsoon broke in mid-May! Bill Smith said he must be 'barmy'. There was a statue of a *nat* in the far corner of our *pongyi kyaung*, its right arm outstretched, pointing north. It was, said Lincoln, yelling, 'Get out! Get out!' On 25 March we

* CO of 2 BURIF with whom I frequently crossed swords, as did the Brigadier.

did, heading for Allanmyo in a large road convoy, mostly American Lease-Lend trucks we had commandeered at Nyaunglebin and guarded like gold ever since. But we were soon to lose them, to the Brigadier's fury. Events in the south, around Prome, were going very badly for us.

After extricating his headquarters and 17th Division from the jaws of the Japanese trap, Alexander had ordered Cowan, now GOC 17 Division, to establish himself firmly on Prome, holding as far south as possible in order to delay the Japanese advance. Although the Japanese 33rd Division had followed up rapidly from Rangoon, the Japanese too required a brief pause in order to reorganize and sort out their logistics. Their 55th Division was pushing us back up the Sittang valley towards Toungoo; reinforcements were being sent to Rangoon. These consisted of 56th and 18th Imperial Guards Divisions from Singapore, together with two tank regiments. To meet the inevitable Japanese offensive in April, Alexander planned to have 17th Division and 1 BURDIV, forming BURCORPS, in the Irrawaddy valley based on Prome; with Vth Chinese Army in the Sittang valley, and VIth Chinese Army extending eastwards in the Southern Shan States.

Alexander realized that Burma Army would be unable to launch a major counter-offensive without substantial reinforcements. The best he could hope to achieve was 'to impose the maximum delay on the enemy and make him expend resources which he might have employed elsewhere'.[13] It should be remembered in this context that at the time there were serious fears of a Japanese invasion of India, although it is clear now that the Japanese had not then included the conquest of India in their plans. Meanwhile, Alexander pressed India Command to extend and improve the indifferent track that led from Imphal into the Chindwin valley.

The tactics he advocated for delaying the enemy bear a marked resemblance to those recommended by Wavell to General Hartley prior to the winding-up of ABDACOM. Strong points were to be established from where mobile forces could sally out to attack the advancing Japanese. Prome and Allanmyo were to be made defended localities, stocked for twenty-one days with food and ammunition. If by-passed, they were to hold out and fight on. Hutton, Alexander's chief of staff, did not agree with these tactics. 'In my opinion,' he wrote, 'such tactics are unlikely to be successful and we shall either have to abandon such garrisons to their fate or else withdraw them at the last moment with severe losses in supplies and transport which we can ill afford.'[14]

Such losses would have indeed been drastic since in Burma Army we were by this stage 'living off our fat'. Had it not been for the prescience of Major-General Goddard, and his remarkable success in back-loading supplies and ammunition to Upper Burma before Rangoon was evacuated, we should have lacked the wherewithal to fight at all. Nevertheless, it was vital to conserve supplies, particularly ammunition. Much had gone astray during the back-loading operation, including the entire stock of maps.

Nor did Hutton agree with the counter-offensive undertaken south of Prome between 28 and 30 March. This was on Alexander's orders, and was intended to relieve the pressure on the Chinese Vth Army around Toungoo. Chiang Kai-shek had specifically asked for it, but all it did was to lose valuable men, and even more valuable tanks, the 7th Hussars losing ten. Of the infantry battalions involved the 'Dukes' suffered the worst, losing five officers and 117 soldiers.

If the Prome offensive was counter-productive, very much worse had befallen shortly beforehand. On 22 March we lost complete control of the skies over the battlefield. It is true that neither the RAF nor AVG had been much in evidence since the Sittang battle, but the occasional sight of a Blenheim flying over us during the weary retreat from Nyaunglebin gave our morale a fillip. However, on 21 and 22 March Japanese fighters and bombers delivered devastating attacks on Magwe where BURWING (as the RAF component was called) had been based after moving from Mingalodon. Magwe had no warning system, protective pens for aircraft, or effective anti-aircraft defences. The Hurricanes and P.40s put up a gallant defence against great odds but could do little against such weighty attacks. The AVG commander withdrew his three remaining undamaged aircraft to Loiwing to refit; Air Vice-Marshal Stevenson, AOC BURWING, flew what remained of his undamaged aircraft to Akyab, where the Japanese soon wrote them off.

There was at the time much criticism of the hastiness of the RAF's departure, the living quarters abandoned with food still on the tables, valuable equipment left scattered all over the place, road convoys filled with ground crews heading north at breakneck pace. General Dorn, who was aide to General Stilwell in Burma, quotes Slim as saying, 'You can thank God, Stilwell, that you don't have a separate air force in your service. I had no authority to stop those planes from going to India, and I have no authority to recall them.'[15] General Winterton, who met Stevenson in Calcutta on his way to join Alexander early in April, found him 'depressing and depressed'. But it is hard to see what else he could have done but evacuate his few remaining aircraft to India. Left in Burma, they would have been sitting ducks.

The effects on those of us on the ground were particularly grim. Hutton was not too wide of the mark when he wrote: 'It was, however, clear that after the Prome operations the morale of the troops, including the British battalions, was very low.'[16] There is a tendency for official historians and for generals when writing their Dispatches to gloss over such temporary aberrations, for fear of giving rise to controversy among those who still survive. There can be, however, no reason to do so nearly half a century later. That there was a serious fall in morale after the RAF's departure cannot surely be disputed. It ceased to be amusing when the mere sound of an aircraft led one to look for the nearest slit trench or patch of cover. Many years later, when serving in West Germany, I sometimes wondered whether the generals and brigadiers who were so blithely moving their regiments and battalions from A to B had ever experienced a time when the air was the enemy's preserve. I had – and I have never forgotten it.

Japanese bombers, now freed from hindrance, ranged far and wide over Burma, reducing town after town to a blazing ruin. Since wood is the most easily available building material in Burma, the towns burnt merrily. The effects, not only on the civilian population but on the troops also, was devastating. Nor were those Burmese operating on the side of the Japanese slow to take their cue from such ruthless activities. It was not uncommon for villages, even haystacks and woodyards, to be set on fire in order to indicate the presence of British troops. In an appreciation, written presumably on Alexander's instructions, Hutton wrote on 26 March: 'Many of the essential services of Burma have practically collapsed. Even at several hundreds of miles from the front, services have already ceased to function, personnel have disappeared and orders are disobeyed or ignored. This applies to both superior as well as to subordinate personnel.'[17] And yet there was no martial law because the Governor and his ministers could not agree.

When I read about the opposition to civil defence in this country today I am reminded of those chaotic days in Burma when the soldiers, with all their faults, alone provided any kind of damage control. It is only when the world is collapsing around us that one realizes how important it is for simple, disciplined men to be in control. At least they can persuade other equally simple men to do what they tell them to do in order to keep the water running, the latrines cleaned, and the dead bodies removed from the sidewalks – and buried. We owed them a lot in Burma.

It was hard to maintain morale in such depressing circumstances. Increasingly, as we retreated north, organized bands of Burmese, well armed and often quite well trained, appeared on the Japanese side. These were not fifth columnists, but the nucleus of what was to become the Burmese National Army (BNA), commanded by Aung San as a Japanese-appointed general. They fought bravely, sometimes fanatically. I remember Sergeant Eteson of the headquarters staff saying to me, 'Why do we bother, sir? If they are so keen to get rid of us, I would much rather be home watching Leeds United than hanging about a shit-hole like Taungdwingyi.' It was difficult to disagree, although when I told Jimmy Green, he told me to put Eteson on to digging slit trenches, his most certain cure for anything touching on 'dangerous thoughts'.

2nd Burma Brigade rolled into Allanmyo on Wednesday, 25 March. I followed next day with the rear party. The town straggled along the east bank of the Irrawaddy, very low at that season, for about two miles. 2 BURIF had already crossed the river to Thayetmyo, moving south to Kama in order to protect the left flank of 17th Division, which we now heard was to move back from Prome to Yenangyaung and the oilfileds. The reason for this change of plan was not immediately apparent to us; I remember the Brigadier relieving his frustration by insisting on moving brigade headquarters nearer the river bank, necessitating the digging of yet another collection of slit trenches. In the meantime Jimmy Green sent me off to find some barbed wire, for which he appeared to have a special regard.

We were not to know about the very serious developments on the Sittang front where the Chinese 200th Division was fighting desperately against the 55th, and elements of the 56th, Japanese Divisions. Stilwell, having obtained Chiang's permission to move the 22nd and 96th Divisions south to assist 200th Division, ordered 22nd Division, as soon as it had reached Pyinmana, to launch an attack. But nothing happened. On 28 March Stilwell, desperate to relieve the pressure on Toungoo, requested BURCORPS to attack the Japanese south of Prome. However, it did not help the Chinese who were forced to cut their way out, abandoning Toungoo but failing to demolish the bridge over the Sittang. *This was a signal disaster*. It left the way open for the Japanese to advance east into the Shan States by the Mawchi–Bawlake road. The 56th Japanese Division was soon rolling along this road, meeting little opposition from the VIth Chinese Army, now deployed in the Southern Shan States. It was to prove the beginning of the end for the Burma Army, *and* for our Chinese allies.

CHAPTER THIRTEEN

The Battle of Yenangyaung

'Dunkirk, compared with Yenangyaung, was a picnic!'
Comment by an NCO in 2nd Royal Tanks[1]

It was towards the end of March that I first met Bill Slim, our newly-appointed Corps Commander. I think it must have been in Allanmyo where he had a meeting with Bruce Scott, GOC 1 BURDIV. 'By a trick of fate, for which I shall always be thankful,' Slim was to write later, 'Scott, Cowan and I all came from the 1st Battalion, 6th Gurkhas. We had served and lived together for twenty-odd years; we – and our wives – were the closest friends . . .'[2] Those of us who served under them had been lucky too.

I found Slim both impressive and reassuring. He was wearing an ordinary army issue *topi*, without embellishment, an ill-pressed khaki bush-shirt without medal ribbons, and a pair of khaki slacks that looked as if he had slept in them (which he probably had). There was none of that trimness in appearance which I always associated with Alexander, and yet, without any obvious effort, Slim dominated the scene. I was to meet him many times in the years to come and he always recalled to mind that remark by Oliver Cromwell, 'If you choose godly honest men to be captains, honest men will follow them.'[3] If I had to compare Slim with any other great British general I think I would select Cromwell, although Slim had certainly more humour and, I suspect, more humanity. He did not have Alex's *panache*, nor Monty's fire, but he impressed by his evident integrity, the absence of any kind of "stuffiness', and by the warmth of his personality. He seemed to me to possess many of the characteristics of Auchinleck, another Indian Army general whom I came greatly to admire, but he was less austere than 'the Auk' and therefore easier to get on terms with.

Slim did not make promises, as Monty did on occasions; promises which, if they failed to materialize, might damage morale. Nor did he convey the impression that our difficulties were only temporary, as Alexander might have done. Slim just gave one confidence that everything that could be done to provide us with a fighting chance would be done. If his effect on my personal morale was any guide, I can only say he stiffened my resolution, and this after only a few minutes' conversation.

God knows he had little enough cause for confidence. The RAF had pulled out. 17th Division had been very badly mauled at Prome, as Hutton, to give him his due, had predicted would be the case; while we in BURDIV lacked almost everything we needed to turn us into a well-balanced force of all arms. Nor, so far as I could see, was there any prospect of reinforcements. Perhaps Bill Slim thought the Chinese would pull our chestnuts out of the fire?

There was, I suppose, just a chance that they might have done had their Vth and VIth Armies moved into Burma in late December rather than during the following January/February. Or, had Stilwell been successful in reinforcing their 200th Division in Toungoo to hold on to the town. As it was, the Japanese, as always quick to seize an opportunity, reinforced their 56th Division with an extra 250 trucks and sent it across the Sittang bridge the Chinese had failed to demolish on a rip-roaring dash into the Southern Shan States. The objective was Lashio, which would effectively cut the Burma Road to China, at the same time destroying the Chinese VIth Army, which was supposed to be covering Alexander's left flank. Simultaneously the 55th Division, now joined by the 18th Imperial Guards Division from Singapore, would press the Chinese Vth Army north towards Mandalay, with the aim of compelling both the British and Chinese to fight at Mandalay with their backs to the Irrawaddy. As part of this plan the 33rd Division, now back in the battle after its capture of Rangoon, would press up the east bank of the Irrawaddy, aiming to capture the oil fields at Yenangyaung *intact*, the Japanese requirement for gasoline being of paramount importance. After Yenangyaung, the 33rd Division would cross the Irrawaddy with Shwebo as its objective, thereby cutting off the retreat of the British and Chinese forces west of Mandalay.

The switch of the Japanese into the Shan States compelled Alex to change his plans. There was no point in trying to hang on to Prome with Toungoo in Japanese hands. It was, however, essential to cover the oil fields, at the same maintaining contact with the Chinese Vth Army now withdrawing slowly north from Toungoo. It was therefore decided to stand on a line running west-east from Minhla (on the west bank of the Irrawaddy) through Taungdwingyi and Pyinmana (an important rail junction fifty miles north of Toungoo) to Loikaw in the Southern Shan States. BURCORPS would be responsible from Minhla to Taungdwingyi, a frontage of more than forty miles; Vth Army for Pyinmana; and VIth Army for Loikaw. The latter town was important because a motorable road ran north from it to Lashio.

Slim, who could not afford to leave the west bank of the Irrawaddy open for a Japanese/Burmese advance northwards, which meant having some kind of force on the west bank of the river, told Alexander that a frontage of forty miles would stretch his corps to its limits; he would have nothing in hand with which to counter-attack, if required. Alexander accordingly asked the Chinese for help in holding Taungdwingyi, the loss of which would expose both the British left flank and the Chinese right. A Chinese regiment was promised but failed to materialize. The truth was that neither Chiang Kai-shek nor Stilwell had any faith in Slim's ability to hold up the Japanese. Stilwell went so far as to tell Dorn that Chiang Kai-shek *hated* the British; Chiang had in fact communicated his feelings directly to Roosevelt, saying that in his opinion the British were not fighting hard enough, a belief that Stilwell vehemently shared.

The time had obviously come for Alexander to reach some kind of arrangement with Chiang. They met in Maymyo where they agreed a strategy. Alexander pointed out that BURCORPS had no reserve. Chiang said he would send a division to Taungdwingyi. Three days later he told Stilwell to do nothing.

'Dealing with Chiang Kai-shek is like trying to make marbles out of mercury,' Colonel St John told me when we were in hospital together in Maymyo. From Chiang Kai-shek downwards, Chinese strategy was essentially defensive, political considerations invariably taking precedence over the military. The almost unbroken succession of defeats suffered at Japanese hands had convinced Chiang that only when the odds were overwhelmingly in Chinese favour was offensive action possible. Therefore, in order to keep his forces intact and also for political reasons, the Chinese traded space for anything more positive. Given their almost unlimited manpower such a policy may be hard to defend, but it should be remembered that they were desperately short of weapons and supplies. Where the ordinary Chinese general was concerned, the loss of a few guns or mortars far outweighed the death or capture of hundreds of soldiers.

An example of this attitude occurred during the withdrawal of Vth Army from Toungoo. A Divisional commander was ordered to counter-attack. When Stilwell visited him in the course of the battle, he found to his annoyance that the entire Divisional artillery, consisting of a battery of obsolescent French 75s, had been withdrawn far to the rear lest they be captured. Their retention was far more important than the overrunning of a complete infantry regiment.

To most of us who came into contact with them, the Chinese seemed to be little more than a rabble. Cooperating with them was desperately difficult. There were the problems of language, as well as the fact that the Chinese had virtually no logistical support of *any* kind. Nor did time mean anything to them. Any plan that depended on a close attention to timing was doomed before battle began. Moreover, many Chinese commanders, from battalions upwards, were at loggerheads with each other. It was not uncommon for a regimental commander to refuse to carry out orders issued by his divisional commander, or to carry them out in such a fashion as to ensure their failure.

Stilwell knew his Chinese, of course. He had been working in China on and off for ten to fifteen years. But he was now endeavouring to conduct operations, rather than just observe them. It was a nightmare. Whatever he might have agreed with

Alexander, whom he did not regard very highly, and however much support he might have been promised by the Generalissimo, whom he regarded even less highly, Stilwell found he just could not deliver. The friction down the Chinese chain of command brought everything to a grinding halt sooner or later. Unless he was personally on the spot – to supervise, cajole or threaten – the Chinese commanders went their own sweet way. Stilwell was much criticized as a general officer for spending so much of his time away from his headquarters; and, when in the field, acting more like a battalion commander than a three-star general. But it was the only way he could get the Chinese to move.

The problem of exercising command and control over wide areas during a time when radio communications were uncertain, helicopters were still in the future, and light aircraft were few and hard to come by, is overlooked far too often by military critics, particularly when writing about the First World War and the first half of the Second World War. Stilwell's headquarters, like Alexander's, was in Maymyo. Chiang Kai-shek was in Chungking, several hours' flight away over some of the most forbidding terrain on this earth. The land fighting was taking place 300 miles to the south, the only means of transportation jeep, car, truck or railway. Many of the towns and villages en route were either burnt out or burning. The air was the enemy's preserve. Gangs of hostile Burmese loitered by the roadside, waiting for suitable victims. Stilwell with his aides made marathon journeys at a season when Upper Burma was at its hottest and driest, trying to shore up a fast crumbling front, but with little or no effect. He deserves full credit for what he was endeavouring to achieve, however much his outspoken Anglophobia led one British officer to inquire on whose side 'Vinegar Joe' considered himself to be. A liaison officer with the Chinese Vth Army, he told me that during his three months at Stilwell's headquarters the general never addressed a single word to him.

Stilwell's bitter tongue, so often employed to express contempt for the 'Limeys', did his military reputation no good, either with his own countrymen or the British. And yet he was brave, resourceful and determined to get to grips with the enemy. 'He really *hates* the Japs,' said Colonel St John. But for a man whose past experience had taught him that the Chinese generals could never be relied on, every day must have been one long frustration. 'To the Chinese,' Stilwell commented, 'concentration of divisions in the battle-zone for a counter-attack meant not only a multiplication of opportunity, but a multiplication of risk of loss. *Reluctance to attack* seemed to drench the spirit of the Chinese command beyond any measure of encouragement I could give.'[4] This was hardly surprising since this defensive attitude emanated from the Generalissimo himself, and woe betide the general who stepped out of line.

There was one lesson we had all learned by the end of March: that the Japanese were never more dangerous than when there appeared to be some kind of a lull in the fighting. They regrouped their troops with remarkable speed, usually moving by night and lying up by day. Their aim was always to outflank us and then cut us off. Their speed of movement was astonishing, bearing in mind that it was the hottest season of the year, the shade temperature at midday ranging between 110 and 120 degrees Fahrenheit. Thirst was a constant problem, for them just as much as for us. But they did receive a lot of assistance from the locals, who either willingly or unwillingly furnished provisions, acted as guides, even murdered for them. A tank crew of the 7th Hussars on outpost duty was approached by a bunch of villagers with eggs and chickens for sale. No sooner had the inevitable bargaining begun than the Burmese whipped out their *dahs* and cut down three of the soldiers; a fourth, who happened to be some distance away at the time, managed to escape to tell the tale.

The Japanese would try any ruse to effect surprise. Many of them dressed as Burma Rifles. One patrol of 2/5th Gurkhas south of Yenangyaung mistook some Japanese for Chinese, after being welcomed in English. They were immediately taken prisoner. Japanese handling of prisoners was almost invariably harsh, more often than not sadistic; it all depended on the mood of the senior officer or NCO in charge. In Burma it was the fear of being taken prisoner, particularly if wounded, that worried us most; one was prepared to take a chance on being killed in battle.

But the Japanese soldier, however sub-human he seemed to be at times, was at least our enemy, and for most of the time could be identified as such. The Burmese villagers came into a different category altogether, as the historian of the 7th Hussars makes clear: 'At a lower level, the troops soon found that now the great British Raj was apparently crumbling, the Burmese villages had few scruples about changing allegiance.'[5] It was about this time that I gave a lift in my jeep to a sergeant in the Cameronians who, noticing my Burma Rifles orderly, asked me with a grin, 'Whose side are you on – ours or theirs?'

The fast deteriorating situation brought Wavell to Burma on 31 March. 17th Division's withdrawal to Taungdwingyi from Prome had not gone well and morale was brittle. It was agreed that BURCORPS should, if pressed, abandon the oilfields (after destroying them, of course). 1 BURDIV should be responsible for covering the escape route to India via Kalewa on the Chindwin; 17th Division should withdraw north up the west bank of the Irrawaddy via Shwebo and Katha, to cover the withdrawal route to India via the Hukawng Valley, north-west of Myitkyina. Alexander proposed that 7th Armoured Brigade, together with one infantry brigade, should withdraw to China via the Burma Road, along with the Vth Army.

This demonstration of allied solidarity horrified the much-tried Brigadier Anstice, commander of 7th Armoured Brigade, and took no account of the logistics problem of supplying the remaining tanks with gasoline on their long march into China – but Alexander never pretended to be a logistician. Alexander's staff were so disturbed by what they felt to be a totally impracticable proposal by the Commander-in-Chief that General Winterton, newly arrived in Maymyo to replace Hutton as Alexander's Chief of Staff, was implored to plead with Alex to make him change his mind. In fact there was no need to do so, the Chinese themselves suggesting that the tanks could be better employed west of the Irrawaddy than on the long haul back to China.

The truth was that the Allies had completely lost the initiative. Although Maymyo escaped being bombed until 6 April,

Mandalay was completely flattened by a heavy raid on Good Friday, followed by an equally heavy raid the following day. An ammunition train loaded with RAF bombs blew up and added to the horrors. On the quayside where Indian refugees were gathered in their thousands, waiting to be ferried across the river, the death roll was devastating. The city was burnt to a cinder, although strangely enough Fort Dufferin was not severely damaged. City by city, town by town, village by village, Burma burned. The Japanese were now calling the tune. Every plan made by Alexander and his staff had to be scrapped almost as soon as agreed upon. Stilwell had proposed an ambitious counter-attack to be launched south from Pyinmana; Slim was prepared to lend him 7th Hussars in support. But it had to be abandoned on account of the rapid advance being made by the Japanese into the Shan States. A similar counter-attack, to be carried out by BURCORPS eastward from Yenangyaung with 200th Chinese Division participating, had also to be scrapped. The 200th Division had to be moved hastily to Meiktila which was threatened by the Japanese.

'I feel like a blind man,' Stilwell said, 'trying to fight with one hand tied behind my back. No troops of my own. Now no air. What I wouldn't give for one American division with all the trimmings.'[6] Slim was in precisely the same situation. No general can make an intelligent plan without information about the enemy. In the absence of air reconnaissance, neither Slim nor Stilwell had any idea of what was happening farther back along the Japanese lines of communication. Burma Army itself had no proper Intelligence service, as General Davies wrote to Smyth: 'I will accept any criticism you care to offer on the complete absence of intelligence about the enemy at Army Headquarters in Rangoon. We possessed no intelligence organization and were completely dependent on you for our information.'[7] It was a case, as Smyth pointed out, of the blind leading the blind.

It takes a great deal of time, and a lot of money, to organize Intelligence; it is not something that can be improvised at short notice. Yet time after time in war, *and in peace*, our Intelligence has been found wanting.[8] A kind of 'Yomas Intelligence Service' was set up after the withdrawal from Rangoon to Prome, consisting chiefly of forest officers and their assistants. But they could function as little more than scouts, or vedettes, and could not guarantee cooperation from the people among whom they were operating. In my experience (admittedly limited) the mounted infantry Frontier Force columns that had been raised for medium reconnaissance purposes were of little value, their radio sets failing to work more often than not whenever there was an urgent piece of information to be passed. The whole thing was so totally amateurish that it beggars belief that the British had managed to govern Burma for more than half a century without seeing the need for (or, more likely, being unwilling to find the money for) a proper Intelligence service.

The oilfields centre of Yenangyaung, where 1 BURDIV went down fighting between 12 and 19 April, is not one of the more attractive places in Burma. Driving from Meiktila, 100 miles to the north-east, one came upon Yenangyaung suddenly, a forest of oil derricks lighting the night sky with their flaming gases. The town straggled across a succession of low, rolling ridges, arid and for the most part treeless, hardly a blade of grass to be seen until one entered the residential area, a succession of houses and bungalows set among green lawns and trim flower beds. With the Irrawaddy close by there was plenty of water, provided the pumping machinery worked. On the Irrawaddy itself there was a constant procession of craft of all kinds. There were two European clubs, one British and one American, and I found the hospitality overwhelming when I visited Yenangyaung at Christmas 1939.

On that visit I was struck by the poor state of the roads until one entered the town itself. Before doing so, coming from the north, one had to cross the Pin Chaung, several hundred yards wide and unbridged, although there was a perfectly passable ford; I wondered how one managed in the monsoon. Again, south of Yenangyaung, we had to cross two other *chaungs*, about forty miles apart, the Kadaung and the Yin. We were warned to stick to the track since there were quicksands above and below the crossing places. These three *chaungs* – Pin, Kadaung and Yin – all flowed from east to west to join the Irrawaddy.

A place we visited on that occasion was Mount Popa, an extinct volcano about 5000 feet high with a crater nearly one mile in diameter. It is a very holy place and a centre for spirit worship. Hamadryads, king cobras, are reputed to live in the dense thickets within the crater but I declined an offer to show me one of them. We had already killed several snakes during that short Christmas visit to Yenangyaung–Magwe and that was quite enough for me. It is only fair to add, however, that I came across a great many more poisonous vipers during my service in the deserts of Arabia than I ever did either in India or Burma.

On 3 April Slim issued orders for BURCORPS to withdraw from the area of Prome to occupy a defensive line stretching from Minhla on the right to Taungdwingyi on the left, some forty to fifty miles of rough, scrubby and blindingly hot countryside where water, other than from deep village wells, was in short supply away from the Irrawaddy itself. The *west* flank guard was to be comprised of 2nd Burma Brigade. 2 BURIF were already across the river, some distance to the south; 8 BURIF were in Minhla under their indomitable CO, 'Bonzo' Bowers. 1st Burma Brigade were ten miles to the south-east of Minhla. East of 1st Burma Brigade was 13th Brigade, covering the road linking Taungdwingyi with Magwe. 17th Division, reported by Alexander as being 'tired and dispirited'[9] were falling back slowly from Prome, covered by Anstice's ubiquitous 7th Armoured Brigade. Cowan's orders from Slim were to turn Taungdwingyi into a strongpoint, the hinge linking BURCORPS with the Chinese across the hills in Pyinmana.

Alexander ascribed much of the drop in morale to the Japanese Air Force which seemed to be overhead throughout the hours of daylight. We were surprised by a Japanese fighter when driving from Taungdwingyi to Allanmyo, took hastily to the paddy fields below the road and found cover behind a convenient bank. To our surprise the pilot ignored the target presented by the jeep, left on the road with its engine still running, and chose instead to fly in tight circles round and round above us, giving us a squirt each time he passed. God knows how much ammunition he had expended before, tiring of the game, he sped off to the south. Our only casualty was a slight graze on my companion's left arm. Alexander begged Wavell for air support, but Wavell, rightly in the circumstances, thought it necessary to conserve his limited air force for the defence of Calcutta, now within striking range from Akyab.

I am not entirely sure that Alexander was correct in blaming the drop in morale on Japanese predominance in the air. That had been a feature of the campaign from the outset. The more likely reason was the heavy casualties we seemed to have suffered south of Prome for no obviously good reason. There was nothing like enough attempt made to explain to us what was happening, and why we were doing the kind of things we were doing. Soldiers fight much better when properly informed. If they are not, rumour then takes the place of information, and if I learnt nothing else from the Burma campaign, I did learn that inaccurate rumours are bad for morale. I also believe that the evident hostility we encountered from so many of the local people, even sometimes from local officials such as schoolmasters, had a very depressing effect.

The Battle of Yenangyaung, which turned out to be a disaster, was fought within an area of about twenty square miles. The northern limit was the Pin Chaung, just beyond Yenangyaung itself; the southern was the Yin Chaung. The Irrawaddy marked the western edge of the battlefield; the Taungdwingyi–Magwe–Yenangyaung road marked the eastern edge. The river itself was very low; there was quite an extensive foreshore in places, and the sand or mud was often treacherously soft. It was the dry season and therefore all the crops had been harvested. Such trees as there were were mostly concentrated round the scattered villages. In some parts the land sloped gently down to the Irrawaddy; in others there were quite high cliffs. From seven in the morning until seven at night the sun beat down with a ferocity I do not recall even in Arabia – it simply blazed. There was little shade and the flies were a torment. Yenangyaung town itself was laid out with good roads, solidly built bungalows and a good shopping area, but everywhere was looted as soon as vacated by the occupants, most of whom had been evacuated by early April. The various roads converged at the village of

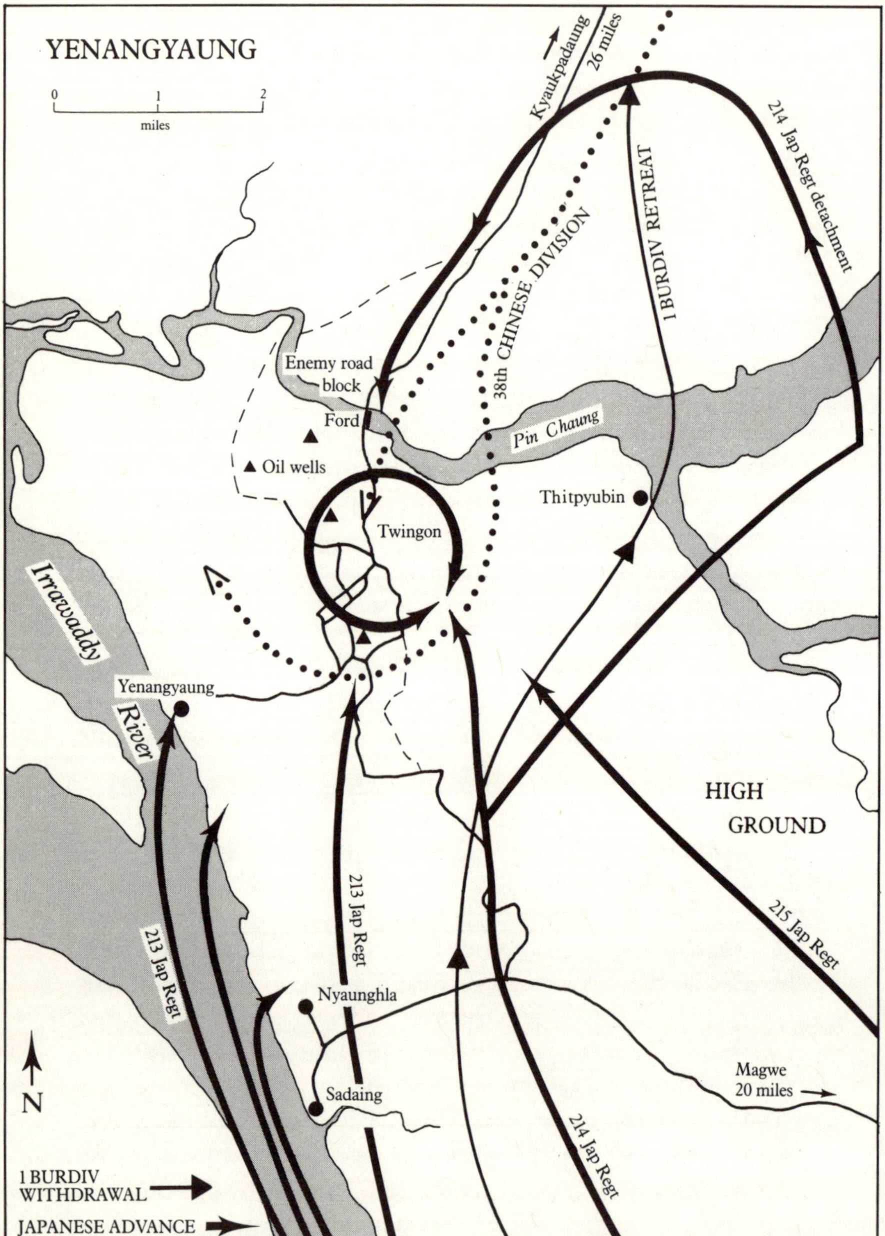

YENANGYAUNG
0
1
2
miles
Kyaukpadaung
26 miles
214 Jap Regt detachment
1 BURDIV RETREAT
38th CHINESE DIVISION
Enemy road block
Ford
Oil wells
Pin Chaung
Thitpyubin
Twingon
Irrawaddy
River
Yenangyaung
HIGH GROUND
213 Jap Regt
213 Jap Regt
215 Jap Regt
Nyaunghla
Sadaing
N
Magwe 20 miles
214 Jap Regt
1 BURDIV WITHDRAWAL
JAPANESE ADVANCE

Twingon on the northern edge of the town, from where a single and not particularly good track led down to the Pin Chaung and the ford across it.

Yenangyaung was both the blooding, and the virtual swan-song, of 1st Burma Division. Rightly or wrongly the Division was cut to pieces for a reason which, when looking back on it, is difficult to understand. Clearly, it was vital that the oil wells and refinery, pumping station and workshops, should not be allowed to fall intact into Japanese hands. But the preparations for the demolitions had been completed as early as 9 April, three days before the Japanese advance guards made contact in any strength with BURCORPS. It is of course possible that Alexander should have thought that at long last he would be able to fight the Japs on ground of his own choosing; or more likely that it was politically essential for BURCORPS to make a fighting withdrawal up the Irrawaddy valley at the same time as the Chinese Vth Army was doing the same up the Sittang valley. As it was, he made it clear that whatever happened Cowan and his 17th Division must hang on tight to Taungdwingyi in order to keep in touch with the Chinese to their east.

As Alexander was later to point out: 'Practically every formation in these two Divisions (17th Indian and 1st Burma) had at one time or another been surrounded by the enemy and had fought its way out. This had a cumulative effect. Further, the 17th Division had fought for five months without rest and practically without reinforcement, and for only one period of three days did it have another formation between it and the enemy. This was a big strain.'[10]

It certainly was, and it would be ridiculous to deny that there had not been adverse effects on morale. There was a shortage of certain types of ammunition, vehicle spares, maps and a host of other things besides. The tanks of 7th Armoured Brigade had long since exceeded the track mileage laid down for workshop attention. There were a large number of mules and ponies for which forage was running short. Gasoline was largely dependent on continued production in Yenangyaung, and in Chauk to the north of it. Large amounts of gasoline had been lost in air raids on Meiktila, Thazi and Mandalay. There was also the cumulative effect of the steady reduction in unit strengths as men were killed, or evacuated as sick or wounded to base hospitals in Maymyo, Meiktila and Shwebo. 2 KOYLI had had one CO killed, another severely wounded, and their third (who brought them out of Burma) had been sick for some time in Maymyo with malaria. Other battalions, British, Indian and Gurkha, were in a similar state. The Burma Rifles, having shed most of their weaker brethren, were rarely more than 200–300 strong.

The Japanese plan for the capture of Yenangyaung was to follow their usual pattern, viz: outflanking the main position, followed by cutting off the main route of withdrawal. 17th Division was to be pinned down in the Taungdwingyi area and kept out of the battle, if at all possible. General Sakurai gave this task to his 215th Infantry Regiment which was forced to fight a bitter battle at Kokkogwa with 48th Gurkha Brigade, supported by 7th Armoured Brigade. The Japanese 213th Regiment's task was to capture Magwe and force 1 BURDIV back into Yenangyaung where it would be trapped by 214th Regiment who would be sent on a wide outflanking march, approaching Yenangyaung from the north-east and establishing a block on the road linking Yenangyaung with Kyaukpadaung (a railway terminus) and Meiktila beyond. Landings would also be made from launches sent up-river from Prome. It was, from the Japanese point of view, more important to capture the oil installations intact than it was to destroy 1 BURDIV. As it happened, it worked out differently. The Japanese 33rd Division started its advance on Yenangyaung from Allanmyo on 9 and 10 April.

There was heavy fighting on 11, 12 and 13 April, most of which took place round the village of Kokkogwa, held by 48th Gurkha Brigade, as the Japanese 215th Infantry Regiment endeavoured to drive a wedge between 17th Division to the east (around Taungdwingyi) and 1 BURDIV in the Irrawaddy sector. By 14 April a dangerous gap had developed between the two Divisions, which could really have only been checked by an attack eastwards by 17th Division. Alexander, however, was reluctant to lose his grip on Taungdwingyi, since it might then mean losing contact with Vth Chinese Army. Since Slim was in no doubt that 1 BURDIV were being outflanked, he ordered Bruce Scott to pull 1st and 13th Brigades back to the line of the Yin Chaung, only ten miles south of Magwe. At the same time he ordered Bourke, who with 2nd Burma Brigade was moving up the west bank of the Irrawaddy, to send 5/1 Punjabis and 7 BURIF across the river to reinforce Bruce Scott.

This left Bourke with only 2 BURIF, 8 BURIF and a hundred or so BMP and BFF he had collected at Thayetmyo. Since the brigade was entirely dependent on animal transport – bullock carts that extended for more than a mile along the dusty tracks – most of its movement had to take place after dark. It had been Slim's original intention to bring what was left of 2nd Burma Brigade across the Irrawaddy at Magwe to reinforce 1 BURDIV, but the reports he was receiving of continuous infiltration northwards by the Japanese between 17th Division and 1 BURDIV led him to leave things as they were.

In the case of all withdrawals conducted in close contact with the enemy, there is inevitably a degree of confusion that can quickly degenerate into panic. Unless contact can be broken cleanly, and there has been sufficient time for a new defensive line to be reconnoitred and prepared, confusion becomes worse confounded. Platoons, even companies, go astray, particularly at night. Transport fails to turn up at the intended rendezvous. Arrangements for food and watering have to be abandoned. No one knows with any accuracy where anyone else is. Messages sent by hand fail to arrive, either because the 'runners' lose their way, or are killed or captured. Worst of all for morale, sick and wounded have to be left behind, for lack of the means to move them rearwards. The enemy is of course often in a similar position, but he is at least moving in the right direction.

The withdrawal of 1 BURDIV from south of Magwe to Yenangyaung provides a typical example of withdrawal under close enemy pressure. Water became a terrible problem, even more for the animals than the men. Communication between units, and even between sub-units, was extremely difficult. The KOYLI, sent down from Yenangyaung at short notice to occupy a village on the Irrawaddy shore south of Magwe, never received the order to withdraw. It should be remembered that almost every man serving with the battalion had had to swim for his life across the Sittang only seven weeks previously, and had been closely engaged on several occasions since. It says a great deal for their regimental spirit that no one who came into contact with the battalion during those difficult days in April failed to be impressed by their dogged determination and pride in themselves. It was tragic that when withdrawing across the Yin Chaung, some of the men missed the ford and were caught in the quicksands where they were machine-gunned to their deaths by the enemy.

In the early hours of 16 April the enemy attacked the Yin Chaung positions. At the outset 5 BURIF, a mere rump of a battalion, fought well, but once the Japanese gained a foothold into their position, the battalion started to disintegrate. This led in turn to the rest of 1st Burma Brigade having to withdraw across country to the Taungdwingyi–Magwe road, covered by the KOYLI. The 2nd Royal Tanks did sterling work, ferrying back the exhausted infantry, picking up the wounded, and constantly counter-attacking to delay the advancing enemy. Moreover, theirs were almost the only reliable communications available to Bruce Scott and his harassed brigade commanders. Two tanks were lost, but it is virtually certain that without the brilliant work of 2nd Royal Tanks, 1 BURDIV would never have got clear of Magwe. That evening, with Magwe in enemy hands, Slim ordered most of his precious 7th Armoured Brigade to withdraw through Yenangyaung to beyond the Pin Chaung.

He had already, at 1300 hours on 15 April, issued the order for the demolition of the Yenangyaung oilfield complex, apart from the power station that was required for the pumping of water from the river. The demolitions were in the capable hands of Mr W. L. Forster who had already sent the Syriam installations at Rangoon sky-high. All preparations had been completed as early as 9 April, the day General Sakurai sent his 33rd Division on their way from Allanmyo, and by 1400 hours on 15 April, their melancholy task completed, Mr Forster and party were on their way up-river to Chauk, by launch or road, leaving behind them a scene of devastation which 2nd Burma Brigade, from across the river, could only describe as 'awe-inspiring'.[11]

The entire eastern horizon was blanketed by an immense pall of thick, black smoke, through which the flames burst through, hundreds and hundreds of metres high. 'It was as if the whole of Yenangyaung was afire',[12] added to which was the dull thud of explosions as building after building was dynamited. Millions of gallons of crude oil burst into flames, signifying, where General Sakurai was concerned, the death to hopes. Yenangyaung might be his for the taking, but without its oil.

On.the night of 16 April the power station was dynamited and water no longer ran through Yenangyaung's pipes. By then the enemy, landing by launches on the river side of the town, had infiltrated through the built-up area, and the vital crossroads in the village of Twingon was under aimed enemy fire. But much, much worse, the enemy had got across the Pin Chaung well to the east and set up a road-block on the road to Kyaukpadaung. Bruce Scott, with 1st Burma and 13th Indian Infantry Brigades, was trapped in Yenangyaung between the Kadaung and the Pin Chaungs, with much of the Irrawaddy east bank in Japanese hands. His only secure communication with Slim was now the command tank of 'A' Squadron, 2nd Royal Tanks.

Fortunately the rear headquarters of 1 BURDIV, under Colonel Basil Amies, had crossed the Pin Chaung before the enemy established the road-block; as had part of the 7th Armoured Brigade and much of the second line transport of the Division. But the bulk of the fighting part of 1 BURDIV was still either holding the line of the Kadaung Chaung or withdrawing towards it, fifteen miles to the south of Yenangyaung itself. Between 17 and 19 April Slim did his best to ease the pressure on Scott by counter-attacking from the east with parts of 17th Division, but the effects were not commensurate with the efforts required to mount such attacks.

1 BURDIV was being attacked from the air, shelled and mortared by the Japanese, and sometimes attacked by bodies of uniformed Burmese operating on the enemy side. The soldiers were exhausted after days of marching in the dreadful heat, thirst being the worst enemy. Men drank from the radiators of abandoned trucks, or lined up to moisten their parched lips from leaking drainpipes. Both Farwell, commanding 1st Burma

Brigade, and Curtis, commanding 13th Indian Brigade, had told Scott that their troops were very close to breaking point. This had been passed on to Slim by Scott, who at the same time asked for assistance from the 38th Chinese Division, reported to be moving down into the battle area.

Scott's predicament by the night of 17/18 April was at least as serious as Smyth's had been prior to the demolition of the Sittang bridge. Although his brigades had now managed to reach the southern outskirts of Yenangyaung, they were separated from most of their transport, now north of the Pin Chaung. Also, the majority of the tanks were across the *chaung*, only one squadron remaining with Scott. Twingon was securely in enemy hands. More and more enemy were landing on the Irrawaddy shore. Every available truck and ambulance was loaded with wounded. Ammunition was running short. Most people would have been happy to trade half a lifetime for a long drink of cool, clear water.

It was at this critical moment that the Chinese came into the scene. The LXVIth Chinese Army was moving slowly into Burma, preceded by the 38th Division which arrived in the Mandalay area early in April. On 12 April Chiang Kai-shek told Stilwell to send a division to support the British. A regiment from 38th Division was sent accordingly to Kyaukpadaung.[13] Chiang cancelled these orders almost as soon as he had issued them, but fortunately Alexander and Stilwell agreed to allow matters to stand. 38th Division was placed under Slim's command. Slim was impressed by General Sun Li-jen, the Divisional Commander: 'He was alert, energetic and direct. Later I found him a good tactician, cool in action, very aggressively minded, and, in my dealings with him, completely straightforward. In addition, he had the great advantage that he spoke good English with a slight American accent, having, as he was rightly proud to tell, been educated at the Virginia Military Academy. The Academy could be proud of Sun; he would have been a good commander in any army.'[14]

The Chinese had neither artillery nor tanks. Slim immediately placed all his available guns and tanks under Sun's command, thereby conferring on him tremendous 'face'. Brigadier Anstice of 7th Armoured Brigade could be excused for being rather less enthusiastic, but in fact he and Sun got on famously. The other subordinate British commanders also cooperated fully. An attack to clear the Pin Chaung was planned for early on 18 April, 1 BURDIV attacking north in support, but although the Chinese fought well, they were unable to take the strongly held road-block dominating the ford. One company of the 1st Royal Inniskilling Fusiliers, attacking alongside the Chinese, were taken prisoner after mistaking some Japanese for Chinese, much easier to do than might seem apparent at this distance in time. Scott, naturally disappointed by the failure of the attempt to clear the block, and knowing that his soldiers were nearing the end of their tether, now requested permission to fight his way out that night, having first destroyed his guns, tanks and transport. Slim's reply was that he must hang on, a fresh attack being planned for the following morning. 'All right, we'll hang on and we'll do our best in the morning,' Scott replied, 'but, for God's sake, Bill, make those Chinese attack.'[15]

As he had said he would, Scott attacked again next morning, but the Chinese attack, promised for 1230 hours, had had to be postponed. The inbuilt Chinese unconcern for time was something which not even Sun could change. It was 1500 hours before the attack took place. By then all communication with Scott had ceased, his desperate situation compelling him to attempt a breakout, in broad daylight, independent of anything the Chinese might or might not do.

His tanks had discovered a rough track, suitable only for tanks and jeeps, that led to the Pin Chaung, a mile or so upstream of the ford. It was hastily improved to take guns and trucks. It skirted Twingon, still holding out against Scott's counter-attacks, and might just provide a means of escape. That morning both brigade commanders had told Scott that their men were completely exhausted. Scott himself was in much the same state. It was time to go. At 1400 hours the long column of tanks, vehicles and guns, marshalled by Scott in person, began to move down to the Pin Chaung, mortared and machine-gunned from across the *chaung* as they went. The wounded, many of them being carried on the tanks, were very vulnerable.

Once the bed of the *chaung* was reached, soft sand compelled the abandonment of most of the vehicles, together with the wounded loaded into them, although as many as possible were transferred to the tanks. The sight of the water flowing through the *chaung* sent both men and animals crazy, everyone throwing themselves down to drink, regardless of the bullets whipping up the sand on every side. 'The haggard, red-eyed British, Indian and Burmese soldiers who staggered up the bank,' wrote Slim, 'were a terrible sight, but every man I saw was still carrying his rifle.'[16] But Scott had had to leave behind two Bofors guns, four 3.7″ howitzers, four 25-pounders, most of his mortars, and all his first line mechanical transport. This included his ambulances and the wounded they were carrying. That evening a young gunner officer who had volunteered to go back to rescue them found that every one of them had either been bayoneted to death or had had his throat cut.

'That our situation should have fallen to such a level that we had to abandon our wounded to the attentions of an enemy notorious for his savagery and brutality, must mark that last day of the Yenangyaung battle, 19th April 1942, as one of the blackest in the long history of British arms,' wrote Pat Carmichael.[17] It would be difficult to disagree.

Carmichael, whose 23rd Mountain Battery had performed as splendidly at Yenangyaung as they did everywhere else, was watching his mules drink their fill from the *chaung* when a bullock-cart passed him, 'with a pair of legs hanging limply out of the back'. Carmichael asked who the casualty was. 'The Divisional Commander,' replied the officer walking beside the cart. 'Exhaustion!'[18] Like his soldiers, General Bruce Scott had stuck it out until eventually he collapsed from the strain.

The Chinese did attack in the end, although too late to help 1 BURDIV. They went in with great *élan*, relishing the rare support of British tanks and guns. Not only did they take Twingon, but they were able to release the men of the Inniskilling Fusiliers taken prisoner the previous day. The unaccustomed tank and artillery support seemed to cause the adrenalin to go coursing through Chinese veins, leading their normally cautious battalion and company commanders to take risks hitherto undreamed of. They got on top of the Japanese – of that there can be no doubt – and by the following morning had fought their way into the ruins of Yenangyaung itself. But Slim decided to withdraw 38th Division before the Japanese counter-attacked at dawn on 21 April. They were too valuable to be frittered away in house-to-house fighting. 'I had expected the Chinese soldier to be tough and brave,' wrote Slim. 'I was, I confess, surprised at how he had responded to the stimulus of proper tank and artillery support, and at the aggressive spirit he had shown. I had never expected, either, to get a Chinese general of the calibre of Sun.'[19]

CHAPTER FOURTEEN

India to be our Destination

'Well, gentlemen, it might be worse . . . it might be raining!'

General Slim[1]

The Burma campaign in 1942, in British terms, was a succession of apparently irretrievable disasters saved by near-miracles. This led to an understandable feeling of euphoria when the immediate danger had passed. After Yenangyaung, where 1 BURDIV only narrowly escaped total annihilation, Alexander and Slim at once began to plan to turn the tables on the Japanese by counter-attacking with 17th Indian and 38th Chinese Divisions, hoping to catch the Japanese 33rd Division off balance and disorganized. Similarly, Stilwell, who required no urging, was planning to counter-attack with Vth Army south of Pyinmana. Alexander seems to have been so delighted at the prospect that he proposed to put the 7th Hussars under Stilwell's command. Meanwhile, the battered 1 BURDIV was withdrawn forty miles north to the vicinity of Mount Popa where it would have to reorganize as best it could, having lost a great deal of essential equipment.

There was by now considerable bitterness among the British soldiers about the conduct of the local population. During the long withdrawal there had been many well-authenticated instances of soldiers being beaten up, handed over to the Japanese, or murdered. There had also been several reports of Burmese, wearing either British or Japanese uniforms, taking part in the fighting on the enemy's side. It was clear that the Japanese, when carrying out their wide out-flanking movements, were helped by local guides, voluntarily or involuntarily. There had been many cases to show that our dispositions were often given away to the enemy by the burning of hayricks or even houses. Single vehicles were ambushed, the occupants butchered and their weapons stolen. The troops became so jumpy that even the thin column of smoke rising from a cooking fire might be taken as being some kind of signal to the enemy.

Nor was it only the British who suffered in this fashion. 'That morning,' writes Pat Carmichael, 'the Chinese had captured three men of the Burma National Army, one of whom was reported to be a lieutenant. All were dressed as Burma Riflemen. The Chinese suspended them by their feet from trees with their hands clear of the ground, and there they were left. The Battery emphatically approved of it and there were many *Shabashes** for the Chinese. I think we loathed the Burmans almost as much as we did the Japanese, for their persistent treachery and murderous attacks on refugees.'[2]

It was inevitable in such circumstances that a good deal of rough justice was meted out, the innocent often suffering for the sins of the guilty. The saffron-robed monks, so easily identifiable, became the focus of suspicion and were often shot out of hand. One of them, a very nice man, told me he had been beaten up three times, twice by British soldiers and once by an Indian who stole his watch and then threw him down a well, which just happened to be dry. But there were also instances when the local people did help those whose lives were in their hands. Second-Lieutenant Ralph Tanner of the KOYLI was leading a patrol south of Yenangyaung when he lost contact with his unit. Although the Japanese were well in evidence in the locality, the villagers provided him with food and temporary shelter. He was fortunately able to get back to his unit without having to put to the test other villagers, who might have acted differently.

The inability by either side to communicate was an insuperable problem. Many British soldiers, after long service in India, acquired some knowledge of 'barrack Hindustani' but this was no use at all when trying to talk to Burmese villagers. Their inability to comprehend what was being said to them was often taken as evidence of non-cooperation. Certainly, those of us who could speak Burmese fared a good deal better than those who

* *Shabash*—Bravo (Urdu).

could not. At Taungdwingyi, for example, where my dysentery necessitated frequent and urgent visits to the adjacent scrubland, I encountered two Burmese villagers armed with *dahs* who looked decidedly threatening until I greeted them in Burmese. They immediately broke into smiles, squatted down beside the track, and we began talking about the weather, the crops, and all the other things Burmese peasants consider important. They regretted their house was on the other side of the town since otherwise they would have provided me with a meal. We parted amicably, although they did warn me not to wander too far afield since there were a lot of dacoits in the area.

The short pause that followed 1 BURDIV's extrication from Yenangyaung proved to be only a matter of days. While Alexander, Stilwell and Slim were concerting their plans for a counter-attack, the Japanese thrust into the Shan States made all such plans nugatory. The Chinese VIth Army put up such a feeble resistance that Stilwell had to move his best Division from Vth Army (200th Division) into the Shan States in an effort to recapture Taunggyi, an important communications centre. VIth Army had abandoned Taunggyi without a fight, and without destroying the large stocks of gasoline collected there. This turned out to be a Godsend for the Japanese who had virtually run out of it, enabling them to press on northwards when otherwise they must have been halted until supplies could be brought up.

The move to the east of 200th Division put an end to the plan to counter-attack south of Pyinmana. Stilwell hurried to Taunggyi in person, offering a bribe of 50,000 Rupees for the town's recapture. It worked. His presence with the forward platoons, an unusual situation for a commanding general, may have provided additional encouragement, but Taunggyi was back in Chinese hands – temporarily. Then the lethargy that seemed to be Standing Operating Procedure where the Chinese were concerned led to a failure to prepare for the inevitable Japanese counter-attack, which drove the Chinese out of the town. Had Stilwell been there, it might have gone differently but he had had to return to the Sittang front where the Vth Army was beginning to fall apart.

On 25 April, Alexander met with Slim and Stilwell at Kyaukse, a small town on the main road thirty miles south of Mandalay. Alexander had already made up his mind to quit Burma, his aim being to keep the Burma Army intact for what might well turn out to be a battle for India. Stilwell, whose military philosophy had much in common with Colonel de Grandmaison's,[3] nursed the deepest suspicions of the 'Limeys'' apparent reluctance to get to grips with the Japanese. 'Are the British going to run out on us? Yes', he had written in his diary on 20 April. That was the day the Japanese 56th Division drove the Chinese out of Loikaw, opening up the way to Lashio. Stilwell also omitted to make it plain that the Shan States were virtually a Chinese-American preserve. Only one general had authority there, Stilwell, but unfortunately his Chinese subordinates refused to acknowledge it.

It was at Kyaukse that Alexander changed the entire thrust of the campaign; it might truly be said that it was the *only* far-reaching decision he made while in command in Burma, apart from changing his mind at the last moment over defending Rangoon. It certainly saved the Burma Army. Had Stilwell been in command, the most likely result would have been another Corregidor, going down in glorious retreat round 'the flag' only to rot for years as prisoners of war.

The Burma Army's goal was Imphal. The Chinese Vth Army could do the same, if it chose. Their alternative was to withdraw up the Mandalay–Shwebo–Myitkyina railway line, making either for China, or for India via the Hukawng valley. The Chinese VIth Army was already falling back towards China as fast as it could, Stilwell having lost control over its operations. It was decided at Kyaukse that the British would cover the withdrawal of the Chinese from Mandalay across the Irrawaddy to the west bank. This would mean moving 17th Division to Meiktila as soon as possible. It was, however, essential to delay the Japanese advance for as long as humanly possible in order to provide time to improve the primitive communications with India via Shwebo and Kalewa. Time was also needed to stock the route with the necessary supplies.

But time was the enemy. It was the third week in April. The monsoon was due to break in mid-May. When Slim made the remark quoted at the head of this chapter, it was at one of the worst moments in the Yenangyaung battle when Burma Division's fate appeared to be sealed, and it was intended to counter the pessimism of his staff (it did in fact rain a few hours later for a short time). But Slim did not know then of Alexander's intention to withdraw to India by an appalling route through dense jungle in one of the regions wettest in the world once the monsoon has broken. The race was now as much against the monsoon as it was against the Japanese.

Somehow or other the administrative machine had been kept ticking over until then. The Governor and his advisers were still in Maymyo where life had been relatively normal until after the bombing on 6 April. As many people as possible had been evacuated to Shwebo, from where evacuation by air had been progressing slowly, but from the middle of April onwards there began a slow but steady collapse. Desertion among the police, non-combatant services and subordinate government officials gathered pace. Slim refers to the fact that 'demoralization behind the line was spreading'; he also says that there had been 'a general and not very creditable exodus'.[4] After it was all over there were those who claimed that control was maintained until the last possible moment but that was not the impression of many of those who were there. Much of the cause for the breakdown in confidence was due to the absence of accurate information and the consequential proliferation of rumours, most of which were false.

On 25 April, when Alexander was making his momentous decision at Kyaukse, the Governor was still in Maymyo. He had sent Lady Dorman-Smith to Myitkyina, assuming that was the route the army would take in its withdrawal. However, the arrival that morning of the US Consul-General to inform him that the Japanese had cut the Burma Road south of Lashio made it plain that Dorman-Smith must leave Maymyo. General Winterton says he was responsible for persuading the Governor to leave Maymyo on 25 April, which he did, arriving in Myitkyina two days later. He was unaware at the time of Alexander's intention to withdraw to India via Kalewa, not Myitkyina.

Mr T. L. Hughes was the Governor's chief civil liaison officer at Headquarters Burma Army. He was horrified to discover that Dorman-Smith had gone to Myitkyina under the misapprehension that Alexander intended to withdraw there. On his own authority he sent Dorman-Smith a message informing him of the change of plan. Winterton was furious when he found out, accusing Hughes of endangering the entire plan, but Hughes was unrepentant. He had a duty towards the Governor, as well as to the Commander-in-Chief, as Alexander later acknowledged. Lady Dorman-Smith was flown out to India on 2 May from Myitkyina. Dorman-Smith left on 4 May, on the Prime Minister's direct instructions. The Japanese entered Myitkyina four days later.

When the generals discussed the plan to withdraw to India on 25 April, it is doubtful whether they had any conception of the difficulties ahead of them. All three had arrived in Burma by air. Most of the fighting since then had been taking place in the relatively open country of central Burma where the road system, however indifferent, was incomparably better than anything to be found in the vast tract of country lying between the west bank of the Irrawaddy and the border with India. Nor had they experienced Burma in the monsoon, when the entire countryside is completely transformed.

There had never been any desire on Burma's part to improve overland communications with India. It was far cheaper to carry on trade by sea. Nor was there any wish to open the floodgates to India's teeming millions, of whom there were more than enough in Burma already. Besides, the terrain was such as to daunt the most enthusiastic road engineer. In a region where the rainfall was the highest in the world, the smallest stream became a raging torrent in a matter of minutes. The mountains were high, razor-backed and matted with jungle. Malaria and every other kind of tropical disease flourished, at their most virulent during the rainy season. The tribesmen who lived there on a subsistence economy – Chins, Shans, Kachins, Nagas, Lushais and others – were too few and too scattered to constitute an effective labour force. Much of their time was spent, in any case, in minor wars against each other.

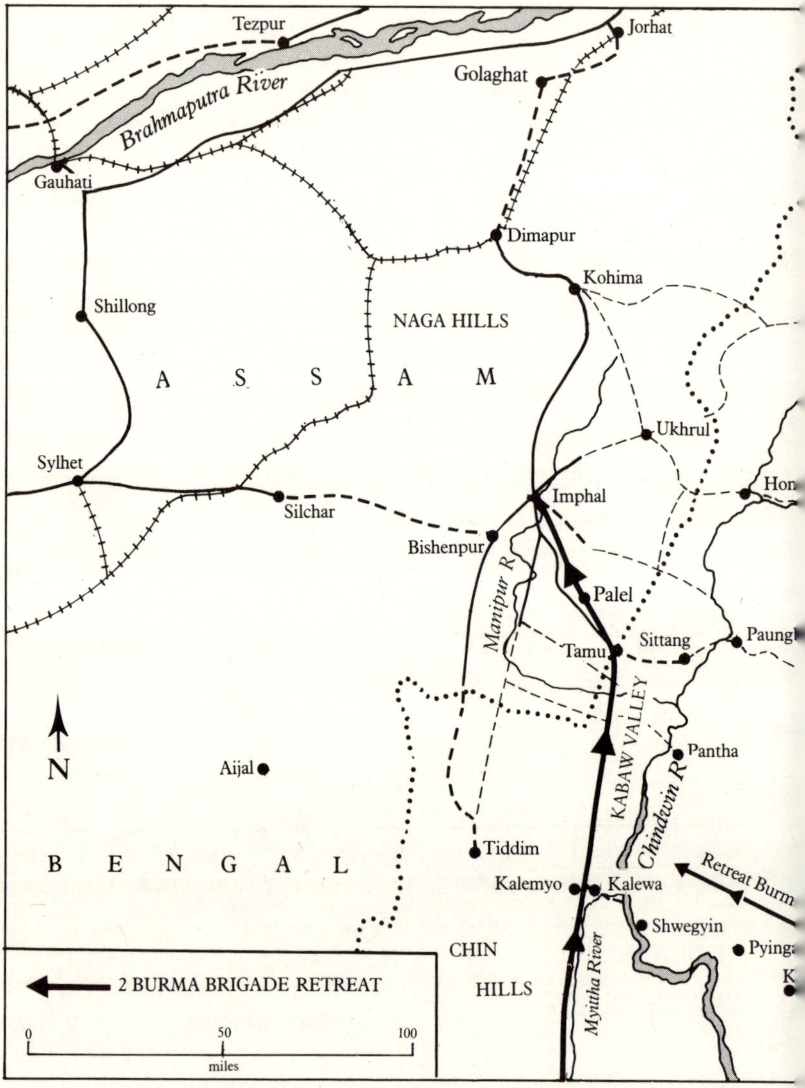
Tezpur
Jorhat
Golaghat
Brahmaputra River
Gauhati
Dimapur
Kohima
Shillong
NAGA HILLS
A S S A M
Ukhrul
Sylhet
Imphal
Silchar
Bishenpur
Manipur R
Palel
Sittang
Tamu
KABAW VALLEY
Pantha
Chindwin R
N
Aijal
Tiddim
B E N G A L
Kalemyo
Kalewa
Shwegyin
CHIN
HILLS
Myittha River
2 BURMA BRIGADE RETREAT
0
50
100
miles

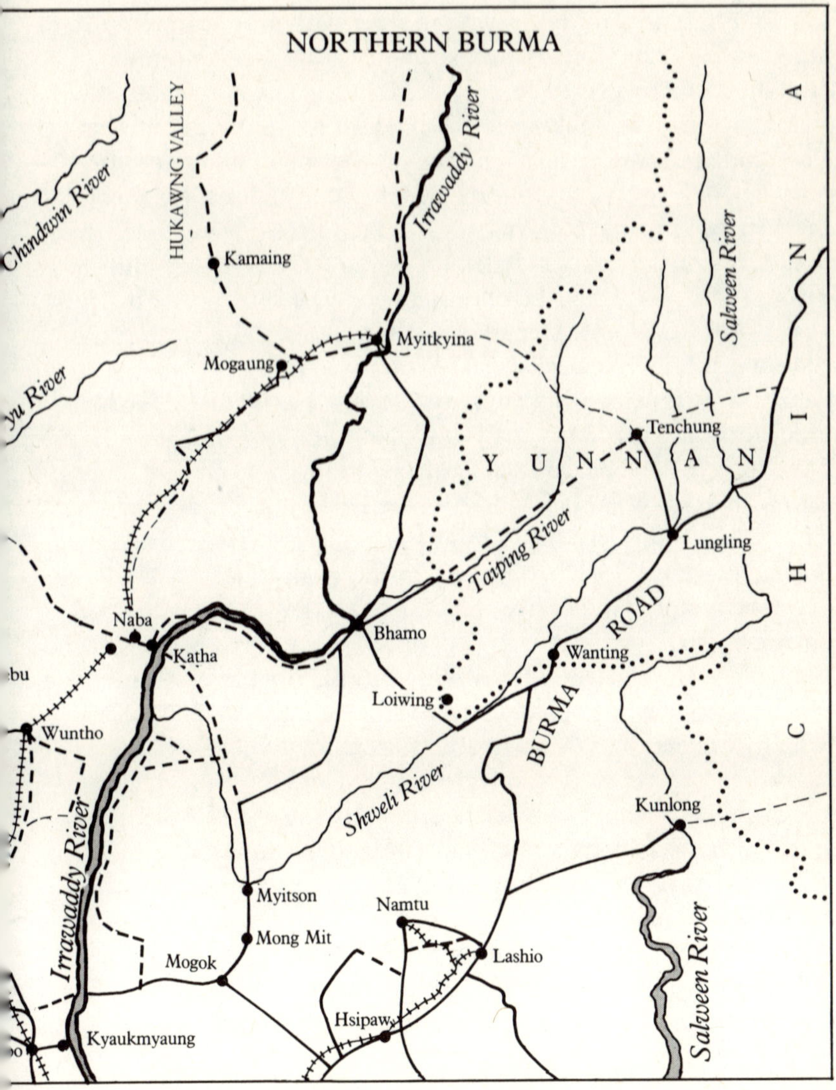
NORTHERN BURMA
HUKAWNG VALLEY
Chindwin River
Irrawaddy River
Kamaing
Myitkyina
Mogaung
yu River
Salween River
Tenchung
YUNNAN
CHINA
Taiping River
Lungling
Bhamo
Naba
Katha
bu
Wuntho
Loiwing
Wanting
BURMA ROAD
Shweli River
Kunlong
Myitson
Namtu
Mong Mit
Lashio
Mogok
Hsipaw
Kyaukmyaung
Salween River

Despite the difficulties, Wavell decided early in December 1941 that a practicable route should be built from Imphal into Burma. Imphal, capital of Manipur state, was itself connected only indifferently by fair-weather road with the Brahmaputra valley and Assam. This is a great tea-growing area and much of the labour force could be recruited from the tea estates, the planters themselves taking an active part in road construction. The roadhead was to be Dimapur on the metre gauge railway, from where a twenty-foot-wide all-weather road would be constructed to run via Kohima to Imphal. From there the road would be continued via Palel to Tamu on the India–Burma border. The task would be undertaken on the Indian side by the Assam Public Works Department, which soon found it could not cope. Major-General E. A. Wood was placed in charge in February 1942, ably assisted by the Assam Tea-Planters Association. As many specialist army engineer units as could be spared from duties elsewhere in India were sent to Assam. By strenuous efforts the fair-weather road had reached Tamu by 28 April, a remarkable effort in the circumstances. A lot was owed to Wavell's intense personal interest in the project.

Unfortunately there had not been a comparable effort on Burma's part. This was due probably to unwarranted reliance being placed on the use of Irrawaddy Flotilla Company steamers, which had been the main carriers since the early days of the British connection. These steamers were very vulnerable to air attack and their crews, who were chiefly Chittagonians, became increasingly reluctant to man the ships. By the end of April 1942 most of the Company's fleet had either been sunk or scuttled.

From Tamu, on the Indian border, where the fair-weather road from Imphal terminated, there was a jungle track running south for seventy miles through the fever-infested Kabaw valley. Virtually nothing had been done to improve it. The track ended at Kalewa, on the *west* bank of the Chindwin, close to the junction of the Myittha and Chindwin rivers. The Myittha, a wide but sluggish stream, rises in the Chin Hills, flowing parallel with the Chindwin, but to the *north* whereas the Chindwin, a mighty stream, flows *south*.

Six miles below Kalewa, but on the opposite bank of the

Chindwin, here about 600 yards wide, is Shwegyin, a jetty used mainly for logging, but also for ferrying to and from Kalewa. In normal times it did not handle a great deal of traffic. Shwegyin lay in a basin, overlooked by high cliffs covered in dense jungle. There was a rough track of some 120 miles linking Shwegyin with Ye-U to the south. It was narrow, twisting and intersected by numerous *chaungs*, dry and sandy in the hot season, torrents in the monsoon. None were bridged. There had never been any requirement to improve this track, used mostly by forest officers, 'teak wallahs' and the local bullock carts, because the Chindwin river was the main artery of communication for 400 miles from its confluence with the Irrawaddy opposite Pakokku. In the dry season water was scarce although there were a few villages in the jungle where wells had been dug; one was Pyingaing; another Kaduma.

Ye-U was separated from Shwegyin to the north by a vast forest. It was a station on the loop railway line which, after crossing the Irrawaddy by the great Ava Bridge at Sagaing, travelled clockwise to Monywa on the Chindwin and then on to Ye-U before doubling back to Shwebo, which was on the main line to Myitkyina, 200 or more miles farther north. Ye-U was linked with Monywa and Shwebo by fair-weather tracks. From Shwebo north to Myitkyina there was, apart from the line of rail, only a fair-weather dirt track without bridges suitable for heavy vehicles.

Many years later Bernard Fergusson, commenting to me on Alexander's selection of this route for the retreat of the Burma Army to India, remarked that had any student at the Staff College done so, he would have been immediately returned to his unit for proposing anything so crazy.[5] But the only real alternative was worse. This was the route from Mogaung, or Myitkyina, through the Hukawng valley to Ledo in Assam. It was much harder going, impassable, for vehicles for most of the way, and in places terribly steep. The main artery, as far as Bhamo, had always been the Irrawaddy, now inderdicted by the enemy air force apart from the occasional *loondwin* (country boat) or motor launch travelling under cover of darkness.

As soon as it was decided to retreat to India through Shwebo and Kalewa, action had to be taken to improve the route through the jungle and stock it with supplies, water etc. General Goddard, whose foresight had enabled the Burma Army to fight in central Burma, now had to face an equally daunting task. Backloading of stores by this route had already started. Now the rush was on, sometimes without much discrimination, as General Winterton found when he came across office files and furniture being loaded on to river steamers at Mandalay. At the same time General Wakeley, commanding the lines of communication, had the task of improving the track from Ye-U to Shwegyin, and then on from Kalewa through the Kabaw valley to Tamu. He was immensely hampered in this task by the thousands of refugees tramping along this route, dying in their scores beside the track from hunger, thirst or disease. The majority were Indians, but there were also Anglo-Indians, Anglo-Burmans, Chinese, Burmese and some Europeans; most of the latter, however, had already been evacuated by the teak firms whose facilities for doing so were far in advance of the army's.

Slim knew it was vital to delay the enemy south of Mandalay. 17th Division seemed to have recovered its cohesion and faith in itself thanks to Cowan's skilful handling. Its 48th Brigade, now under Brigadier Cameron, had given the enemy a hard knock at Kokkogwa. 17th Division began to withdraw slowly towards Meiktila, covering 1 BURDIV which was still recovering from Yenangyaung. Slim decided to send Bruce Scott, with 1st Burma and 13th Indian Brigades, both very tired, across the Irrawaddy by ferry at Sameikkon. Scott was then to dig in around Monywa, fifty miles farther up the Chindwin, which Slim correctly recognized as the key to movement up the river. Against the possibility of the Japanese carrying out an outflanking movement west of the Chindwin, by way of the Myittha valley, Slim decided to use 2nd Burma Brigade, still west of the Irrawaddy, as his left flankguard. Meanwhile 17th Division would hold the enemy south of Mandalay for as long as possible. Slim moved his own headquarters to Sagaing, west of the Ava Bridge, following after Alexander's headquarters which had been established at Shwebo, with a rear headquarters at Kalewa.

It was the end of April, the rains were at most three weeks away, the Japanese had taken Lashio, and the sands were running out fast for the Burma Army.

It was a time when no one seemed to know what was happening, not even, I suspect, the generals. The Governor certainly did not. The Chinese, falling back, behaved like the rabble they were, plundering, looting, and obeying only the orders that suited them. Some of the British and Indians were little better. Orders were issued only to be disobeyed. Other orders, hard to understand by hindsight, were obeyed only to cost us dear. Michael Calvert, sent by Alexander to prepare the vital Gokteik Viaduct, on the railway line from Maymyo to Lashio, for demolition, sat there for days waiting for the order to blow, but it never came. Returning to Maymyo, he was astonished when Alexander expressed surprise that the viaduct had not been blown, although he had given Calvert orders that it was only to be blown on his, Alexander's, express instructions.[6] Similarly, Lieutenant-Colonel Tony Mains, then on Alexander's Intelligence staff, was sent by him to destroy a dump of high octane petrol near Mandalay, which would have been a gift from the Gods for the hard-pressed 7th Armoured Brigade. 'In the growing confusion,' writes Slim, 'mistakes of this kind were almost inevitable, but none the less damaging.'[7] His forbearance does him credit, but he could hardly have felt it at the time.

Despite the confusion that always accompanies retreats in war, Slim's withdrawal of BURCORPS west of the Irrawaddy was successfully accomplished by one minute to midnight on 30 April, when the two centre spans of the great Ava Bridge were satisfactorily blown. The successful breaking of contact with the advancing Japanese had been largely due to the very successful action at Kyaukse, fought by 48th Gurkha Brigade on 28/29 April, when the advance of the Japanese 18th Imperial Guards Division was stopped dead in its tracks. It was the view of those who fought there that this *elite* formation, which had been in the van in Malaya, did not compare with 33rd Division, still reorganizing after its capture of Yenangyaung. The 1/7 Gurkha Rifles, who had been in the thick of the fighting ever since Kawkareik at the outset of the campaign, particularly distinguished themselves at Kyaukse. There were more than 500 Japanese casualties for the loss of only ten killed and wounded in 48th Brigade, despite dive-bombing and almost continuous shelling. Contact with the enemy was successfully broken by last light, the Gurkhas passing through 63rd Brigade, which was holding the bridgehead on the east bank. Slim later described the action as 'a really brilliant example of rearguard work'.[8]

It was while I was in hospital in Maymyo in early April that I first met Michael Calvert. He had come to visit someone in the next bed to me. I knew that he commanded the Bush Warfare School in Maymyo, a cover name for an establishment intended to train officers and NCOs to lead parties of guerrillas in China. He had recently led a raid on Henzada, with a mixed force of so-called "Commandos" and Royal Marines, transported across the Irrawaddy by Captain Rea[9] in the Irrawaddy Flotilla Company's *Hastings*. Unfortunately, although the raid on Henzada was successful, with few casualties, Calvert was recalled to receive a rebuke for 'endangering the lives of civilians of the Irrawaddy Flotilla Company and damaging property of the Burmah Oil Company'[10] during his operations. Meanwhile his force was surprised and several of the wounded were taken prisoner, later to be tied to trees and used to demonstrate bayonet fighting by the Japanese. It was an unhappy episode, for which Calvert was in no way to blame.

Paradoxically the British, who have since the time of Sir Francis Drake produced unconventional warriors of the highest quality, find it difficult to reconcile their gift for guerrilla warfare with the rigid conventional frame within which most of us find ourselves fitted. Muddling through may be the national virtue, but it is costly in lives and money, and often kills initiative. 'This, "I'll 'ave to ask me Dad" attitude of the British Army is its worst feature in my opinion,' wrote Calvert on 11 October 1945.[11] This is probably why we make such heroes of Nelson, Gordon, T. E. Lawrence and Orde Wingate, uncomfortable characters though they may have been.

Michael Calvert's later distinguished career as a Chindit requires no encomium from me. His worth was proved ten times over in battle. But his zest for the unconventional led him into curious scrapes. Having to his chagrin failed to blow up the Gokteik Viaduct, he returned to Maymyo to find Burma Army Headquarters hastily packing. After winding up what was left of the Bush Warfare School, Calvert followed suit, across the Irrawaddy to Shwebo, where he fell in with Peter Fleming, another unorthodox warrior with a nose for trouble, and Sandy Reid-Scott of the 11th Hussars, one of Wavell's ADCs. They were engaged in an operation of a kind which was very much up Calvert's street.

Wavell, outwardly the conventional soldier, had a very unconventional mind. It had conceived the deception outside Beersheba, in Palestine, in 1917, when a satchel was dropped near the Turkish lines containing bogus plans. A simple enough ruse, one would have thought, but it worked. In April 1942, after his disastrous experience in Java, and with Burma fast following Malaya into defeat, Wavell's principal concern was the defence of India. He was short of guns, tanks, trained soldiers, and above all aircraft. India was in fact wide open to invasion and totally unprepared for war. If the Japanese had planned to roll on from Burma, they must somehow be deterred – by any means including deception.

Thus was conceived the plan whereby an attaché case belonging to Wavell, as Commander-in-Chief in India, should fall into enemy hands. Within it would be papers contaning false Orders of Battle in India Command (two armoured divisions, for example, where not even one existed), details of reinforcements due from the United Kingdom and the Middle East, and much other misleading information. But how to get it into enemy hands? Finally it was decided that Fleming, accompanied by Reid-Scott, whose zest for action had survived the loss of an eye in the Western Desert, should somehow contrive to crash a staff car bearing Wavell's flag and "stars" in the enemy's path, abandoning it but in their haste leaving behind the attaché case. There is a *Boy's Own Paper* ring about the whole business, but simpler ruses have worked in war. Calvert fell in with Fleming and Reid-Scott soon after his arrival at Shwebo, agreeing to accompany them on what might reasonably be described as a mad escapade. He took with him Private Williams of the Welch Regiment, one of his men from the Bush Warfare School, to drive the car; Williams, who had survived being bayoneted by the Japanese, was in Calvert's words, 'a wonderful type and just the man to take on a job like this'.[12]

Somewhere between Mandalay and Kyaukse they ran into the Japanese. Coming under fire, Calvert, who was at the wheel, turned the car, braked sharply, and managed to skid off the road and down the embankment. The occupants baled out, Fleming throwing the suitcase away from the vehicle, lest it should catch fire. Then the four men ran for safety through very thick cover, pursued by the Japanese. It was getting dark, which helped them to get away, and they managed to reach the Ava Bridge only shortly before it was blown. When one reads of escapades of this kind, John Buchan's Richard Hannay seems almost true to life.

It was of course only a part, and a comparatively minor part, of a much more sophisticated deception scheme. We know now that the Japanese had no plans to invade India in 1942. They were much more concerned with China, and had in any case far outrun their supplies. Besides, the monsoon was about to break, and there were still pockets of resistance to be cleared up elsewhere in Burma.[13]

Mike Calvert has always had, of course, a salamander-like quality for attracting fire. Not long afterwards, prior to swimming the Chindwin, he and a few companions were engaged in trying to delay any Japanese who might be following up the retreating Burma Army. A company of Gurkhas were supposed to be operating with him, Calvert having arranged a rendezvous with them in a jungle hut that night. Accompanied by a sergeant and corporal Calvert walked up to the hut, talking loudly in English as he did so, lest they be mistaken for Japanese, knocked on the door and entered. Seated round the table, strewn with maps, were several Japanese. Both parties stared at each other, astonished, until Calvert said quickly, 'Excuse me, gentlemen, good night', closing the door firmly behind him. They then ran for cover, finding relief in laughter. Behind them, they thought they heard the Japanese laughing too.

Every war throws up characters like Mike Calvert, men of

imagination and courage who find danger a challenge, and who have the personality and the leadership to inspire men and women to do great deeds. Inevitably unorthodox in attitude and in thought, they are not invariably patient with those who lack their burning zeal, their desire to get things done, and the need to get to grips with the enemy. If in wartime they find themselves more often than not in conflict with the vast majority, who find safety in orthodoxy, it is hardly surprising that they should fare even worse in peacetime. But it will be a sad day for this nation, and for the British Army, if we should ever cease to produce men like Michael Calvert, with such fire in their bellies as sets lesser men's flaming.

CHAPTER FIFTEEN

Monywa – Slim's Costly Miscalculation

> 'I reproached myself bitterly for having allowed 2 Burma Brigade on the west bank to continue its march.'
>
> *General Slim*[1]

When General Slim ordered Bourke to take his brigade across the Irrawaddy from Allanmyo on Saturday 4 April 1942, it was not Bourke's understanding that 2nd Burma Brigade would remain as flank guard to BURCORPS until India was reached. His immediate task was to fall back to the little town of Minhla, seventy-two miles upriver from Allanmyo, and prepare to defend it against attack. Having been ordered to leave all his mechanical transport on the east bank, he had to arrange transport for the four days' worth of supplies he had brought with him. This involved the collection of some 350 bullock-carts, together with their drivers, his staff captain from now on becoming in Dick Lewin's words, "a bullock-master extraordinary".[2]

The west bank of the Irrawaddy was not as thickly populated as the east bank; there were few metalled roads and villages were connected by cart-tracks virtually impassable in wet weather. *Chaungs*, both large and small, criss-crossed the countryside on their way to the Irrawaddy, most of them dry between November and May. Those that were bridged were intended principally for bullock-carts. The population was scattered among small villages; there were only a few towns like Pakokku and Pauk where substantial buildings had been constructed. The main highway was of course the river, low at that season, with steep banks, more correctly cliffs, that made access difficult in certain places. Since the Irrawaddy was the chief source of water at that stage of the dry season, its accessibility had to be taken into account when planning each stage of the march. The Army had not been much in evidence in this area previously, law and order being maintained by the civil police, backed up by detachments of the BMP in the few towns, and farther north by the Chin Hills battalion of the BFF, with headquarters at Falam.

Thayetmyo, a medium-sized Burmese town, had yet to be burnt to the ground by Japanese bombers. It had acquired an unsavoury reputation during the Burma Rebellion in the 1930s as a trouble spot, but 2nd Brigade encountered no trouble. In fact Bourke was surprised to discover that the local club was making preparations for the usual weekly 'guest night'. His first action was to recall 2 BURIF, now forty miles to the south, and dispatch 5/1 Punjabis to Minhla, with orders to get there as quickly as possible. The Punjabis' CO, Lieutenant-Colonel K. D. Marsland, took Bourke at his word, his battalion marching the last thirty-nine miles along an appalling track in only sixteen hours. Not a man fell out, a record which the Mountain Gunners, the army's champion marchers, would have found difficult to beat. Arrived at Minhla on 8 April, the Punjabis, without pausing for food, at once set about digging trenches. It was a fine effort. Their reserve ammunition, rations and kit were carried by pack mules, of which the brigade had about 150 at this time.

It took some time to collect the bullock-carts. Fortunately there was no shortage of cash with which to pay for them. The Nyaunglebin sub-treasury, handed over by the sub-divisional officer before he decamped, proved to be a Godsend. However, a great many years had passed since the East India Company's army had conquered India, with bullock-carts, elephants and camels comprising the baggage train. Certainly no British officer had the slightest idea how far or how fast a bullock cart would go, nor how much it could carry. To begin with there was a tendency to overload the carts, inevitably slowing the pace of the convoy, and there was always the likelihood of the drivers running away and not returning after an air attack. Nor was it possible to conceal a column one mile or more in length, trundling along slowly under a dense cloud of dust; it was visible for miles. 7 BURIF were detailed to escort the baggage convoy which left Thayetmyo on the evening of 5 April, arriving in Minhla two days later.

Before leaving Thayetmyo the cement factory was put out of action and a small oil well nearby was fired. Bourke took under his command the BMP and BFF detachments he found in Thayetmyo, amounting to about 150 men, and also a garrison company consisting almost entirely of Burmese and Karens who soon deserted. Strangely enough, many men who deserted returned later only to desert again. 2 BURIF had never had any Burmese, but many of their Karens had deserted. Those who remained proved very staunch. 7 BURIF had lost all its Burmese and most of its Karens; those men who remained were chiefly Indians and Gurkhas,[3] amounting to not much more than 250 rifles. 8 BURIF was of course wholly Indian (Sikhs and Punjabi Mussalmans) from the outset. It too had been reduced to less than half strength (about 250) but this was largely due to battle casualties; it had fought very well at Moulmein, and again on the Sittang, and was undoubtedly the best of the BURIF units.

The brigade remained at Minhla until 13 April, withdrawing north on 14 April to conform with the movements of 1st Burma Brigade, deployed at the time near Magwe. 5/1 Punjabis had already been ordered to cross the Irrawaddy and join 1st Burma Brigade, which they did on 13 April, a great loss to Bourke's brigade since they were a very good battalion. 7 BURIF and part of the Field Ambulance were sent across the river on 15 April, the intention then being that the rest of 2nd Burma Brigade, still operating under command of BURCORPS, would reinforce BURDIV at Yenangyaung. However, Slim had decided that it was by then too late to make much difference to the desperate situation and Bourke's orders were countermanded. In the light of what happened, it was a wise decision.

The intense heat, coupled with the danger of attack from the air, meant that almost all movement had to be carried out by night, but this did not mean that the daylight hours could be devoted entirely to rest. Slit trenches had to be dug against air attack; water had to be fetched, sometimes from a considerable distance; animals and men fed; patrolling carried out; and foraging parties sent to purchase supplies. It soon became clear that rest was essential, particularly since most of the marching by night was over very rough ground. Bourke therefore decided that movement would not begin before 0200 hours, so that everyone had three or four hours' sleep after the night 'stand-to'.

It had been the intention to resupply the brigade at regular intervals by launch from the river, but this became impossible after the fall of Yenangyaung. In fact the brigade received no supplies at all after 13 April. 'Although we had no government rations,' wrote Bourke, 'we managed to purchase what we wanted, including an odd chicken, and occasionally vegetables. We had plenty of money and two good officers who knew local conditions to make purchases. All the same a continuous diet of local food did not agree with European stomachs. I got very tired of cold rice out of a mess tin at about 2 am, even though it might have a Jap sardine in it and was washed down with tea.'[4]

The brigade was able to maintain communication with Headquarters BURCORPS for most of the time, although there were occasions when it lost contact, sometimes for as long as forty-eight hours. The brigade signals section had only been formed shortly before the outbreak of hostilities and consisted mainly of Karens, who seem to have an aptitude for this kind of work. Their equipment was laughable by today's standards and they had to be masters of improvisation, but it can be said without equivocation that the Burma Army Signals fully deserved the praise they received in General Alexander's Dispatch.[5] In the case of 2nd Burma Brigade, we were fortunate in our Brigade Signals Officers, first Dick Kemp (of Burmah Oil) who left us early on for higher things; then Joe Kirby; and finally Bill Smith.

General Slim understandably had more pressing problems on his mind than 2nd Burma Brigade while the battle of Yenangyaung was being fought out between 1 BURDIV and the Japanese 33rd Division. From across the Irrawaddy, the brigade watched the huge columns of smoke and flames mounting into the sky as the oilfields were denied to the enemy. Occasionally they were mortared or shelled as they marched steadily northwards, encountering little hostility from the local inhabitants, but a good deal of bewilderment at the turn of events. There were occasional air attacks, the worst on 16 April when there were several casualties. The Brigadier and his Brigade Major in their haste to find cover ended up in a very prickly cactus bush.

The heat and thirst caused more problems than anything else. As much kit as possible was shed *en route* and kit was reduced finally to a blanket, a mosquito net and a groundsheet. Spare shirts and socks were also essential. As far as was known, the brigade was to march to Pakokku, and from there probably to Monywa, where it would rejoin BURDIV. Not much was known of events taking place across the river, other than the fact that things seemed to be going badly.*

The vital significance of the river port Monywa to the retreating Burma Army must be evident from the map. Situated on the east bank of the Chindwin, some fifty miles above its confluence with the Irrawaddy and 150 miles below Kalewa where the track to India via the Kabaw Valley began, Monywa in Japanese hands meant the virtual denial of the Chindwin as a means of logistical support for the Army. Its loss also meant that the enemy could use the river to land troops to outflank Alexander and Slim, their favourite tactics when employed in conjunction with a road-block. Moreover, Monywa was connected with Ye-U (from where the jungle track to Kalewa began) by a railway line, and also by a reasonable fair-weather road. 'The denial of Monywa meant the denial of retreat to India,' wrote the historian of *The First Punjabis*.[6] It is hard to understand why neither Alexander nor Slim seem to have appreciated how vital it was that Monywa should be strongly held from the very moment that Alexander decided to withdraw the Burma Army to India.

As it was, on 30 April 1942, as the rearguard of the Burma Army was preparing to cross the Ava Bridge prior to its demoli-

* Brigadier Bourke recalls one occasion when they managed to hear a broadcast from the BBC's Overseas Service. But instead of News they heard the Archbishop of Canterbury offering up prayers for the seriously beleaguered Burma Army!

MONYWA

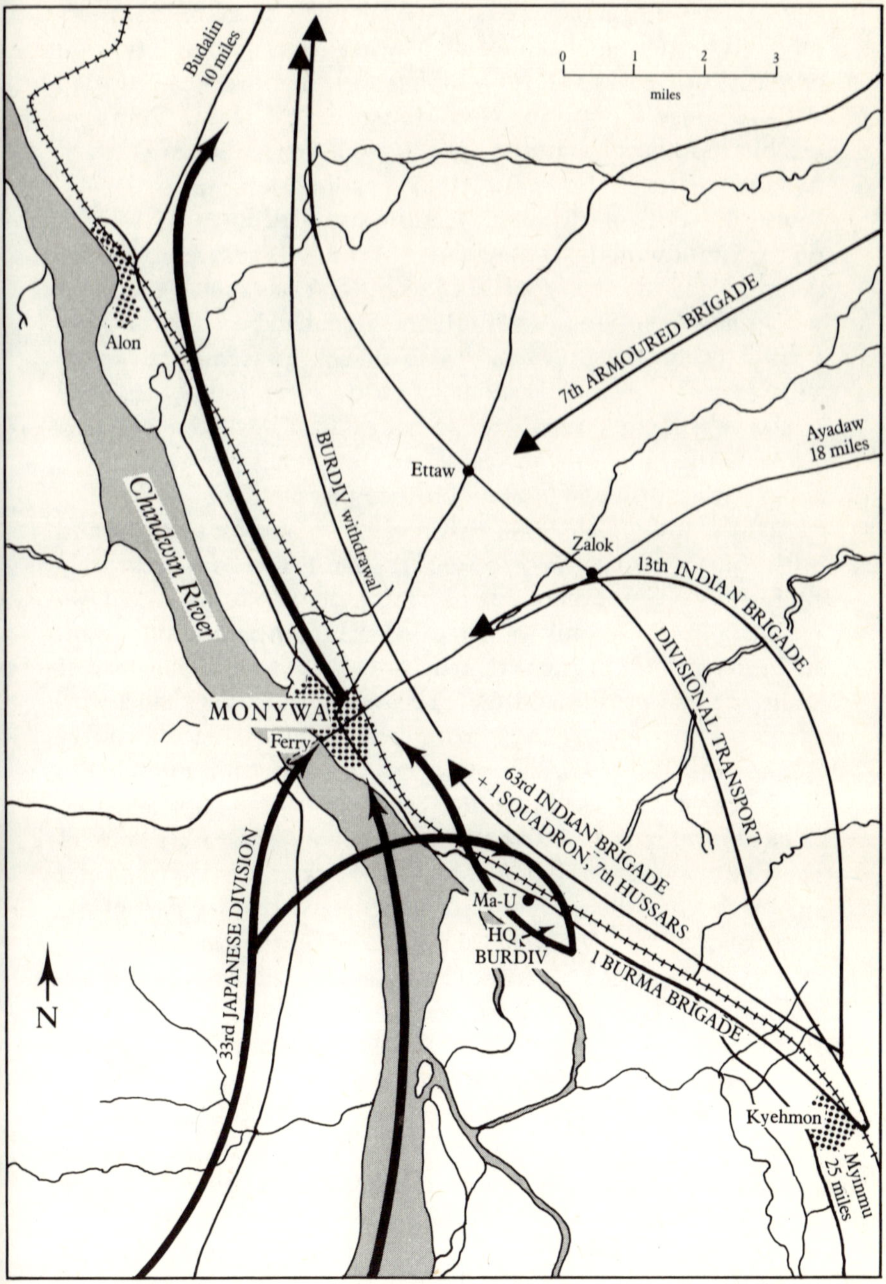
Budalin
10 miles
0 1 2 3
miles
7th ARMOURED BRIGADE
Alon
Chindwin River
BURDIV withdrawal
Ettaw
Ayadaw
18 miles
Zalok
13th INDIAN BRIGADE
DIVISIONAL TRANSPORT
MONYWA
Ferry
63rd INDIAN BRIGADE
+ 1 SQUADRON, 7th HUSSARS
Ma-U
HQ
BURDIV
1 BURMA BRIGADE
33rd JAPANESE DIVISION
N
Kyehmon
Myinmu
25 miles

tion, Monywa's garrison consisted of all that was left of 1 Glosters (about 150 men) and the Royal Marines river patrol. The civil administration was still functioning and the town was crowded with refugees waiting for river transport to Kalewa. Slim had established his corps headquarters about sixteen miles north of Monywa. Bruce Scott's BURDIV headquarters was at Ma-U, four miles south of Monywa. At Alon, six miles north of Monywa on the Chindwin, there were 2400 subordinate staff from Burma Army Headquarters together with their servants, many of whom had their families with them. They had been sent to Alon from Shwebo the previous day to be transported by steamers upriver to Kalewa. Alexander's headquarters, greatly reduced in size, was moving into Shwebo before starting on the long trek through the jungle to Shwegyin, from where there would be a short river journey to Kalewa on the opposite bank.

Scott's two depleted and very weary brigades, 1st Burma and 13th Indian, who had crossed the Irrawaddy two days previously by ferry, were still marching along the dusty Sagaing–Monywa road, about twenty miles south of BURDIV headquarters. Slim had intended to lift them by trucks to Monywa but shortage of transport had prevented this. The troops were too exhausted to be forced-marched in the blazing heat and there had to be frequent halts. As soon as Monywa was reached, Slim intended to send one of the two brigades across the river to protect that flank. He already had 2nd Burma Brigade on the west bank of the Chindwin. Bourke had entered Pakokku on 28 April after a march of forty-three miles in thirty-three hours, for part of the time followed by what were thought to be Burmese collaborating with the Japanese. Pakokku was in fact definitely hostile, according to Lewin. It was quite a large town.

Bourke could certainly have reached Monywa by 30 April, the mere presence of Burma Army forces in the area almost certainly slowing down a Japanese advance. However, Slim was concerned by reports coming in of hostile Burmese gathering in the Myittha valley, sixty miles west of the Chindwin and leading directly to Kalewa. Conscious that he might well be out-flanked if the enemy utilized this route, Slim ordered Bourke on 28 April to turn north-west from Pakokku to Pauk, and from Pauk to advance north up the Myittha valley via Gangaw, to protect the western flank of the retreating Burma Army. Bourke did as he was told, the consequence being that for a vital twenty-four hours the approaches to Monywa from the south-west were unprotected. It might easily have turned out to be a fatal mistake but for a great deal of luck and some very tough fighting by all the troops involved.

General Sakurai had allowed his 33rd Division little rest after their capture of Yenangyaung. Pausing only long enough for essential replenishment of supplies and ammunition – and doubtless bitterly regretting his failure to seize intact the vital stores of gasoline – Sakurai pressed on at the heels of the retreating 1 BURDIV. He moved out of Yenangyaung on 25 Qpril, sending his 215th Infantry Regiment across the river with orders to take Pakokku. The advance was slowed down owing to the intense heat but Pakokku was entered on 29 April, less than twenty-four hours after Bourke had marched out. Sakurai, who had the advantage over Slim and Bruce Scott of almost unlimited air support during the daylight hours, must have been made aware by air reconnaissance of the virtually open right flank of BURCORPS. He managed to get trucks across the Irrawaddy, loaded 215th Infantry Regiment into them, and sent them off to Monywa. 'After driving a distance of 50 kilometres,' according to the Japanese report,[7] 'the Regiment arrived at the bank opposite Monywa at sunset. Monywa was silent in the dark and the enemy situation was not known. However the Regiment Commander judged that the enemy would eventually retreat back to Monywa and decided to occupy the town, ordering the 1st battalion to cross the river by surprise during the night and attack Monywa from the south.'

As had come to be Burma Army's bitter experience where the Japanese were concerned, they had appeared out of nowhere and when least expected. Just before last light they opened fire on Monywa with machine guns, mortars and infantry cannon, capturing a steamer moored on the west bank. It was Thursday, 30 April, a little after 1900 hours.

The report that reached Slim shortly after his evening meal was, as it turned out, greatly exaggerated. He was told that the

Japanese had captured Monywa. They were in fact still on the west bank. However, Slim ordered Scott to concentrate his two brigades as quickly as possible at Chaungu, fifteen miles south of Monywa; and 17th Division were ordered to rail 63rd Indian Brigade, which had just crossed the Irrawaddy, to Chaungu also. He then collected about 300 men and dispatched them down the road towards Monywa, with orders to delay the enemy for as long as possible. Meanwhile news of the disaster was reported to Alexander, bringing General Winterton driving down the road from Shwebo in the middle of the night to consult with Slim.

Slim, who was still under the impression that Monywa was in Japanese hands, advised that every truck, every jeep and every other kind of vehicle that could be secured should be ordered to dump all loads and be loaded instead with personnel, including sick and wounded, and hurried along the jungle track to Shwegyin without further delay. Winterton hastened back to Shwebo to do as Slim had advised. It is his opinion that it was this action that, above all else, saved the bulk of the Burma Army from being captured.[8] As it was, the Japanese were beaten to Shwegyin, where transhipment across the Chindwin had to take place, by the very shortest of short heads.

While Scott was trying to concentrate his division during the small hours of 1 May, Slim was bitterly reproaching himself for having sent 2nd Burma Brigade on its long march up the Myittha valley. But such are the fortunes of war. In the absence of concrete information, a general has to work on what can only be described as 'a best guess'. In Slim's case, his 'best guess' could neither be confirmed nor denied by air reconnaissance. There was none on the British side. A single helicopter, had such a machine existed at the time, would probably have made all the difference. As it was, Slim had decided there was more danger from a wide outflanking movement up the Myittha valley than there would be from an attack on Monywa itself; indeed, it seems almost as if he had discounted any immediate threat in that direction.

The Japanese crossed the Chindwin before first light on 1

May, establishing a road-block on the road between Monywa and Headquarters 1 BURDIV at Ma-U. They had collected country and rubber boats for the crossing. At 0500 hours a considerable force of Japanese and Burmese attacked Scott's headquarters, scattering it and forcing Scott himself, with a mixed body of staff officers, clerks, a handful of Indian sappers and anyone else who could be gathered up, to beat a fighting retreat down the road towards Chaungu. They lost all their kit, so painfully gathered together after the Yenangyaung disaster two weeks previously, and almost all the divisional headquarters equipment. They did however succeed in saving their ciphers and secret papers. Major Marcus Witherow, commanding 23rd Mountain Battery, lost his false teeth, but fortunately recovered them forty-eight hours later.

The Japanese account of the early stages of their attack on Monywa is interesting: 'The 1st battalion . . . crossed the Chindwin River in silence. By sunrise the battalion advanced to the Mandalay–Monywa road without knowing the enemy situation. At sunrise several hundred enemy soldiers were found resting in Maigon [Ma-U?] village on the road and the battalion opened out and attacked them. The enemy were surprised and fled . . . the leading company followed them up and charged into the village.'[9] The account goes on to say that the British counter-attacked, leading to a temporary Japanese withdrawal. It says that enemy tanks were met, one being destroyed and another damaged. The battalion then advanced north, 'charged into the town of Monywa and occupied its southern part. It was a little before 1 p.m. on 1st May'.[10]

Clearly this was the surprise attack on Headquarters 1 BURDIV, followed by the partial occupation of Monywa. The crossing of the Chindwin by the main body of the Japanese 215th Infantry Regiment is described as follows:

> Observation by binoculars at dawn revealed no enemy in Monywa. The 2nd battalion had its artillery and machine guns deployed in case of enemy reaction, the crossing being made during daylight and the river being 600 metres wide. At 10 a.m. the first group in three boats began to cross. Half way across they were met by heavy

> fire, the enemy being concealed in the jungle. Our mountain cannon and machine guns destroyed the enemy machine gun posts and the first wave crossed the river successfully. Thereafter the battalion continued with the crossing without further difficulty, the central and northern part of Monywa being occupied by around noon . . . The regimental headquarters advanced to Monywa in the afternoon.[11]

The rest of the day was spent establishing a strong defensive cordon round Monywa, in the face of what appear to have been strong counter-attacks.

> The enemy alongside the southern railroad facing 1st battalion, and those facing 7th Company east of the town were gradually strengthened in the afternoon and their fighting spirit was high. Shells started to burst all over the town and tanks approached 5th Company in the northern part of the town. Every group tried to strengthen their position and repelled the enemy attacks. On the morning of 2nd May, however, the enemy began to launch full-scale attacks from every direction . . .[12]

The first British brigade into action at Monywa was 63rd Indian which had been hastily dispatched from Sagaing by rail, after covering the demolition of the Ava Bridge. The two leading battalions detrained eight miles south of Monywa and began at once to advance towards the town. There was stiff fighting, two tanks of 7th Hussars being knocked out and the 2/13 FFRif suffering serious casualties. Since it was late in the afternoon and the troops were exhausted, a halt was called for the night of 1 May. Meanwhile 13th Indian Brigade had come up to join 63rd Brigade. 1st Burma Brigade was expected to arrive early in the morning of 2 May, and 7th Armoured Brigade, then supporting the 38th Chinese Division on the Irrawaddy line, was about to be switched to Shwebo.

This had been decided at the last conference Alexander was to have with General Stilwell, on the evening of 1 May. Both generals agreed that the situation at Monywa had drastically altered the situation. It would be necessary as a result to withdraw immediately from the line of the Irrawaddy opposite

Mandalay, Stilwell deciding to fall back on Katha on the Irrawaddy, rather more than halfway between Mandalay and Myitkyina. Thereafter he was keeping his options open, the alternatives being either a withdrawal through Myitkyina into China, or north-eastwards into India. Alexander and Stilwell were not to meet again until they were both in India.

Both Alexander and Slim would have liked to retain the 38th Chinese Division under General Sun, who had won for himself such a high reputation among the British. Sun himself was anxious to remain under Slim's command, but Stilwell was naturally reluctant to lose the best of his Chinese subordinates. When, therefore, Sun arrived at Alexander's headquarters to press his case for remaining with the British, General Winterton feared that Alexander might well agree, failing to see the political implications of doing so. Leaving the room, Winterton sent another officer to ask Alexander if they could have a word in private. When Alexander came out, Winterton spoke strongly against falling in with Sun's request. Alex replied that he knew Stilwell would accuse him of stealing his best Division, but how could he manage to save Sun's face? 'Then suddenly,' said Winterton, 'Alex's face lit up. "I know," he said, "I'll give him a British decoration." He borrowed a pair of scissors, cut the ribbon of the CBE from his string of medal ribbons, went into the next room and pinned it on the chest of the gratified General Sun, who left us beaming all over his face. Later, I understand, Alex received a rocket from Buckingham Palace when the King came to hear of the incident.'[13]

Sun Li-jen was unusually cooperative for a Chinese general. He did eventually succeed in withdrawing his 38th Division to India, independent of either Alexander or Stilwell. Most Chinese generals behaved very differently, one of them commandeering a train which was to transport women and children from Shwebo to Myitkyina for air evacuation to India. 'Stilwell behaved very well when we explained about this,' says Winterton. 'He provided U.S. planes to evacuate the families from Shwebo.'[14]

While Alexander and Stilwell were conferring at Shwebo on the evening of 1 May, General Bruce Scott, in his hurriedly improvised headquarters south of Monywa, was planning the battle for Monywa, due to begin at dawn on 2 May. It should be remembered to the eternal credit of 1 BURDIV, and above all of Scott himself, that they had only got out from the hell of Yenangyaung two weeks previously. No infantry battalion amounted to much more than half strength, some considerably less than that. Many were suffering from dysentery or malaria; all, both officers and soldiers, were exhausted, as much from the heat as from the marching and fighting. And yet they fought as well at Monywa as they had done at any time since the campaign began.

As was almost always the case during that campaign, the battle began with a cross-country march at night, always an exhausting performance. 'Night marching in these conditions was a game of follow my leader,' writes Pat Carmichael of 23rd Mountain Battery. 'Each man had to stick to the one in front at all costs throughout the column, and God help anyone who lost touch, for it was easy for men to do so and wander off, and in floundering about put an operation at risk.'[15]

The plan was for 13th Indian Brigade, under Brigadier Curtis, to attack westwards, astride the track from Zalok to Monywa. 63rd Indian Brigade, which had retaken Ma-U late the previous day,[16] was to advance up the road and railway from the south, joining hands with 13th Brigade, it was hoped, in Monywa itself. 1st Burma Brigade, coming up from Chaungu, would reinforce 63rd Brigade if required. One squadron of 7th Hussars was supporting 63rd Brigade, the rest of 7th Armoured Brigade moving to Ettaw, eight miles north-east of Monywa, ready to support the attack.

The Japanese had had twenty-four hours to dig themselves in, and had made full use of it. The ground was flat, there was little cover and there was excellent observation from the built-up area over the surrounding countryside. Machine guns, mortars and infantry cannon had been skilfully sited to cover all likely approaches. The Japanese had the advantage of almost continuous air cover, although their fighters and bombers found it difficult to intervene owing to the proximity of the two sides. 'From the morning of 2nd May, the enemy started a full strength attack from all directions,' states the 215th Japanese Infantry Regiment record. 'The enemy infantry advanced under artillery cover, shells bursting all over the town. They were supported by tanks and tried to break through our 1st battalion several times, but were repelled . . . The enemy (Indian and Gurkha soldiers) attacked very bravely, many falling under our fire, but they kept coming on over their dead.'

13th Brigade fought their way with great *élan* into the town, 5/1 Punjabis and 1/18 Royal Garwhal Rifles particularly distinguishing themselves. There was a ding-dong struggle for the railway station, one moment in the Punjabis' hands, then back again to the Japanese. 63rd Brigade in the southern approaches to Monywa were less successful, meeting stiff opposition. General Scott therefore decided to pass 1st Burma Brigade through 63rd Brigade to maintain the momentum of the attack. It was the old story of a road-block, cleverly positioned and desperately defended by well-concealed machine guns and mortars. However, when 1st Burma Brigade attacked in mid-afternoon on 2 May, the two leading battalions advanced to the east of the road-block, thereby outflanking it, 2/7 Rajputs making good progress on the right. On the left, 1/4 Gurkha Rifles were held up by heavy fire from the area of the railway station.

There was now a distinct possibility that 1st Burma Brigade and 13th Brigade would meet head-on in the middle of Monywa. 1st Burma Brigade had in fact attacked without artillery support, for fear of firing on their comrades, which was to happen when the Rajputs mistook the Garwhalis for Japanese and shot them up, causing several casualties. It was of course yet another example of how difficult it was to pass information quickly and accurately during the 1942 campaign. In close-quarter fighting, as had been the case at Yenangyaung and was to be again at Monywa, it was almost impossible to identify friend from foe often until too late. Also the Japanese, who were masters of deception, frequently wore British uniforms.

Nevertheless, despite all the difficulties, things seemed to be going reasonably well for General Scott's 1 BURDIV. Large numbers of Japanese had been observed recrossing the Chindwin, several launches and country boats being sunk. The commander of 1st Burma Brigade was planning the capture of the railway station when he was ordered to stand fast. It was 1700 hours. Two hours earlier an officer of 7th Armoured Brigade passed a message, purporting to have come from Alexander, to the effect that 13th Brigade was to halt its attack and withdraw to Alon, six miles north of Monywa. This was reported to General Scott by 13th Brigade. Scott accordingly ordered 1st Burma Brigade to withdraw north-east of Monywa, and then take up a defensive position astride the track from Monywa to Ye-U, behind 13th Brigade at Alon. Meanwhile the divisional transport had been successfully by-passed round Monywa, via the cart-track linking Zalok-Ettaw with the main road to Ye-U. The battle of Monywa was over.

The message calling it off has never been satisfactorily explained. That it was delivered by an officer of 7th Armoured Brigade to Headquarters 13 Brigade is certain. He claimed that he received it in clear from the Army Commander (Alexander). Both Alexander and Slim were to state later that they knew nothing about it. The most likely explanation, as accepted in both the British and the India-Pakistan official histories, is that the message was false and was passed by the Japanese. That it was not queried at the time can be explained by the fact that by that stage of the campaign the only reliable means of radio communication within Burma Army were the tanks of 7th Armoured Brigade.

BURDIV's disengagement from Monywa was satisfactorily accomplished, the Japanese having been fought to a standstill. However, by capturing Monywa they had managed to seize several shallow draught vessels which were invaluable for following up the Chindwin, always difficult to navigate at that stage of the dry season, and enabled them to deny the British the use of the river as a means for withdrawal. Fortunately, when the Japanese arrived opposite Monywa on 30 April, the six largest sternwheelers of the Irrawaddy Flotilla Company's Chindwin fleet were upriver, having been operating for twenty-four hours a day evacuating refugees from Monywa to Kalewa. As soon as the Japanese started to bombard Monywa, thereby giving the game away, the Flotilla party made for Alon, six miles upstream, where they managed to intercept the first of the returning steamers. They then turned the steamer and set off for Kalewa, intercepting and turning round the other five steamers *en route*. Had they not been able to do this, there would have been no steamers to transport the Burma Army across the Chindwin from Shwegyin to Kalewa.

On 3 May, at sunset, the 215th Japanese Infantry Regiment set off from Monywa in pursuit of the retreating British.

> The advance guard was the 2nd battalion . . . and the division's tank company, which was composed of six enemy tanks captured at Shwedaung. The tank company led the column since we anticipated meeting enemy tanks. The night was dark, without moonlight. When we passed Alon, we heard a lot of shooting to our front. Our tanks had bumped into enemy tanks. One of our tanks was destroyed. Nevertheless our tanks kept on advancing, destroying two enemy tanks and forcing the others to retreat. *This was a fight between British-made tanks, and we won.** We often came across tired and lost enemy soldiers in the dark. After sunrise the leading battalion was fired on from the direction of Budalin and was forced by enemy tanks to deploy. The 2nd battalion continued to advance, supported by our tanks and mountain guns. The enemy artillery was very accurate, its fire directed by tanks acting as observation posts . . . Many casualties resulted, including the battalion commander. However, the 2nd battalion and tank company advanced from the left, charging into Budalin village about noon. Then the main body of the regiment came up and occupied the village completely. The enemy were thought to be the rearguard for their retreat. They withdrew north-west. This battle featured cooperation between infantry, tanks and artillery, which had occurred very rarely during our operations in Burma.[17]

The Japanese had indeed run into the rearguard of BURCORPS, consisting of 7th Armoured Brigade and 1st West Yorkshire Regiment. The British official account does not tally exactly with the Japanese, particularly in not mentioning that the Japanese tanks were captured British ones. One tank of 2nd

* Author's italics.

Royal Tanks was lost through falling into a *chaung* in the dark, and another was destroyed in action on 4 May. All the official history has to say of this incident is: '7th Armoured Brigade had several encounters with enemy tanks supported by anti-tank guns near Budalin, but no infantry action developed and the withdrawal was completed by nightfall without further incident.'[18]

By 4 May the majority of Slim's Corps had reached Ye-U, preparatory to the long slog through the jungle to Shwegyin. Once again disaster had been narrowly averted, but only at considerable cost. Would they now be able to reach the Chindwin before the Japanese? And even then, would they be able to get to India before the onset of the monsoon?

CHAPTER SIXTEEN

By the Skin of our Teeth

'It was a damned nice thing, the nearest run thing you ever saw in your life.'

Wellington commenting on the battle of Waterloo

If, in Wellington's opinion, his victory over Napoleon was the 'nearest run thing', the Burma Army's narrow escape from the Japanese was an equally close call. The battered, bruised and bewildered Burma Division had fallen back from Monywa to Ye-U leaving behind, according to the Japanese, 790 dead, 403 taken prisoner, two tanks, two armoured cars (probably Bren Gun carriers), 158 trucks, six anti-tank guns and thirty-seven machine guns of various calibres. Also among the booty were 'plenty of rifles and ammunition'.[1]

Ye-U was crammed with troops, refugees and the flotsam and jetsam always to be found in the tail of a retreating army. There were men who had become separated from their units and who were desperately looking for them. There were others who had abandoned all pretence at discipline and whose only aim was to get out to India as rapidly as possible; looting came as second nature to them. The 38th Chinese Division was still at Shwebo, thirty miles south-east of Ye-U, acting as rearguard to the Vth Chinese Army which was withdrawing north along the railway to Myitkyina. Alexander had ordered Scott to hold on at Ye-U until the Chinese were clear of Shwebo. Meanwhile he had ordered his own headquarters, slimmed down to only a handful of staff officers, clerks and signallers, to move to Kaduma, twenty miles along the jungle track to Shwegyin; the balance of Headquarters Burma Army had already been moved by river steamer and overland to Kalewa.

Alexander was beset by two terrible fears at this time, although no one who engaged him in casual conversation would have known it.* The first was the very real possibility of his escape route being cut by the Japanese hooking in from the Chindwin which they now virtually controlled. To guard against this a boom was erected by what remained of the Royal Marines' contingent two miles south of Shwegyin. Alexander also asked for air support to delay the Japanese moving upriver. This was forthcoming on 3, 4 and 5 May, imposing considerable delay as had been expected. The Japanese had become so accustomed to operating without hindrance from the air that to be served out with their own medicine must have come as a nasty shock.

Nevertheless, with this brief exception, their Air Force had everything their own way. Shwebo had been very badly bombed during the last week in April, the inevitable fires completing the destruction begun by high explosive. The most serious effect was the enforced abandonment of Shwebo airfield for the evacuation to India of the wounded, sick and refugees, many of whom were European families who had been sent to Shwebo for the purpose.[2] With Shwebo unusable the only alternative was Myitkyina, 200 miles farther north, but movement by rail was hideously complicated due to attacks from the air and the general collapse of peacetime administration. The Chinese, in their wayward fashion, contributed to the disorder by commandeering at pistol-point trains intended for the movement of wounded and refugees to Myitkyina. And Myitkyina airfield was rendered unusable on 6 May when three out of the five aircraft were destroyed by bombing while loading. After that there was only one way to India – overland through some of the most difficult country in the world.

The route to India, whichever one was chosen, might just be possible during the dry season. With the coming monsoon,

* Chief Engineer William Hutcheon of the Irrawaddy Flotilla Company, who played a gallant part in ferrying Burma Army across the Chindwin from Shwegyin to Kalewa, recorded in his diary: '7th May – General Alexander on board one trip today. Came up on flying bridge and had a yarn. Plenty of planes overhead and we are bombed – but he thanked me for a pleasant voyage!' (*Irrawaddy Flotilla* by McCrae and Prentice, James Paton Ltd, Glasgow, 1978, p. 146.)

however, the situation would be drastically changed. Jungle tracks would disintegrate into muddy bogs, impassable to all vehicles including bullock-carts. Even mules would find it difficult in places to retain their footing. There would be malaria, blackwater fever, jaundice, typhus and the dreaded cholera. The jungle would become a sodden, dripping mess, shrouded for much of the time in a dank and penetrating mist, making it impossible to stay dry. It is usual in Burma for the monsoon to arrive in the middle of May. This was the second of Alexander's anxieties as he daily scanned the sky; far better the Japanese Air Force than the thunderclouds heralding the monsoon. As it was, there had already been heavy showers as a foretaste of what was to come.

The withdrawal plan was for Scott, as soon as the Chinese had cleared Shwebo, to send 16th Brigade at best possible speed up the 120 miles of track to Shwegyin and then across the Chindwin to secure Kalewa and, farther west, Kalemyo, towards which Bourke's brigade was steadily plodding 'at best bullock-cart speed'[3] up the Myittha valley. 17th Division was to take up a series of layback positions along the track at Kaduma and Pyingaing, after which BURDIV and 7th Armoured Brigade (less 7th Hussars) would fall back through them to Shwegyin, from where they would be ferried to Kalewa. 48th Brigade and 7th Hussars were to form the rearguard.

This was a nice, tidy staff officer's plan, but there were several complicating factors. Firstly, there were the wounded, some 2300 of whom had not been evacuated by air from Shwebo. Next, there were the refugees, mostly Indians but also many Europeans, Anglo-Indians, Anglo-Burmans, and some Burmese. Few were prepared for the arduous miles ahead, many were sick, others were pregnant, all were terrified of the Japanese. There were thousands of them. Finally, there was the condition of the troops themselves.

'Like the animals,' writes Pat Carmichael, 'men and officers had lost condition badly. Men were under-weight with cheeks and eye-sockets hollowing out. Some of the *jawans** also had

* *Jawan*—lad (Urdu). The usual expression used by British officers for their Indian soldiers.

jungle sores and dysentery. But our main concern was for the *khattchars* [mules] who . . . would have to do the long stretch to Shwegyin under full loads. During the march from Alon Tom had had to shoot four of them, and warned me there were bound to be more casualties each day we marched.'[4]

Carmichael was writing of 23th Mountain Battery, a unit which had retained its cohesion ever since those early days in March south of Toungoo. It was well commanded, had excellent officers, British and Indian, and a fine pride in itself. There were other units less fortunate. If the overall state of health was poor, morale too was a brittle quality. Nor was it helped by the wretched state of the refugees, lying beside the track as they died from thirst, or hunger, disease or sheer exhaustion. It was a sight likely to lower the highest spirits.

Every possible effort had been made to improve the track to Shwegyin. Wherever it could be done, the track had been widened and graded, the steepest slopes improved, the sandiest *chaung* crossings made firmer by the laying of bamboo or wooden planking. But the surface was still dusty and loose, hard going for all but four-wheeled drive and tracked vehicles. Supplies of food and water had been dumped at regular intervals. There was sufficient petrol for all the vehicles but the troops were put on half rations as a precaution. Alexander had been told not to halt the Burma Army at Kalewa but to press on up the Kabaw valley to Tamu, where the dry-weather road to Imphal via Palel began. The bottleneck was still Shwegyin where there were only six sternwheelers available to transport men and vehicles the six miles upriver to Kalewa, each with a capacity of 600 men and four vehicles at most. Vulnerable to air attack not only when loading and unloading but also when on passage, the steamers were crewed by Chittagonians who deserved every praise for remaining at their posts. The congestion at Shwegyin itself, and at Kalewa too for that matter, was another limiting factor in a race against time, making it almost inevitable that the majority of the transport, and also the tanks, would have to be left behind. It was the Sittang all over again.

The Japanese had not rested on their laurels after capturing Monywa. Their 215th Regiment continued to maintain pressure on BURDIV south of Ye-U while arrangements were being made to send their 213th Regiment upriver. General Sakurai had been told by XVth Army's Chief of Staff on 5 May 'Not one Allied soldier is to get back to India.' On 9 May General Iida, the Army Commander, met Sakurai near Shwebo, urging him to press on; Sakurai embarked that night with his divisional headquarters, 213th Infantry Regiment and a battalion of mountain artillery. A fleet of forty launches had been collected at Monywa for the purpose. The objective was Shwegyin.

Sakurai had of course been preceded upriver by other, but smaller, parties with the task of causing as much trouble as possible for the retreating Burma Army. On the British side Major Mike Calvert, with what remained of his Bush Warfare School, was operating under much the same kind of instructions, his main problem being his failure to persuade many of the retreating British to join in the game with him. In a report he wrote after the war ended, *à propos* the formation of the SAS Regiment, he said:

> A force consisting of two Gurkha Coys and a few British troops of which I was one was left behind in 1942 in Burma to attack the enemy in the rear if they appeared. The Commander, a good Gurkha officer with a good record, when confronted with a perfect opportunity (Japs landing in boats onto a wide sandy beach completely unaware of our presence), avoided action in order to get back to his Brigade because he was 'out of touch', and could not receive orders. By avoiding action, the unit went into a waterless area and more perished this way and later by drowning than if he had attacked.[5]

Later, after unarmed combat with a Japanese officer whom Calvert killed (they came upon each other while bathing in the Chindwin), swimming the river, and making his way through the Japanese-infested jungle with a party of Indians who insisted he disguised himself and his companions as women, presumably to hide their faces, Calvert and his two companions managed to reach Kalewa.[6] One year later he was back – with Wingate.

Notwithstanding all Calvert's efforts to delay the Japanese, Sakurai's swift move upstream on the night of 9 May nearly destroyed the Burma Army. By the following morning a large part of Burma Army was west of the Chindwin, the troops remaining at or near Shwegyin consisting of Headquarters 17 Division (much reduced in strength), Headquarters 7 Armoured Brigade, 48th Brigade and 1/9 Royal Jats. These troops, together with their vehicles and supplies, were either in, or overlooking, a basin about 400 yards in width with the Chindwin on one side and on the other, steep cliffs about 200 feet high. Beyond the cliffs was jungle. Refugees were everywhere, some giving birth, some dying, all utterly exhausted and without hope. Over all hung the stench of human excrement, decomposing bodies, burning trucks and tanks, but despite all the apparent confusion Cowan had his Division under tight control. Having halted overnight two miles short of the basin, he hastened towards it when firing broke out early in the morning of 10 May.

Slim had come down by launch from Kalewa to confer with Cowan, leaving while it was still dark. As he stepped ashore from his launch at 0530 hours, he was greeted with rifle, mortar and artillery fire. Sakurai, his old opponent, had reached the southern rim of the basin with his Araki Force, and was ready for the kill. There followed one of the fiercest battles of the entire campaign. The Japanese could see victory in their grasp, resisting counter-attack after counter-attack launched with all the desperation of men finding themselves caught in a trap. And amidst all this mayhem, the work of loading the steamers continued. The wretched refugees huddled under any cover from fire they could find, and as many wounded as could be embarked were loaded aboard the steamers, handled so gallantly by their captains and crews. There was, however, a limit to the crews' endurance and by early afternoon they had made it plain that where Shwegyin was concerned, they would sail no more. Cowan then made the only possible decision: to withdraw upstream by the narrow up-and-down jungle track skirting the east bank to Kaing, opposite Kalewa. But first he destroyed his vehicles and tanks, and fired off all his ammunition in one last awe-inspiring *Götterdämmerung*.

The corps commander had left in the early afternoon, believing he would be better employed organizing what help could be provided from Kalewa. He took with him Brigadier Roger Ekin, who had been responsible for organizing the embarkation arrangements at Shwegyin. Once again Ekin was withdrawing across a broad river, with the enemy hot on his heels, but compared with Shwegyin, Moulmein had been a picnic. The noise of that last bombardment, every available gun firing for twenty minutes, reached as far as Kalewa. It stunned the Japanese crouching in the jungle and left them with no stomach to follow up Cowan's retreating men. Instead they went down into the basin to count the booty.

The successful outcome of what can perhaps be best described as the 'Custer's Last Stand' of the Burma Army was largely a consequence of the gallant performance of the rearguard, without whose self-sacrifice and devotion the withdrawal of 17th Division up the narrow track to Kaing might well have proved impossible. It consisted of the 1/9 Royal Jats and the 1/7 Gurkha Rifles, both of whom first met the Japanese at Kawkareik, five months and nearly one thousand miles previously. Since then both battalions, although sorely reduced in strength, had gained confidence in battle. Their commander was Lieutenant-Colonel Brian Godley of the Jats whose brilliant leadership wrested victory from defeat.

They were supported by 'A' Troop of 3rd Indian LAA Battery whose Bofors guns were employed in both an anti-aircraft and a ground role. Raised only twelve months previously by Major Charles MacFetridge, RA, 3rd Battery had already distinguished itself at Moulmein, Sittang, Pegu, Prome and Yenangyaung, but it surpassed itself at Shwegyin. No one had visualized the Bofors guns in a ground role but 'A' Troop (under Captain F. D. Webber) demonstrated at Shwegyin what could be done given the will and the leadership. They gave covering fire to the infantry struggling to hold back the Japanese, firing often over open sights, and destroyed a Japanese infantry cannon, a mortar and two aircraft. 'The chief contribution came from the Bofors,' records a war diary, 'whose tracer shells lit up the descending darkness. It was a cheering sound the like of which we had not heard during our time in Burma. At 8.15 the guns ceased fire, and five minutes later we received the order to go.'[7]

There was of course no hope of saving the guns, which had to be destroyed, but the gunners took their packs and rifles and marched away under their battery commander, their morale still high and conscious that together with the Jats and the Gurkhas they had secured the retreat of 17th Division. They were the last unit to engage the enemy in Burma. As Compton Mackenzie was later to write: 'The Royal Regiment of Artillery can be proud of those Indian gunners who have inherited its own incomparable traditions.'[8]

Shwegyin was the last battle BURCORPS was to fight, although no one knew it at the time. 17th Division made the crossing from Kaing to Kalewa without interruption, most of the troops making the long march thereafter through the Kabaw valley to Tamu on the Indian border where some transport had been assembled for the onward journey to Imphal. It was just in time. On Tuesday, 12 May, the monsoon burst with all its fury.

'With the exception of some guns, very little in the way of armament, ammunition or equipment had been brought out of Burma,' records the Official History; 'all the tanks and motor vehicles, except fifty lorries and thirty jeeps, had been destroyed or abandoned as unserviceable.'[9] Out of forty-eight artillery pieces – field, mountain and anti-tank – twenty-eight were brought out to India.[10] And only one tank! The 7th Hussars had managed to get one of their tanks across the Chindwin, contriving to drive it thereafter all the way to Imphal. It was to have its revenge for the indignities suffered during the retreat. Named 'The Curse of Scotland', it was acquired in some fashion by the 7th Light Cavalry, Indian Armoured Corps, and as their commanding officer's command tank was fought all the way back to Rangoon in 1945.

Throughout this terrible period, 2nd Burma Brigade was 'out of the battle', although fulfilling its role of protecting the far western flank of BURCORPS. After leaving Pakokku on 29 April it met with no opposition other than at Pauk where there was a sharp little engagement with a body of Thakins. The inhabitants there were definitely hostile, according to Lewin, bridges having been destroyed and Pauk itself having been looted and burnt. Merton, carrying out his duties as Brigade Intelligence Officer, was lucky to get away with his life when he encountered a large body of armed Burmese some miles east of Pauk. He was alone at the time but his command of the language probably saved him. When, later, Bourke's Frontier Force column (FF8) engaged this party, FF8 largely disintegrated, so it proved impossible to establish whether they were Japanese or Burmese, more likely the latter.

In the course of the march 8 BURIF were caught in the open by Japanese planes but suffered surprisingly few casualties. A BMP *subedar* was, however, killed. Since almost all movement was confined to night-time, Japanese air activity was not very troublesome, their Air Force's attention being in any case concentrated far to the east. Desertion was a problem; there was a continuous trickle of Karens from 2 BURIF, and later Chins as they drew nearer to their home districts. The Kachins remained staunch on the whole, as did the Indian soldiers in 8 BURIF, now pitifully reduced in strength.

After leaving Pauk, the brigade continued to march north, flanked on the west by the great jungle-covered mass of the Chin Hills, rising tier after tier like waves in a rough sea. No Japanese had reached there yet but the time would come when they would be fought over as bitterly as any other part of Burma. The Myittha itself was not a very fast-flowing river at that late stage of the dry season, and the cart track ran parallel with it for most of the way. There were innumerable *chaungs* flowing down from the hills to the Myittha, most of them bridged, however primitively. However, the Chin Hills Battalion of the BFF, whose bailiwick this was, had taken it upon themselves to destroy most of the bridges, earning for themselves the curses of every man from the Brigadier downwards. It meant, more often than not, unloading every cart, manhandling the contents across the *chaung*, finding a way across for the cart and bullocks, and then reloading on the other side. This became an increasingly tiresome and exhausting exercise as the combination of excessive heat and lack of nourishment took its toll of men's stamina.

The Burmese drivers took to their heels soon after Pauk, their places taken by soldiers who had at least the benefit of riding rather than plodding through the dust. The Brigadier rode a horse according to Lewin, who says he himself preferred to walk, although at night there was always the risk of being kicked sideways by a bullock. For the most part the valley was open, but not highly cultivated; Gangaw was the principal town. Bourke remembers it as being, with Minhla, the pleasantest place they passed through in the course of their odyssey. Although Compton Mackenzie describes the Myittha valley as 'hate-haunted' in *Eastern Epic*, Lewin recalls the inhabitants as being mostly friendly, only surprised to see their British masters on the run.

Nevertheless, Compton Mackenzie probably put the brigade's services into proper perspective when he wrote:

> It was only possible to move at night, and during the day defensive positions had to be manned. At last after marching 216 miles in 14 days the 2nd Burma Brigade made contact with the Chin Hills Battalion of the Burma Frontier Force near Natchaung, a few miles south of Kalemyo beside the dark green waters of the Myittha, on the edge of some of the wildest country in the world. This long indomitable march by the 2nd Burma Brigade through the insufferable hot dankness of that hate-haunted valley after an exhausting campaign of over three months was one of the notable feats of the Second World War.[11]

At Sihaung Myauk, twelve miles south of Natchaung, Bourke was astonished to find an impeccable Quarter Guard drawn up for inspection. It was provided by the Chin Hills Battalion whose commandant, Lieutenant-Colonel Moore, was a brother officer in the 92nd Punjabis. Later they sat down to a delicious dinner, more than welcome after a diet of cold and soggy rice. Bourke was less pleased on reaching the Manipur River to find the bridge destroyed by order of 'an officer of the line of communication services retiring ahead of the corps'. The carts had to be burnt and the 400 bullocks slaughtered, lest they fell into enemy hands. Bourke could not bring himself to do this, turning the animals loose instead. The Manipur was wide and the crossing was made with difficulty. 'It [2nd Burma Brigade] rejoined us at Kalemyo, west of Kalewa, tired, hungry, and angry,' wrote Slim.[12]

Since leaving Thayetmyo on 5 April, the brigade had marched 513 miles altogether, although for the last sixty miles or so those who were too sick, or too exhausted to march any farther, were ferried forward in trucks. The brigade reached camp at Milestone 109 on the Imphal road on 24 May, and was inspected by Wavell at 1 pm the following day. When we went into battle at Moulmein at the end of January, the brigade was about 5800 strong. The strength on arriving in India was 480, although this was not due only to battle casualties. 2 BURIF was the only Burma Rifles battalion to reach India at reasonable strength, but on arrival at Imphal those who had marched out were given the option of returning to their homes, together with three months pay, their rifles and fifty rounds of ammunition per man. Naturally enough, a large number took the opportunity to do so, but to their credit 500 Karens, Chins and Kachins remained 'true to their salt'. They were later, under Wingate, to win great renown, demonstrating that if properly trained and motivated they were to be numbered among the finest jungle-fighting men in the world.[13]

2nd Burma Brigade suffered few casualties compared with 1st Burma Brigade, and it certainly had to experience fewer calamities. But it retained its cohesion throughout the retreat and carried out efficiently whatever was asked of it. In the Burma Army the composition of brigades changed almost weekly, sometimes daily, and it followed that a brigade's spirit owed a great deal to its commander. We were lucky in 2nd Burma Brigade because we had in John Bourke, a very sound, courageous and determined leader, never afraid to speak his mind when he thought the occasion required it. He ended the retreat a good deal lighter in weight than when he began it, but his spirit was unquenched. He, too, was fortunate in his right-hand man, the Brigade Major, Jimmy Green, who was later to win the DSO commanding 6/13 FFR in Italy. Together they made a very well-balanced team and represented for me the very best of the old Indian Army. Green's services in Burma were rewarded with the award of the MBE, Bourke's with a Mention in Dispatches. It seemed little enough after one of the longest withdrawals in the Army's history, but retreats are notoriously ill-rewarded.

On 20 June 1942, by a stroke of some staff officer's pen, 2nd Burma Brigade ceased to exist, and was reborn as 113th Indian Infantry Brigade. Only a handful of those who had served in the headquarters at Moulmein still remained, Brigadier John Bourke being one of them.

It has been generally conceded that the treatment received by the Burma Army on arrival in India is difficult to condone. Slim, in measured language, compared adversely this treatment with that given to the British army returning from Dunkirk: 'My men had endured a longer ordeal with at least equal courage; they deserved an equal welcome.'[14] He says that it was due to Scott and Cowan, and to General Savory, GOC 23rd Indian Division at Imphal, that the resentment was largely contained; but Slim's own part was if anything more important. Nor was the resentment confined to officers and soldiers almost at the very end of their tether. Davies, Slim's Chief of Staff at BURCORPS, was moved to comment: 'The slogan in India seems to be, "Isn't that Burma Army annihilated yet?"'[15]

There are several reasons to account for the apparent total lack of preparation to deal with thousands of battle-weary, sick and exhausted men, in no physical state to endure the incessant monsoon downpours in leaky tents or rain-sodden bamboo huts. Firstly, the Indian authorities were simply overwhelmed by the magnitude of the problem. For more than a century the North-West Frontier preoccupied the minds of the staffs, both civil and military, at Army Headquarters. The north-eastern frontier, at the extreme end of the most rickety communications system in the sub-continent, was completely ignored. It was too late to rectify this when war with Japan broke out; indeed, it took the best part of two and a half years to do so.

Secondly, it has to be admitted that there was something of a *sauve qui peut* after Alexander's decision to cut his losses and retreat to India. Large numbers of officers and soldiers found their way back to India, giving all sorts of reasons for doing so, spreading alarm and despondency in their trail, and undoubtedly conveying the impression of a complete breakdown in morale, of a lack of will to fight. Some of the officers were senior in rank. There can be no doubt that Lieutenant-General Noël Irwin, GOC IVth Corps and therefore responsible for the defence of India's north-eastern frontier, formed the very worst impression of the morale of Burma Army as a result of his contacts with these fly-by-nights.

Thirdly, the medical problem was beyond description. Most men had dysentery, that horribly debilitating disease; those who had not were probably suffering from malaria, much of it contracted while marching through the Kabaw valley, one of the most malaria-infested regions in the world. The Burma Army's battle casualties – 1354 killed and 2534 wounded – were vastly outnumbered by the casualties from disease. The medical staffs simply could not cope, their only remedy to backload as many men as possible to hospitals in India along a railway system that was rapidly creaking to a halt.

Finally, but probably most significantly, India was totally unprepared for a war on its doorstep, both psychologically and in terms of organization. General Winterton, on his way across India at the end of March to join Alexander as his Chief of Staff, was appalled by the apparent lack of concern. Coming from a Britain which had just survived the Blitz, he found it astonishing that people were going about their everyday affairs 'almost as if there wasn't a war on!'[16] My wife was similarly struck by this when she arrived in Peshawar after escaping from Burma in February. Even as late as the end of 1942, after discharge from hospital for 'light duties', I found it remarkable that only two out of the forty-odd officer instructors at the Indian Military Academy had been in action against Germans, Italians or Japanese. It was remedied in the end, of course, but it took much longer than it should have done.

For the Japanese it had been, undoubtedly, 'a famous victory'. In five months they had out-manoeuvred, out-fought and out-marched an army no less well equipped than themselves. They had secured dominance in the jungle and in the air – the two elements vital for success when campaigning in Burma against a road-bound enemy. They had destroyed the myth on which so many European empires had been built, that in some way the white man is superior to all others. They had conquered a province rich in so much the Japanese lacked – oil, teak, minerals – while as for rice, Burma was the granary of South-East Asia. They may not have won the 'hearts and minds' of those they claimed to have liberated – their brutal behaviour and national arrogance saw to that – but at least they had rid the Burmese of one kind of foreign domination. Moreover, although no one could realize it at the time, they had set the Burmese on the road to Independence, something which every Burman in his heart of hearts truly craved.

Those of us who fought against them recognized their courage and strength of purpose, but at the same time we were repelled by their savagery and ferocity. Before we met them in battle many of us admired the Japanese for what they had accomplished since emerging from their seclusion in the middle of the last century. I used to play golf with a Japanese in Mandalay and found him a delightful companion. Therefore it came as all the more of a shock to discover that beneath the outward veneer there was a viciousness almost beyond our comprehension. No amount of special pleading by those who understand the Japanese character far better than I do, will ever convince me that it did anything other than to damage Japan's good name, at least for as long as those of us who fought against them survive to tell the tale.

The reasons for the British defeat will be discussed in the final chapter, but it may be as well here to end on a slightly higher note after such a catalogue of disaster. Throughout the retreat from Burma two formations stood out for their *esprit* and professional excellence. They were the 7th Armoured and 48th Gurkha Brigades, both of which arrived in India with their spirit unimpaired, although the 7th Hussars and 2nd Royal Tanks had to complete the final miles on their feet. Of the Gurkhas, Slim was to write: 'The reputation of the Gurkha remains unsurpassed in the field.'[17] In his Dispatch, Alexander was equally complimentary regarding 7th Armoured Brigade. I do not believe that any one who had the privilege of fighting alongside either of these two brigades would disagree.

CHAPTER SEVENTEEN

Against All the Odds

> 'I shall never go back. There are no more jungle paths or wild river crossings for me . . . But I shall go on thinking about them, and remember with gratitude the friendship and loyalty of two very great races, the Karen and Kachin . . .'
>
> Desperate Journey *by Francis Clifford*[1]

If the extracts from his letters to his wife, edited but unwisely published after Stilwell's death, are anything to go by, he must have been one of the most disagreeable officers in the United States Army. Nonetheless, his very curtness of speech and obvious determination never to give in won him the respect of many people who otherwise found it difficult to stomach his too-often violently expressed Anglophobia. It would seem that the picture he wanted to present to the outside world was that of a man with the root of the matter in him, but hindered and harassed at every turn by a collection of pygmies lacking in every human virtue, including courage. Among those he found particularly detestable were Chiang Kai-shek, whose Chief of Staff in Burma he ostensibly was, and General Alexander, whose two principal failings in Stilwell's eyes were that he was British and an aristocrat; it would have been difficult to produce a worse combination.

Where Chiang Kai-shek was concerned, Stilwell could justifiably claim that he never knew from one moment to the next what plots were being hatched against him. President Roosevelt's insistence on treating Chiang as head of a 'Great Power', disregarding the fact that he ruled over less than half of China, placed Stilwell in a very difficult position. It does not seem that his relations with Chiang were warm, and in the end Chiang succeeded in getting rid of him, but not until 19 October 1944. Long before that it had been suggested to Stilwell by the President, according to General Dorn, that Chiang should be got rid of 'once and for all'.[2] He was to be replaced by a Chinese general whom Stilwell could manage.

This bizarre affair came to nothing, as Stilwell predicted to Dorn, but not before Dorn had worked out a plan for Chiang's elimination. An air accident was to be staged *en route* to India and Chiang's parachute, and if needs be Madame Chiang's, was to be 'doctored'. For verisimilitude the American aircrew would have had to be sacrificed, together with the rest of Chiang's entourage. The CIA in its wildest moments has yet to come up with anything quite so fantastic.

Stilwell's own escape from Burma in 1942 was a remarkable story. He had parted from Alexander at Shwebo on 1 May, with the news of Monywa's capture ringing in his ears. There were still Chinese troops holding the west bank of the Irrawaddy opposite Mandalay, the intention being that they should retreat up the line of rail to Myitkyina. Thereafter they could withdraw either through the Hukawng valley into India, or across the wild mountains north of Myitkyina to Yunnan. The route to China via Bhamo and Lashio was blocked. When Stilwell left Shwebo he was undecided as to which route to take.

It was not until Stilwell's convoy had reached Indaw, roughly midway between Shwebo and Myitkyina, that he decided to turn west towards India. The journey so far had been a nightmare, the dusty track clogged with vehicles fleeing north, refugees begging for lifts or simply lying down to die, bridges destroyed, Chinese and other looters roaming the towns, and Japanese air attacks at regular intervals. The railway was blocked, General Lo Cho-ying, Stilwell's Chinese Chief of Staff, having seized a train at pistol-point and ordered the driver to head north. The line was single-track and there was a collision with a southbound train. Stilwell hoped that Lo would have to walk every inch of the way to Chungking in just retribution.

Stilwell's party consisted of his American staff, including a radio operator; Dr Segrave's Quaker Ambulance Unit, with Karen, Shan and Kachin nurses; a Chinese guard; and various cooks, sweepers and other helpers. It amounted to about eighty people at the outset, increasing in numbers as it was joined by other refugees, British, Indian, Chinese and Burmese. Throughout it was controlled with drill-book meticulousness by the elderly American general (he had his sixtieth birthday on the way out), who refused to take 'No' for an answer and was unforgiving with anyone who failed to abide by his rules.

They marched due west from Indaw, making for Homalin on the Upper Chindwin, nearly 200 miles away, across what the Japanese were later to call (wrongly), the Arakan Yomas. It is some of the most difficult terrain in Burma, formerly known only to the people who lived there (Shans and Kachins), and to forest officers, and 'teak wallahs' of the Bombay-Burma Trading Corporation and Steel Brothers. Stilwell's party had to jettison their trucks and jeeps when the jungle tracks petered out into slippery footpaths. They climbed the knife-edge ridges, to slither and slide down the other side. For part of the way they walked knee-deep down the Chaungyi river, boating the last part of the journey down the Uyu river to the Chindwin on bamboo rafts. That they arrived in the end in India, in one piece and relatively unscathed, was entirely due to the leadership, courage and determination of the man who led them from beginning to end, General 'Vinegar Joe' Stilwell. They arrived on 15 May 1942 in Imphal after a journey none of them would ever forget.[3]

They were more fortunate than the nearly one million Indians who sought to escape from Burma. Only the very fit, very tough, or very lucky got through, most of them leaving by the roadside the corpses of members of their families to mark their trail. The governments of India and Burma were to be severely criticized for their alleged mishandling of the refugee problem, a natural reaction after disasters. The truth was that the magnitude of the refugee problem was not foreseen until it was too late to do anything about it; and also that the military priorities conflicted with the civilian, the latter having to give way, whatever the human consequences.

It all began in Rangoon, after the first Japanese air raid on 23 December 1941. Astonishingly, the after-effects of such an attack on the civilian population appear to have taken the administration by surprise. Nearly everyone fled the city, paralysing the essential services and the docks. The military were frantic to get people back, partly because of the risk to public health, partly because of the succession of troop transports due in Rangoon at any moment. The Governor and his ministers were worried because they knew that the majority of the refugees were Indians (Rangoon was virtually an Indian city), who would be at the mercy in the countryside of the Burmese who hated them. There was therefore a grave risk to law and order.

Every attempt was made to persuade the Indians to return to Rangoon, both by bribes and a variety of other inducements. The wiser among them carried on, plodding their way from Prome across the Arakan Yomas to Akyab, and thence to Chittagong and Calcutta. They were fleeced every inch of the way – so many rupees to cross the Irrawaddy from Prome, so much for a passport, so much for the ferry to Akyab, and so much more for the sea trip to Calcutta. If any of them had doubts about the wisdom of continuing, these were soon put at rest by the attacks of Burmese gangs, hovering in the jungle to cut off stragglers. But those who left by the end of 1941, overland to Akyab or by sea from Rangoon, were the wise virgins. The route over the hills may have been rough, but at least it was dry; and sea passages were still available for those able to pay for them.

Those who listened to the siren voices seeking to reassure them, who returned to Rangoon to help unload the ships, cleanse the streets and fight the fires, were the foolish virgins. By the time they decided to flee for the second time, the enemy was within striking distance of Rangoon, the army was falling back, the monsoon was that much closer, and the Japanese Air Force was reducing every important Burmese town to a smoking pyre. By then it was too late for them to reach India by any other means than on foot, and the routes that most of them were bound to take had already been bespoke for the retreating Burma Army.

Wherever they went, the story was the same. Filthy camp sites, shortage of water, lack of food, the absence of medicines.

Volunteers, both Europeans and others, did their best to help, but the vastness of the problem was far beyond them. The Government of Burma in Maymyo had completely lost control of events. Across the border in Assam the magnitude of the problem had yet to be appreciated. There, as in Burma, the military had priority. Civilians would have to take their chance, and as is always the case in such circumstances, the dice was loaded in favour of those who could either afford to buy their way, or could claim priority on account of their special position in the community. It was later to be asserted, with great bitterness, that Europeans, including Anglo-Indians and Anglo-Burmans, were given priority over Indians and others.

The ability of the Assam Government to cope with the problem was not self-evident. Assam is one of the more remote of the Indian provinces, dependent for its revenues almost entirely on tea and oil. Its communications are poor and liable to seasonal interruptions, whenever the great Brahmaputra overflows its banks. East Bengal (now Bangladesh) was similarly situated, besides being prone to more natural disasters than anywhere else in the world. As was the case with Burma, Assam was a military backwater, with little cause hitherto to anticipate invasion, least of all by hundreds of thousands of refugees on top of a defeated and debilitated army amounting to many more thousands. It is hardly surprising that the handful of British, Indian and Burmese officials charged with handling the refugees in Burma and Assam should have found themselves incapable of dealing with the situation.

The mistake lay in leaving it so late. This was to some extent due to the conflicting military and civil requirements in Rangoon; and also to the priority given to the military to clear the Irrawaddy and Chindwin and get back to India. One consequence of the latter was that large numbers of refugees were collected in Mandalay, only to be bombed or incinerated on Good Friday, 1942, with the consequential panic flight that followed. There were just not the means to control such a mass exodus of human beings, terrified out of their wits.

In the latter part of the Retreat, most of those who managed to get back to India preceded, or followed, the Burma Army by way of Kalewa, Tamu, Palel and Imphal. Those who went ahead of the Army were the lucky ones, although thousands died on the way. Those who came after suffered the monsoon, as well as other hazards, and died in even greater numbers, cholera being the most certain killer. Hugh Tinker, a Civil Servant, who played a prominent part in dealing with the refugees, has estimated that between 10,000 and 50,000 of them may have died. The exact figures will never be known although some estimates reckon as many as 100,000. The Government of India calculated that 500,000 Indians reached India, roughly 50 per cent of Burma's Indian population in the 1931 census.

It meant the virtual end of Indian influence in Burma, a consummation devoutly desired by almost every Burmese, whatever his political sympathies. Some Indians did remain, notably in Tenasserim where the tide of war swept over them too rapidly for them to react by taking to the road. Those who remained do not appear to have been badly treated, probably because the Japanese, who had cause to sweeten their 'Indian National Army', saw to it that the Burmese behaved reasonably. British officers taken prisoner in Burma, and subsequently confined in Rangoon Jail, emphasize the fact that the Indians with whom they came into contact were much friendlier than the Burmese. Captain H. B. Toothill of the 7/10 Baluch Regiment, seriously wounded at Pa-an on 7 February and subsequently confined in Moulmein Jail until moved to Rangoon, wrote in his diary: '. . . friendly Indians outside the gaol would press cheroots on the men. I stress Indians, as the Burmese were not as a rule friendly, the difference between them and the Indians being most striking.'[4]

There were other ways out of Burma to India, ranging from the appallingly difficult to the well-nigh impossible. General Sun Li-jen, who had wanted all along to accompany Burma Army to India, fell back with Vth Chinese Army as far north as Naba on the Irrawaddy before turning south and fighting the Japanese at Wuntho. Then he turned west via Pinlebu, crossing the Chindwin at Paungbyin, but losing his rearguard in the process. He reached Imphal safely on 24 May, much to Slim's relief.

Of the many accounts of escape from Burma, Francis Clifford's *Desperate Journey* is probably the most graphic. Starting in the Southern Shan States, where he had been operating successfully against the Japanese with a detachment of Karens from 1 BURIF, Arthur Thompson (Francis Clifford was his pen-name) and his party of British, Karens and Indians eventually reached Fort Hertz, 250 miles north of Myitkyina, after surviving many mishaps and adventures. They were flown out from Fort Hertz by the RAF.

It may sound macabre to those survivors of the Burma Army who struggled their way through the fever-haunted Kabaw valley, past the dead and dying refugees, but those refugees who had chosen this route to India were the lucky ones. There was at least a modicum of organization. Those who chose, or were compelled, to go north via Myitkyina were faced with even more appalling conditions. There seemed to be thousands of them milling around the airfield when I was in Myitkyina towards the end of April. Those of us whose wounds or sickness were considered to require evacuation by air were taken down daily to the airfield where we were dumped on our stretchers to await the arrival of the aircraft. There was very little cover and no facilities whatsoever. The airfield perimeter was one huge latrine, men, women and children squatting down regardless whenever the necessity overtook them. Since most of us were suffering from dysentery or worse, this happened pretty frequently. I noted at the time: 'Aerodrome about 3 miles from town in jungle, and still being built. Dry-weather "runway" finished, but "all-weather" runway still uncompleted . . . No arrangements at all for shelters and no slit trenches. By 10 a.m. aerodrome was crowded with refugees waiting for planes – thank God no Japs came over! Foul day and bitterly cold. It started to rain and we had to shelter in workmen's huts – stinking! . . . No planes came as flying conditions very bad.'

I can still remember my amazement at the total abandonment under those conditions of what we assume to be normal civilized behaviour. One man, a civilian whom I had known in happier times, sat down on my stretcher weeping copiously as he estimated his chances of obtaining some priority for the air trip to India. Another, a woman whom I had met in Mandalay, beseeched me to take her fur coat with me. She was wearing it at the time. Since I could barely stand, let alone walk, a fur coat was the last thing I wanted to be encumbered with.

The people I most admired were the Anglo-Burmans, of whom there must have been many hundreds in Myitkyina. Without them there would have been no trains driven, sick nursed, or crowds marshalled under the constant threat of air attack. Most of them had held subordinate positions in the police, railways and other public utilities. Those I came across were not only extremely loyal, but also very brave. It gives me great pleasure to pay tribute to them after all these years. They were splendid people.

Very few of them could have succeeded in getting away by air, since the airfield at Myitkyina ceased to be usable after Japanese air attacks on 6 May. Most had then to make their way up the Hukawng valley and over the high passes, Pangsau, Chaukan or Diphu, into Assam. It is some of the wildest country in the world, difficult enough in the dry season for men in the peak of condition, impossible in the monsoon for people already debilitated by sickness and hunger. But, despite the difficulties, some 500 Europeans and 10,000 Indians perforce chose this route, among them Eric Battersby, ADC to the Governor, who had remained behind after Dorman-Smith's departure on 4 May. Battersby, who was in the Burma Police, joined a party of seventeen led by Robin McGuire of the BCS, Deputy Commissioner in Myitkyina. McGuire had at least some knowledge of the route, as well as authority with the Kachin tribesmen who inhabited that wilderness.

An account of this journey is given in *Last and First in Burma*.[5] It makes grim reading, but Battersby was one of the lucky ones. The Indian refugees in particular suffered appallingly, dying in thousands as the monsoon rains turned jungle tracks into quagmires and reduced normal human resistance to vanishing point. Even Major E. H. Cooke, an original 20 BURIF who had become an expert with the Kachins, had a terrible journey, arriving in India racked with the disease that eventually killed him some years later.[6] Many were drowned attempting to cross the swollen rivers; I recall being told of one instance when no less than twenty men, women and children, embarked on a rickety bamboo raft, were swept away to their deaths when the raft disintegrated in midstream.

The behaviour of the numerous army deserters added to the horrors. One report talks of them behaving 'like an armed rabble',[7] seizing at rifle-point anything they needed – boats, rafts, mules etc. Even on the Tamu–Imphal route Tinker was critical of the behaviour of some army units, remarking that 'Senior officers seemed to be leading in the manner of the Duke of Plaza Toro.'[8] Bourke recalls meeting a *subedar* of the Kokine Battalion, BFF, in Shillong, who had deserted his post when the Japanese attacked Tavoy in mid-January. He says the Indian greeted him like an old friend only to be disabused when placed under arrest and court-martialled. He was dismissed the service without pension.

When emotionally involved, it is easy to assume that one's own case is unique. But there were similar scenes in Europe in the aftermath of the Second World War, as there were to be later in Palestine as the Arabs fled terrified ahead of the advancing Jews. Even more recently we witnessed the scenes in Saigon as the Americans pulled out, leaving to their fate the thousands of Vietnamese who had put their trust in them. Expediency is a dirty word, in more ways than one, but it never fails to be used by politicians to explain away their failures. It never was 'expedient' in Burma to face the hard facts – that the Japanese were better motivated than we were, and far better trained, and that the Burmese did not much care who won, provided they regained their independence. Nor were the civil authorities anxious, at any stage, to abdicate their powers in favour of the military.

Whether the army would have been able to cope is another story altogether. But when the world one knows is crumbling into ruin, when law and order ceases to prevail, when lawless men have it all their own way, then only draconian measures are of the slightest use. When the house is blazing, it is useless to consider whether the use of a chemical fire extinguisher will irreparably damage the carpets. Only the sternest measures, unhindered by the financial and other considerations beloved by the bureaucrats, will save the lives of people, which I would have thought is what civilized government is all about.

Judged by this, we failed in Burma in 1942 – lamentably.

CHAPTER EIGHTEEN

The End of the Beginning

'As Taffy Davies so rightly said, the Angel Gabriel could not have saved Burma in 1942.'

General Smyth to General Hutton, 29 December 1955[1]

All defeats are bitter, the more so in war when the consequences will be humiliating and tragic. As Slim was to write later, with characteristic honesty, 'The outstanding and incontrovertible fact was that we had taken a thorough beating.'[2] He omitted to add that we had suffered it at the hands of an enemy whom Wavell had persisted in describing as overrated. In his Dispatch, however, Wavell, when giving some of the reasons for our defeat, seems to have changed his mind about the Japanese. 'In Burma itself,' he wrote, 'more might have been done, in spite of all the deficiencies, to place the country on a war footing. Political considerations, the climate, *under-estimation of the enemy*, over-estimation of the natural strength of the frontiers, the complacency of many years of freedom from external threat, all combined to prevent the defence problem being taken sufficiently seriously.'[3]

Sir Reginald Dorman-Smith, the Governor, suffered a great deal of criticism when it was all over. His critics, mostly European civilians, accused him of failing to react soon enough, or positively enough, to the Japanese threat. Scurrilous and totally unfounded accounts of his conduct, or misconduct, were given circulation wherever European escapees from Burma happened to congregate in India. There may have been those in the Burma Army who held similar views, but I never met them. Certainly General Hutton would not have agreed.[4] He praises the Governor for his support of the Army, and for his cooperation, although he does mention in his Dispatch that '. . . the Government were opposed to the institution of Martial Law', without going on to say whether he was himself in favour of it. Whether it would have made any difference is difficult to say, but probably not. The army already had its hands full, and was totally lacking in provost services. It is doubtful if it was in any way capable of dealing with the administration of martial law.

Where Dorman-Smith might be considered blameworthy was in deluding himself, and perhaps some of his officials, that the majority of Burmese were on our side. He even believed early on that they would rise in their wrath against the Japanese. This is the less excusable since he was essentially a politician, dealing almost daily with Burmese politicians, from whom he must surely have gained some understanding of Burma's national aspirations. He would have been naive, if not worse, to assume that the country at large was contented under British rule. The reports he received from the police CID must have made it clear that this was far from being the case. Nevertheless, he persisted in administering the country in the normal peacetime fashion long after it had become clear that a considerable number of Burmese were actively aiding the enemy. The railways were not placed under the army, nor for that matter was the Irrawaddy Flotilla Company, and it was only after law and order had completely broken down in Rangoon that the army was permitted to take over from the civil police.

It was indeed a serious misjudgement, but Dorman-Smith was not alone in under-estimating the seriousness of the Japanese threat. His culpability was shared with the British War Cabinet and the Chiefs of Staff in London. 'Invasion came almost at the same moment as the realization was a probability,' said Mr T. L. Hughes, a prominent Burma official. He went on to say, 'Burma was not in fact organized for total defeat.'[5] That is understandable; less so is the fact that Burma was not organized for *war*, either physically or psychologically, which made the impact when it came so much greater.

That there was complacency, together with a marked disinclination to face the facts, cannot be denied. The governmental machine, like all bureaucracies, creaked on as usual, with apparently little or no sense of urgency. Tight budgetary control restricted the kind of action essential for war preparations, but so had it done in Britain during the early months of the war. The possibility that the bombing of Rangoon might lead to a mass exodus seems to have occurred to only a very few; certainly little was done beforehand to cope with it. If war was to be conducted in Tenasserim, communications with that distant province assumed overriding importance, but here again little was done, and too late, to improve road communications or convert the Sittang railway bridge to make it usable for wheeled traffic. 'Business as usual' remained the popular slogan, any suggestion to the contrary being regarded as defeatist. Meanwhile Burma, despite many urgings by Army Headquarters in India, remained at the bottom of the Chiefs of Staff priority list until it was far too late to do anything significant to improve matters.

If we except Wavell's extraordinary failure to judge the worth of the Japanese as soldiers, and his over-estimation of the ability of his own troops to defeat them, British generalship in Burma was no better and no worse than it had been anywhere else at that stage of the war. Hutton, tied to Wavell's apron-strings, made mistakes, but he cannot be accused of failing to appreciate the magnitude of the threat. The fact that he lacked the personality to impress himself on his troops as a fighting commander was hardly his fault, the blame lying with Wavell who selected him in the first place. By the time Alexander arrived to succeed him, Rangoon had been virtually lost and defeat was inevitable. Smyth was a sick man, and in any case he was never allowed to fight his Division in the way he wanted. Scott and Cowan were both competent professionals, displaying quite remarkable resilience as disaster followed disaster. Slim, too, retained the confidence of his soldiers despite a succession of defeats. Air Vice-Marshal Stevenson was severely criticized for the bombing of 17th Division during the withdrawal to the Sittang, and again for the 'over-hasty' removal of BURWING from Magwe on 22 March, but he too had been given an impossible task, with too few planes and virtually none of the means necessary to protect his aircraft while on the ground. It is highly unlikely that any other senior RAF officer at that time would have done any better. One other senior officer certainly merits special mention. This was Major-General E. N. Goddard, whose foresight and energy in stocking Upper Burma with the munitions of war alone enabled the Burma Army to fight for as long as it did. God knows where we would have been without him.

Wavell's lack of touch in the war against the Japanese is difficult to understand. Until his replacement by Auchinleck in Cairo in July 1941, Archie Wavell had been our 'only general'. Every victory gained by the British Army since the beginning of the war had been won by him. He was robust, determined and experienced. No one who met him could fail to be struck by his personality or not be awed by his long silences. He had imagination, and the farsightedness to support those who favoured an unorthodox approach to fighting the enemy. And yet, in almost every instance in Burma, he got it wrong. Why?

Firstly, because he knew nothing about the Japanese and confused them with Mussolini's miserable conscripts who had surrendered in their scores in Cyrenaica. Secondly, because his long years in Cairo, making bricks without straw, conducting several campaigns simultaneously, and fighting his corner against Churchill, had lost him his touch with his troops. His victories in Cyrenaica, Abyssinia, Iraq and Syria had been won chiefly by the old regular Army, British and Indian;* he had no conception of how the expansion of that army, particularly the Indian, had reduced its immediate battleworthiness. The 17th Indian Division which began arriving in Burma towards the end of 1941 bore little resemblance as a fighting formation to the 4th and 5th Indian Divisions with whose help Wavell had won his victories at Keren and in the Western Desert. This was because the expansion in 1940/1 had bled the Indian Army white.

In the Soviet Army everything depends on the officers; in my experience the same holds true of the US Army. In the British and Indian Armies, it was the senior NCOs and the VCOs who were the backbone. They were (and still are) the long-service career men who hold the unit together. Officers

* And of course African, South African, Australian and New Zealand volunteers.

can come and go – to the staff, extra-regimental employment etc. – and the soldiers disappear to the reserve after five or seven years; but the senior NCOs and VCOs remained year after year to provide stability and to 'guide young officers and soldiers into the paths of military righteousness'.*

Wartime expansion wrought havoc with this system. In British units the senior NCOs were taken away to be commissioned, to help raise new units or to be instructors at Cadet and other Schools of Instruction. Those promoted in their place lacked their experience and authority. The same was true of the Indian Army. The 1st battalion of the 11th Sikh Regiment, as distinguished a regiment as any in the Indian Army, contained 400 recruits with less than five months' service when it landed in Rangoon early in March 1942. Most of the British officers had been only recently commissioned, the same being true of the Indian officers. 'Hardly anyone, officer or man, had seen a three-inch or a two-inch mortar, a Bren gun or anti-tank rifle, a radio set or an armoured carrier . . . There were not more than twenty trained men to a company.'[6] It is hardly surprising that their first encounter with the battle-experienced Japanese, at the Taukkyan road-block on 8 March 1942, was little short of disastrous. But it is pleasant to be able to record that once the Sikhs had found their feet, they became a first-class fighting battalion again.

The British units that fought in Burma were all regular battalions, also much reduced in efficiency by the 'milking' to which they had been subjected. Added to this, long years of garrison duty in a hot climate might have blunted their cutting edge. Moreover, many of them were not soldiers from choice but as a means of escaping from the dole queue, or from some unwelcome entanglement. The morale of British troops remained a problem throughout the Burma Campaign, at no time more so than during the retreat in 1942. Fortunately there is a streak of stubbornness in the British character that comes to the fore when conditions are at their worst, making the British soldier, along with the Turk, one of the most enduring fighting men on earth. The pride with which they dubbed themselves

* This was how my first Platoon Sergeant explained his role to me!

'The Forgotten Army' is only one manifestation of this, a form of masochism peculiar to themselves.

The Indian soldier was very different. In the first place there is a strong martial tradition in India, the warrior being highly regarded throughout India's long history, irrespective of religion. The Indian Army was a tightly-knit organization, son following father into the ranks, generation after generation. The same was true of the British officers. The relationship between officers and soldiers was closer than in the British Service, despite the barriers of different religions, traditions and cultures. It was paternalistic, of course, a word which seems to have a pejorative meaning nowadays, but it did bind together men of completely different backgrounds in the service of a common cause. Moreover, both officers and soldiers were volunteers. They were in the army because they wanted to be, not because they had been conscripted or as a last resort. The *lingua franca* was Urdu, spoken by everyone with greater or less facility,* creating a bond between the leaders and the led. Inevitably, the influx of a large number of British Emergency Commissioned Officers, unable to converse as fluently as their predecessors, weakened this relationship.

Although Field Marshal Montgomery would not have agreed with me, I sometimes felt that the Indian Army between the two World Wars was a more professional organization than my own. The officers were given responsibility much earlier, enjoying opportunities for active service that came but rarely in the British Service until Palestine erupted in 1936. What is more, the power of the purse played little or no part in determining choice of regiment, which was emphatically not the case in the British Army. Promotion was quicker, too. It is true that the influence of the North-West Frontier on military thought in India tended to give officers one-track minds, as became manifest when a large part of the Indian Army had to fight in the jungle; nor can it be denied that India was far removed from the mainstream of military thought in Europe. The great horse-

* It is often overlooked that Urdu was not the native tongue for many of the soldiers enlisted into the Indian Army, the Gurkhas being the most obvious example. There were many others like them in this respect.

versus-tank debate took a very long time to reach India. The effects on the European of long periods of service in an unforgiving climate must also be borne in mind. But by and large I envied my Indian Army contemporaries for the opportunities that were denied to me.

If General Smyth's comment, quoted at the beginning of this chapter, is to be taken at its face value, it would seem that he had had very little confidence in his ability to hold up the Japanese, which may account for Hutton's belief that Smyth's principal preoccupation was to get his Division back behind the River Sittang as soon as possible. However, Hutton's refusal to let him do so was probably the worst of the many bad decisions made by our High Command.

Almost as bad was Wavell's failure to accept in full Chiang Kai-shek's offer of Chinese troops at the end of 1941. His reasons for not doing so seemed sound enough at the time, but they had disastrous consequences. It is strange that neither Churchill nor Alanbrooke put pressure on him to change his mind. In February 1942 the Director of Military Operations & Plans minuted the CIGS: 'The necessity for the relief of our forces in the North by the Chinese forces and their consequent availability to thicken our troops West of the River Salween has become all the more important . . .'[7] Perhaps Wavell at the time was so preoccupied with Singapore that the CIGS forbore to add to his problems, but an earlier introduction of the Chinese into the fight, regardless of the logistical difficulties they would have brought with them, might well have made a great difference. They were well experienced in fighting the Japanese, and although seldom successful had nevertheless managed to survive.

Another decision hard to justify was Alexander's insistence on holding on to Taungdwingyi at a time when 1 BURDIV was fighting for its life in Yenangyaung. Alexander was under great pressure at the time from Chiang Kai-shek and Stilwell to protect the right flank of the Chinese Vth Army, but his sacrifice of one of his only two Divisions was a very high price to pay for Allied solidarity. It can be said with absolute certainty that had the boot been on the other foot, the Chinese would have abandoned their ally without a moment's thought. As it was, Cowan only managed to extricate 17th Division because he had had the foresight to order his Sappers to destroy the railway line between Taungdwingyi and Kyaukpadaung and make the permanent way motorable.

But mistakes, or miscalculations, are inevitable in war. The control of armies is not a science but an art, luck playing a vitally important part. Not every one of Alexander's subordinate commanders would have agreed that he was a great captain but few would have disputed that he was a remarkably lucky one.

The soldiers who fought in Burma in 1942 were for the most part ill-trained and badly equipped. They were also far too dependent on wheeled transport in a country where roads are few and far between. By contrast the Japanese 33rd and 55th Divisions were well experienced in battle, nearly all their officers, and a great many of their soldiers, having fought in China. They were tough, highly motivated, skilful in minor tactics and the use of ground, making up for their indifferent marksmanship by their clever handling of mortars. They seemed to be able to endure adverse climatic conditions for longer than we could, covering great distances through difficult terrain and yet being fit to fight at the end of it. They enjoyed, of course, the tremendous advantage of air support, as well as far more active assistance from the local population than we did, but they undoubtedly proved themselves to be among the most formidable soldiers the British Army had fought in the course of its long history. It has to be admitted, although reluctantly, that an unusually high sense of motivation was the principal cause of their psychological superiority over us.

It will come as a shock to many people to learn that the Japanese did not rate us very highly in 1942. Colonel Miyawaki Kosuke, the commander of 213th Infantry Regiment in the Arakan in October 1942, 'knew, as his men did, that the British were weaker than the Chinese'.[8] Those of us who saw the Chinese shambling around in Toungoo may find this shaming, although it is true that their 200th Division fought well there, as did their 38th Division at Yenangyaung. Nor, as we have seen, was General Stilwell to be numbered among our admirers, although his splenetic outbursts seldom took account of the true facts of the case.

I have often since asked myself how it was that we did not do better. The Japanese did not outnumber us until the later stages of the campaign; nor were they better provided with guns and tanks. The main reason for our failure, I believe, was a lack of motivation. Until war broke out, those of us serving in Burma were living under what were virtually peacetime conditions. The possibility of war appeared remote until it suddenly burst upon us. The general atmosphere was very, very different from that prevailing in Britain at that time. It has to be admitted that too many of us were far too soft, physically and mentally. Much the same was true in India and Malaya. Long years of overlordship must have had their inevitable effect.

This is, of course, a generalization. Those whom the cap does not fit, such as the late Major Seagrim and Brigadier Michael Calvert, are not expected to don it. But, speaking for myself, I cannot recall feeling any motivation regarding Burma in 1939 and 1940; so much so that I was anxious to get back to my British regiment in France or Britain and play some part in the war. At regimental duty in Burma during those years it was difficult to discern much difference in our way of life from that which we had enjoyed prior to Hitler's invasion of Poland.

When battle began, it was hard to avoid the feeling that we were fighting to defend a country whose inhabitants were on the whole glad to see us go. They may have regretted this later, but not in 1942. My few Burmese friends were plainly 'on the other side', and I had some sympathy for their aspirations. The ease with which the Japanese out-flanked us, set up their road-blocks, cut us off and compelled us to fight for our lives, was horribly depressing. If it depressed me, what must have been its effect on the ordinary British soldier, Indian *jawan* and Burmese rifleman? Why had no one given us the slightest inkling of the Japanese soldiers' 'Dare to Win'? They were not pure automatons, fighting like robots, but men with a purpose which we lacked. If, later on, we discovered the answer, it should not blind us to our failure to do so in the early stages of the campaign.

How was it that three years later, and under two of the same generals, Slim and Cowan, we reconquered Burma? Where was the motivation then? I believe it to have been two-fold. First, it is much more satisfying to take part in the reconquest of a former possession than it is to seek to defend it when the odds seem to be weighted against one's doing so. Also, the advantage to be gained from air power was ours, not the enemy's. The part played by the RAF and by the USAAF in bringing about the reconquest of Burma was certainly not less than that of the XIVth Army.

Secondly, we were better trained and could count on better support from the Burmese themselves. They had had enough of the Japanese; like Hitler's minions in the Ukraine they antagonized, rather than tried to win over, the hearts and minds of those they claimed to have liberated. It was strangely short-sighted, since the Japanese had originally operated along very different lines. It is probably inevitable for those who initially claim some kind of racial or ideological superiority that sooner or later they actually come to believe they are superior, and act accordingly. Perhaps it is because of this human failing that few empires succeed in surviving for much more than two centuries.

The Wingate expeditions in 1943 and 1944 went a long way towards destroying the myth that the Japanese were some kind of supermen, able to dominate the jungle without apparent effort. Oceans of ink have been spilt about Wingate, and the Chindits, some praising him, some decrying. But that one fact about him is incontrovertible: he put an end to the myth of the Japanese superman.

One other consequence of the 1942 campaign which took some time to realize was a radical revision of training for war within the army in India. Two men can claim the principal credit for bringing this about. The first was Sir Claude Auchinleck, almost certainly the greatest of *all* the British officers who held the high appointment of Commander-in-Chief in India. Auchinleck instituted a complete overhaul of the training machine in India; his appointed instrument, the Director of Military Training at Army Headquarters, was Major-General R. A. Sabory.[9] Jungle training became the army's first priority. Two Divisions, the 14th and 39th, were converted from an operational to a training role, their task to prepare officers and soldiers for the ordeal of battle – in the jungle against the Japanese. Curtis, who had commanded 13th Brigade throughout the retreat, commanded 14th Division; Bruce Scott commanded 39th Division for a time. John Bourke commanded a brigade under the latter.[10] They may have chafed at the bit, wanting an operational command, but the task they were carrying out in preparing British and Indian soldiers for war with the Japanese was probably far more important then anything else they could have done.

In the end we reconquered Burma, but certainly not in the way envisaged either by Churchill or Mountbatten. Both men favoured an amphibious operation, landing at Rangoon and cutting off the considerable enemy forces in Upper Burma. But they would have preferred to bypass Burma altogether, seizing the northern tip of Sumatra and from there assaulting Singapore from the sea. Only Slim's success in repelling the Japanese offensive against Imphal, and Stilwell's in establishing a foothold in Myitkyina, brought about the decision to reconquer Burma the hard way, from top to bottom. If nothing else, this demonstrated to the Burmese that the Japanese too were on the run, as the British had been three years previously, but it brought with it further devastation of their country, which only increased their determination to rule it themselves.

Was it worth it? Almost certainly not if judged from hindsight, forty years on. Many good men whose worth we miss today lie buried at the other end of the globe for a cause which the present younger generation find difficult to comprehend. Professor Raymond Callahan, with that perception denied to those of us who were at the time emotionally involved with Burma, has no doubts. 'In the end, in spite of everything,' he has written, 'Auchinleck, Savory and Slim forged an army that won a victory immense but almost meaningless, except that it vindicated the Indian Army's honour and traditions before that army marched into the shadows. It certainly yielded no tangible fruit.'[11]

This may be true, but could we have afforded to leave the Japanese in peace in Burma? India was seething with discontent and there was always the fear that the Japanese might invade

Assam, as General Mutaguchi set out to do in March 1944. There was also the question of British prestige, the *izzat* (honour) that had been lost in 1942. Finally, and unquestioningly, any suggestion that Burma should not be regained as an imperial possession would have received short shrift from Churchill. Whichever way we did it, we were bound to go back into Burma, and if that may make no sense today, it certainly did at the time.

It was a particularly unpleasant campaign, partly on account of the terrain and climate, partly because few people wanted to die on behalf of a country whose population seemed content to see the back of us, and partly because we were fighting an enemy whose apparent savagery was beyind our comprehension. As Micky Merton said to me one day at Nyaunglebin: 'It's one thing fighting to create an empire, but it's entirely different fighting to prevent one bursting open at the seams, particularly when so many Burmese seem to prefer the Japanese to us.'

Those of us who took part in the Retreat from Burma are unlikely to look back on that experience with anything but regret. It was a humiliating defeat. God knows, the British Army is familiar enough with retreats, thanks to its governments that so often send it into battle unprepared and ill-equipped, but the Burma retreat was in a class of its own. It was horrible to witness a beautiful country being ravaged; to see innocent men, women and children dying by the roadside; to experience the total collapse of a civilized administration; and to have the feeling that so many of the Burmese were glad to see the backs of us after more than half a century of British rule. I think it was this that humiliated me the most.

Because the British are so familiar with retreats at the beginning of their wars, we have a tendency with the passage of time to turn them into victories, Dunkirk being an obvious example. It is therefore salutary to recall Winston Churchill's comments on that particular episode – 'We must be very careful not to assign to this deliverance the attributes of a victory. Wars are not won by evacuations.'[12]

The same was true of Burma, of course, but it can be said that we learnt our lesson, found out what had caused it, and went back and recaptured Burma, as General Stilwell had said we should. It reminds me of a verse in a book of poems I found in Nyaunglebin, which I carried with me until I lost it in one of the many hospitals I inhabited after my evacuation from Burma. I remember sidelining the verse as I lay on a stretcher in the plane which bore me away from Myitkyina, and showing it to a wounded companion who nodded his head vigorously. I feel it must have represented our feelings at the time:

'Fight on, my men!' says Sir Andrew Barton,
'I am hurt, but I am not slain;
I'le lay me downe and bleed a-while;
And then I'le rise and fight again' –[13]

and in the end that is what we did!

POSTSCRIPT

In war fortune is a remarkably fickle jade. Neither the most gifted general, nor the most dedicated and well-trained soldier, can be certain how the battle will go. It will depend on far too many imponderables, as the following two examples may show.

The first is taken from Field Marshal Slim's *Defeat into Victory* and describes the arrival of the last of the Burma Army in India:

> On that last day of that nine hundred-mile retreat I stood on a bank beside the road and watched the rearguard march into India. All of them, British, Indian, and Gurkha, were gaunt and ragged as scarecrows. Yet, as they trudged behind their surviving officers in groups pitifully small, they still carried their arms and kept their ranks, they were still recognizable fighting units. They might look like scarecrows, but they looked like soldiers too.[1]

The other is taken from Louis Allen's *Burma: The Longest War 1941–45* and describes the retreat of General Mutaguchi's XVth Army after his much-trumpeted 'March on Delhi' had been held, and then thrown back:

> The tatterdemalion divisions staggered back along the mountain roads. Weapons gone, clutching a stick in one hand and a rice tin in the other, the Japanese stumbled painfully through the torrential rain. The lucky casualties were taken to the Chindwin on horse-drawn sledges, others bounced to and fro on sodden stretchers. The more seriously wounded lay by the sides of the tracks. The pain from untended wounds, the frantic hunger, and the inward racking of malaria and dysentery pushed them inexorably to the moment when they would beg passers-by for a hand-grenade with which to finish themselves off.[2]

It was indeed a strange reversal of fortunes – one that few of us would have believed possible two years previously.

GLOSSARY OF BURMESE AND HINDUSTANI WORDS

Chaung:	Watercourse that becomes a raging torrent in the monsoon.
Dah:	Jungle knife.
Lu-zo:	A criminal.
Oozo:	Elephant-handler.
Pongyi:	A Buddhist monk (sometimes a priest).
Pongyi kyaung:	Monastery (sometimes a temple).
Saya:	Teacher, often used as an honorific.
Sepoy:	Soldier.
Sowar:	Cavalry soldier.
Subedar:	Indian/Burmese officer.
Thakin:	Literally 'master', used as a polite form of address (= *Sahib* in Urdu). Also the name of political party whose goal was Independence; members called themselves Thakins.
Yomas:	Hills.

MILITARY ABBREVIATIONS

AA and QMG:	Assistant Adjutant and Quartermaster General (Lt-Col)
AVG:	American Volunteer Group
BM:	Brigade Major
BGS:	Brigadier General Staff
BURCORPS:	Burma Corps
BFF:	Burma Frontier Force
BMP:	Burma Military Police
BURIF:	Burma Rifles
20 BURIF:	20th Burma Rifles 1922–37
BURWING:	RAF component in Burma
CGS:	Chief of General Staff
CIGS:	Chief of the Imperial General Staff
'Dukes':	Nickname for the Duke of Wellington's Regiment
FF 1 etc:	Columns formed from Burma Frontier Force and numbered 1–8
13 FFRif:	13th Frontier Force Rifles (Indian Army)
Glosters:	Gloucestershire Regiment
GOC:	General Officer Commanding
GSO 1:	General Staff Officer 1st Grade (Lt-Col)
KOYLI:	King's Own Yorkshire Light Infantry
West Yorks:	West Yorkshire Regiment

NOTES TO THE TEXT

Introduction

1. *Wellington* by Arthur Bryant (Collins, 1971), p. 330.
2. Cowan to General Hutton, 31.5.42 (Hutton Papers, Liddell Hart Archives, King's College, London).
3. *The Lacquer Lady* by F. Tennyson Jesse (Heinemann, 1929).
4. The excessive force employed by Brigadier-General R. E. H. Dyer to disperse a crowd assembled in the Jallianwallah Bagh in the centre of Amritsar City on Sunday, 13 April 1919, was seldom absent from the minds of those of us responsible for keeping the peace in that turbulent capital of the Sikhs, whose Holy City it is. As I wrote in my diary at the time: 'Whenever I take my platoon on a flag march through the city, I seem to hear a ghostly voice calling from the rooftops – "Remember Dyer! Remember Dyer!"' I certainly never forgot him.

Chapter 1: Uneasy Burma

1. *Imperial Sunset* by James Lunt (Macdonald, 1981), p. 354.
2. I recall my embarrassment when shortly after my marriage I took my bride to visit Mandalay's celebrated covered bazaar. There, behind a stall in the silversmiths' section, a pretty girl with whom I had from time to time exchanged pleasantries inquired about my companion. I explained the relationship. 'Thank goodness,' she replied. 'Now we poor virgins will feel safer when you are around!' Such as interchange would have been unthinkable in India – and as it was I was greatly relieved that it was conducted in Burmese.
3. Sir George White ended his career as a Field Marshal and as Governor of the Royal Hospital at Chelsea.
4. *Arabia Deserta* by Charles M. Doughty (CUP, 1888).
5. *Naga Path* by Ursula Graham Bower (John Murray, 1952).
6. *The Jungle in Arms* by Balfour Oatts (William Kimber, 1962), p. 41.

Chapter 2: Before the Battle

1. *Official History of the Indian Armed Forces in the Second World War: The Retreat from Burma 1941–42*, ed. Bisheshwar Prasad (Calcutta, 1952) p. 42.
2. *The Union of Burma: A Study of the First Years of Independence* by Hugh Tinker (OUP, 1961) p. 316.
3. The Indian Army raised battalions for special duties in Burma, all of them in the Punjab and attracting a good type of man by the offer of special allowances. They were numbered the 89th, 90th, 91st, 92nd Punjabis and 93rd Burma Infantry, amalgamated in 1922 as the 8th Punjab Regiment. Their badge was the *chinthe*, the legendary

beast standing guard outside Burmese temples and *pongyi kyaungs*, which was later adopted by Wingate for his Chindits. Brigadier John Bourke commanded the 4/8th Punjab Regiment, formerly the 92nd Punjabis.

4. The Gurkhas from Nepal are great mercenaries. They enlisted in large numbers in the BMP, many of them settling after discharge around Maymyo where they became market gardeners. The 10th Princess Mary's Own Gurkha Rifles, which now forms part of the British Brigade of Gurkhas, was originally raised in Maymyo from Gurkhas domiciled in Burma.
5. *Some Experiences of an Irish R.M.* by Edith Somerville and Martin Ross (Longmans, Green, 1899).
6. Brooke-Popham Papers (Liddell Hart Archive, File V, No. 7/18/2).
7. The Kokine Battalion, BFF, was raised in 1940, with the specific task of defending Burma's airfields (more appropriately termed, no doubt, landing grounds). They were not very well trained, and even less well equipped for their task.
8. L. B. Oatts, *op. cit.*, p. 40.

Chapter 3: The Japanese Invade Burma

1. Wavell, *Dispatch: Operations in Burma from 15th December 1941 to 20th May 1942* (Public Records Office WO/106-2666).
2. Comment by CIGS on Wavell's Dispatch, *ibid.*
3. *Walkout: With Stilwell in Burma* by Frank Dorn (Thomas Y. Crowell, New York, 1971), p. 20.
4. Major E. H. Cooke: 9 BURIF Diary (National Army Museum).
5. Comment on Wavell's Dispatches by War Office (PRO WO/106 2666).

Chapter 4: Moulmein

1. *Before the Dawn* by Sir John Smyth (Cassell, 1957), p. 140.
2. On 16.1.42 Headquarters 2 Burma Brigade and 4/12 FFR were railed from Moulmein to Ye in order to reinforce 6 BURIF, then about to be attacked in Tavoy. Lt-Col I. A. J. Edwards-Stuart, commanding a company in 4/12 FFR, has written: 'At Ye, again, there was absolute chaos, as the only method of getting across the river was by *sampans*, of which only a few were available, and each one carried only about eight men . . . It actually took two full days to get the battalion across the river.' All trucks had to be left on the far side. (National Army Museum, Monograph 7711–232).
3. *India–Pakistan Official History*, p. 31.
4. Major E. H. Cooke: 9 BURIF Diary.
5. The 6th Gurkha Rifles, a regiment of two battalions, had a remarkable record during the 1942 campaign. Lt-Gen. W. J. Slim (later Field Marshal Viscount Slim) was the Commander of BURCORPS; Maj-Gen. C. Bruce Scott was GOC 1 BURDIV throughout; and Maj-Gen. D. T. ('Punch') Cowan was GOC 17th Indian Division from March onwards. All three had served together as captains and subalterns in the

6th Gurkhas and were personal friends.

6. *Wavell: Supreme Commander* by John Connell (Collins, 1969) p. 41.
7. National Army Museum Monograph 7711–232.
8. C-in-C Far East Telegram 276/4 of 13/8/41.
9. One of whom has since become Quartermaster General and another GOC in the Falklands.
10. *India–Pakistan Official History*, pp. 54–5.

Chapter 5: Confusion Worse Confounded

1. PRO WO/106–2634.
2. Wavell explained to McLeod his reason for relieving him by emphasizing that the extensive reorganization within Burma Army required a commander with more experience of organization and administration of troops on a large scale. Much the same reason was given for the replacement of Hutton ten weeks later. It is however fair to point out that McLeod was approaching sixty and a very tired man.
3. A Chinese 'Army' was an army only in name. In strength it might amount to a weak British Division, its equipment a weird hotch-potch of weapons of foreign manufacture. Much of its transportation was by porters, its logistics were virtually non-existent, and its equipment – guns, mortars and machine guns – rarely amounted to that of a British brigade. One British liaison officer attached to the VIth Army used to refer to it as 'Genghiz Khan's horde'.
4. Hutton Papers.
5. PRO WO/106 2659 (Abraham Diary).
6. *Ibid.*
7. In discussion with General Winterton, Alexander's Chief of Staff in the later stages of the campaign, we both felt that landing the 18th British Division would not have made all that much difference to the outcome of the campaign.
8. The 18th Indian Division was re-numbered 19th to avoid confusion with its British equivalent (which was captured at Singapore). The 19th Indian 'Dagger' Division went on to win fame and recapture Mandalay under its dashing commander, Maj-Gen. Pete Rees.
9. Smyth, *op. cit.*, p. 110.
10. *India–Pakistan Official History*, pp. 82–3.
11. *Burma 1942–1945* by Raymond Callahan (Davis-Poynter, 1978), p. 32.
12. 'I admit quite frankly that I misjudged the situation and never expected the Japanese to get along as fast as he did, or in such strength.' Wavell to Hutton, 2.7.42 (Hutton Papers).

Chapter 6: The First Shocks

1. *The Virginians* by William Makepeace Thackeray (1899), p. 636.
2. *Milestones* by Sir John Smyth (Sidgwick & Jackson, 1979), p. 157.
3. *Ibid*, p. 169.
4. Smyth Papers (Imperial War Museum).

5. *Defeat into Victory* by Field Marshal Sir William Slim (Cassell, 1956), p. 25.
6. Hutton Papers.

Chapter 7: We Abandon Moulmein

1. In *Milestones* (p. 170) Smyth makes it clear that Hutton thought Jones should have been removed from his command for the disaster at Kawkareik. Smyth, who thought Jones had been given 'a very raw deal', declined to do so, and in fact Jones proved himself to be a very dependable brigade commander, later being awarded the DSO.
2. Japanese Report in translation (Imperial War Museum).
3. The Three Pagodas Pass by-passed the main Kawkareik–Sukli position. It was later that the Japanese constructed their railway (*Bridge over the River Kwai*) across this pass. The jungle was dense and the Gurkha company encountered no enemy during their withdrawal to the Salween and thereafter to join the rest of their battalion west of the river.
4. The BFF detachment defending the airfield put up a very stout defence, undoubtedly delaying the Japanese for several hours. Lt N. R. Watts, commanding the detachment, was awarded the MC.
5. Letter from Maj-Gen. R. G. Ekin to Official Historian (Hutton Papers).
6. Manuscript account by Lt-Col I. A. J. Edwards-Stuart (National Army Museum).
7. 4/12 FFR (4th Sikhs) was an 'Indianized' battalion with only a handful of British officers. It was a first-class unit. Captain Atiq Rehman, then the Adjutant, achieved high rank in the Pakistan Army, retiring as a Lieutenant-General in the appointment of Adjutant-General.
8. Maj. L. G. Wheeler later rejoined 3 BURIF. An original Burma Rifle, he was an excellent officer with a fluent command of Burmese. He was killed during the first Chindit operation, receiving a posthumous DSO (see Bernard Fergusson's *Beyond the Chindwin*, Times of India Press, Bombay, p. 207).
9. Ekin to Official Historian (Smyth Papers). In an interview in September 1984, General Ekin told me that Bourke had been 'disgracefully treated by both Hutton and Smyth, neither of whom had had the manners to apologize to him. Anyone else but Paddy Bourke would have pushed off and left me to muddle my way through,' he added, 'but, thank God, we had always been good friends.' It ought to be added that Roger Ekin was an exceptionally nice man himself.

Chapter 8: We Move to Nyaunglebin

1. *High Command in War* by Field Marshal Montgomery, C-in-C, 21 Army Group, Germany, 1945, p. 17.
2. Connell, *op. cit.*, p. 117.
3. *Ibid*, p. 133.
4. Lt-Col Humphrey Purton, an original Burma Rifle, writes on 11.2.85: 'You are quite right when you say we were very badly trained. My own battalion (5 BURIF) had done hardly any collective training at all before

the retreat started. They were barely past the stage of being recruits. The Burmans deserted *en masse* after their first action but the remainder behaved extremely well and, in spite of all the temptations, we had very few desertions.'

5. Ekin to Official Historian (Smyth Papers).
6. Smyth, *Milestones*, p. 176.

Chapter 9: The Sittang Disaster

1. At the Battle of Aliwal during the First Sikh War, the Sikhs elected to fight with their backs to the Sutlej River. When driven back by the British, they drowned in their thousands while attempting to escape.
2. Official History: *The War Against Japan* by Kirby, etc. (HMSO), 1958), p. 61.
3. General Ekin in an interview on 4.9.84 said he still could not understand why Smyth refused to send his brigade back to strengthen the bridgehead. Ekin said that all the information he was getting from his patrols made it plain that the enemy were outflanking 17th Division through the jungle.
4. Captain S. H. J. F. Maneckshaw was to end his career as India's only Field Marshal (to date).
5. PRO WO/106–2659 (Abraham Diary).
6. Cowan to Smyth 8.10.55 (Smyth Papers).
7. Smyth, *Milestones*, p. 190.
8. The officer who actually pressed the exploder was Lt (later Major) Bashir Ahmed Khan of the Malerkotla Sappers & Miners.
9. *India–Pakistan Official History*, p. 177.
10. Cowan ('Punch') and Jones ('Jonah') had served together in the 6th Gurkha Rifles, as had Slim and Bruce Scott. On 18.11.42 Slim wrote to his old friend, Lt-Col H. R. K. Gibbs: 'There were times when I didn't feel too good in Burma but the old 6th Gurkha party always held me up and I was very sorry when it was broken up.' (Imperial War Museum – Misc 824).
11. Taken from 'The Iron Duke' (*Duke of Wellington's Regimental Magazine*, April 1984). Mr Crowther was not to meet his companion again until 1972 when one night, while helping with the parking of lorries outside a café in Staffordshire, the driver of one of them leant out of his cab, saying, 'I remember you.' It was Bandsman Les Williams whom he had last seen thirty years previously on the banks of the Sittang. Williams was a prisoner until the end of the war in Burma.
12. *The Longest Retreat* by Tim Carew (Hamish Hamilton, 1969), p. 145.
13. Lt-Col H. B. Owen of the 'Dukes' became separated from his battalion in the jungle during the withdrawal from Kyaikto. With a small party he reached the river which they swam in complete darkness. On the far bank, exhausted, Owen and his batman lost touch with the others. Making their way to the nearest village to seek food and rest, Owen was murdered while sleeping. His batman escaped with severe injuries.

Chapter 10: Wavell Shuffles the Pack

1. *The Age of Louis XIV* by Voltaire (Everyman's Library, 1961), p. 193.
2. Hutton Papers.
3. Cowan to Smyth, 8.10.55 (Smyth Papers).
4. Smyth, *Milestones*, p. 141.
5. Smyth to Hutton (Smyth's Papers).
6. Hutton Papers.
7. Smyth to Hutton 4.2.42 (Smyth Papers).
8. *The Chief* by Ronald Lewin (Hutchinson, 1980), p. 176.
9. Hutton Papers.
10. Official History, p. 82.
11. Hutton Papers.
12. Hutton Papers.
13. Bryant, *op. cit.*, p. 114.
14. Connell, *op. cit.*, pp. 180–81.
15. Interview, 4.9.84.
16. Hutton Papers.
17. Smyth, *Milestones*, p. 203.
18. *Chief of Staff: The Diaries of Lieutenant-General Sir Henry Pownall* ed. Brian Bond (Leo Cooper, 1974).
19. Connell, *op. cit.*, p. 190.
20. Ibid.
21. Ibid.
22. *India–Pakistan Official History*, Appendix U, p. 463.
23. Tuker Papers (Imperial War Museum).
24. Hutton Papers.

Chapter 11: Retreat to Toungoo

1. Interview with Maj-Gen Sir John Winterton on 15.6.84.
2. Lt-Gen W. J. Slim was appointed GOC Burma Corps on 19.3.42.
3. There is an excellent account of the chaotic state in Rangoon in Lt-Col Tony Mains' *The Retreat From Burma*, (Foulsham, 1973); also in *Red Moon Rising* by George Rodger, (Cresset Press, 1943). I recall that Sub-Conductor Collet, our Ordnance Warrant Officer at Headquarters 2 Brigade, gave me invaluable assistance in trying to control the situation on Nyaunglebin station.
4. Hutton Papers.
5. Smyth Papers (there is a manuscript copy of the unpublished memoirs of Maj-Gen H. L. Davies included with these papers).
6. *Observer*, 3.6.84, p. 5.
7. There were two Karen officers serving in 2/1 Punjabis in Multan when I was there in 1938. Originally enlisted in 20th Burma Rifles, they had been the first Burmese selected to attend the Indian Military Academy at Dehra Dun, from where they were commissioned as King's Indian Commissioned Officers (KICOs). One was Milton Kyadoe; the other was merely named Smith. He did in fact win the Sword of Honour, and when it was pointed out to him that he must possess a first name, he elected to call himself Dun (after Dehra Dun), being known thereafter as Smith Dun. After the war he was for a time Commander-in-Chief of the Burma Army, publishing *Memoirs of the Four-Foot Colonel* (Cornell University Press) in 1980. Kyadoe, whom I knew better than Dun, was an extremely nice man and an able officer but he was later tricked into joining the Burma National Army in charge of organization and training. After the Karen mutinies in 1949 he disappeared into obscurity.

8. *Mountain Battery* by Pat Carmichael (Devin Books, 1983), p. 68. This provides an excellent account from a subaltern's point of view of the Burma Retreat.

Chapter 12: Vinegar Joe

1. Stilwell to his wife, 10.3.42 (*The Stilwell Papers*, ed. T. H. White, Macdonald, 1949).
2. Memoir (Imperial War Museum). Brigadier L. F. Field was Alexander's Senior Liaison Officer with the Chinese in 1942.
3. Although promotion was stagnant in the British Army between 1919 and 1938, the US Army was if possible worse. In 1969, when serving at SHAPE, I congratulated General Lemnitzer for having been a general officer since 1942. 'Thank you,' he said, 'but don't forget I was a lieutenant for twenty years before that!'
4. Memoir (Imperial War Museum).
5. Dorn, *Walkout*, p. viii.
6. Memoir (Imperial War Museum).
7. Arthur Thompson, writing under his pen-name, Francis Clifford, described his escape from Burma in *Desperate Journey* (Hodder & Stoughton, 1979). His novel, *A Battle is Fought to be Won* (Hamish Hamilton, 1960), is a thinly disguised account of the attempt to hold up the Japanese advance into the Shan States. Seagrim's story was told by Ian Morrison in *Grandfather Longlegs* (Faber, 1947); it is a fitting tribute to a brave man and fine soldier. The bravery of the Karens, both with Seagrim and Thompson, demonstrates what splendid soldiers they were when properly employed in their own element, and when fighting for a cause they could understand.
8. 'Toungoo, 21 March 1942' from *Charge to Glory* by James D. Lunt (Harcourt Brace, NY, 1960), pp. 9–10. The 'Guides' referred to were Queen Victoria's Own Corps of Guides (cavalry & infantry) of the British-Indian Army. 'Bobs' was the affectionate nickname for Field Marshal Earl Roberts of Kandahar, Commander-in-Chief in India 1885–93.
9. Carmichael, *op. cit.*, p. 79.
10. PRO WO/106–2693.
11. Hutton, *Dispatch* (PRO WO/106–2666).
12. Wavell, *Dispatch* (PRO WO/106–2666).
13. Alexander, *Dispatch* (PRO WO/106–2666).
14. Hutton Papers.
15. Dorn, *op. cit.*, p. 72.
16. Hutton Papers.
17. Hutton Papers.

Chapter 13: The Battle of Yenangyaung

1. The corporal and I were in hospital together. He had been wounded at Yenangyaung.
2. Slim, *op. cit.*, p. 23.
3. Cromwell to Colonel Robert Hammond, 25 November 1648 (*Letters & Speeches*, Vol. I ed. Thomas Carlyle, 1846) p. 148.
4. *Stilwell Papers*, *op. cit.*, p. 76. At a particularly critical moment, Chiang sent Stilwell an order to provide every soldier with a watermelon as a boost to morale (Dorn, p. 72).

5. *The 7th Queen's Own Hussars* by J. M. Brereton (Leo Cooper, 1975) p. 187.
6. Dorn, *op. cit.*, p. 72.
7. Smyth, *Milestones*, p. 170.
8. One of the most recent examples of a failure was General Galtieri's success in gathering together, transporting and landing 9000 or more Argentinian soldiers at Port Stanley in the Falkland Islands without apparently giving Her Majesty's Government any prior cause for concern.
9. Official History, p. 161.
10. Alexander, *Dispatch* (PRO WO/106–2666).
11. Brigadier Bourke in discussion with author, 1984.
12. Mr Lewin in conversation with author, 1984.
13. The branch line from Pyinmana ran through Taungdwingyi and Natmauk to Kyaukpadaung which was really railhead for the two oil towns, Chauk and Yenangyaung. After 17th Division arrived in Taungdwingyi from Prome, General Cowan had the foresight to make his Sappers lift the rails and provide him with a motorable track.
14. Slim, *op. cit.*, p. 65. There were three Chinese in my company when I was a cadet at Sandhurst in 1936–7. We never knew their ranks in the Chinese Army (they were Nationalists) because none of them spoke English and I failed to see what possible advantage they could have obtained from the course. Two years later, however, I was told that one of them was promoted to Lt-Gen. on his return to China.
15. Slim, *op. cit.*, p. 68.
16. *Ibid*, p. 71.
17. Carmichael, *op. cit.*, p. 168.
18. *Ibid*, p. 165.
19. Slim, *op. cit.*, p. 72. Sun Li-jen distinguished himself later under Stilwell during the battle for Myitkyina in 1944. He was one of the only Chinese generals (possibly *the* only one) to be rated highly by both the Americans and the British. Sun followed Chiang to Taiwan on the Nationalists' withdrawal from the mainland and became Chief of Staff of the Nationalist forces. In 1952 he accepted responsibility for the actions of a subordinate who had been involved in a plot against Chiang Kai-shek. The subordinate was executed but Sun was too popular to be dealt with summarily. Instead he was stripped of office and placed under house arrest. According to General Dorn, a great admirer of Sun's who visited Sun six years later, he was a shell of a man. Dorn was convinced he had been subjected to long periods of physical and mental torture.

Chapter 14: India to be our Destination

1. Slim, *op. cit.*, p. 69.
2. Carmichael, *op. cit.*, p. 177.
3. Colonel de Grandmaison's notorious Plan XVII, based on *offensive à outrance*, caused the French High Command to squander hundreds of lives in futile attacks during the first weeks of the First World War.
4. Slim, *op. cit.*, p. 86.
5. Bernard Fergusson, Lord Ballentrae, author of *Across the*

Chindwin, The Wild Green Earth, A Trumpet in the Hall, etc.

6. In *Fighting Mad* (Jarrolds, 1964, p. 85), Calvert says that for political reasons, presumably connected with the Chinese, Alexander could not *order* the Gokteik Viaduct to be blown. It was precisely for this reason that he had chosen Calvert for this task, believing that such an independent-minded officer would act on his own initiative. For once in his career, Calvert waited for orders!
7. Slim, *op. cit.*, p. 86.
8. *Ibid.*
9. Captain Rea was awarded the Military Cross.
10. Calvert, *op. cit.*, p. 71.
11. *A History of the S.A.S. Regiment* by John Strawson (Secker & Warburg, 1984) p. 281.
12. Calvert, *op. cit.*, p. 94.
13. According to Louis Allen no Japanese general he questioned in 1945 had even heard of this escapade. (*Burma: The Longest War 1941–45*, J. M. Dent, 1984) p. 71.

Chapter 15: Monywa – Slim's Costly Miscalculation

1. Slim, *op. cit.*, p. 94.
2. Captain R. Lewin, 2 BURIF, took over from me as staff captain on 28 March when I was admitted to hospital. I was evacuated by air to India from Myitkyina on 27 April, suffering from amoebic hepatitis and weighing by then less than eight stone. I never really got rid of the dysentery until after my return to England at the end of 1944, but survived six years in Arabia thereafter without any recurrence.
3. Many Burma-born Gurkhas enlisted in the BMP, BFF and Burma Police, but were not enlisted in the Burma Rifles other than as clerks or bandsmen. Our band in 4 BURIF was almost entirely Gurkha in content. They were better disciplined than the local Burmese but lacked the *élan* of their cousins from Nepal.
4. Manuscript notes made by Brigadier Bourke in 1954.
5. 'I must pay tribute to the Burma Army Signals which had a large proportion of Karens and some Burmese personnel. This unit did magnificent work and was completely reliable.' Alexander, *Dispatch.*
6. *The First Punjabis* by Major Mohammed Ibrahim Qureshi (Gale & Polden, 1958) p. 382.
7. Translation from the War Records of the *215th Infantry Regiment, Japanese Imperial Army*, by Kazuo Tamayama, compiled by Kazuo Imai on 3 November 1972 (by courtesy of Dr Ralph Tanner).
8. Interview with General Winterton, 15.6.84.
9. 215 Infantry Regiment, *War Records, op. cit.*
10. *Ibid.*
11. *Ibid.*
12. *Ibid.*
13. Interview with General Winterton 15.6.84.
14. *Ibid.*
15. Carmichael, *op. cit.*, p. 188.
16. When the leading troops re-entered Ma-U late on 1 May, the tin box containing Major Witherow's false teeth was miraculously retrieved. He was luckier than 2 KOYLI, who

never recovered their regimental silver which had been buried in the jungle prior to their withdrawal across the Chindwin to Kalewa. Two or three pieces were traced after our return to Burma, but the rest has vanished.

17. 215th Infantry Regiment, *War Records*, *op. cit.*
18. Official History, p. 202.

Chapter 16: By the Skin of our Teeth

1. 215th Infantry Regiment, *War Records*, *op. cit.*
2. 'In the event only a small proportion of the wounded were evacuated from Shwebo and the remainder had to be sent by rail to Myitkyina under conditions of great discomfort and evacuated from there. It seemed to those on the spot that the authorities in India never fully appreciated the urgency of the air transport problem.' (Governor of Burma, *Dispatch*, para. 131.) The truth was of course that there were so few transport planes in India at that time.
3. Captain R. Lewin's description. Interview 11.10.84.
4. Carmichael, *op. cit.*, p. 206.
5. Strawson, *op. cit.*, p. 281.
6. Calvert, *op. cit.*, p. 98.
7. *Eastern Epic* by Compton Mackenzie (Chatto & Windus, 1951) pp. 498–9.
8. *Ibid.* 14th LAA Battery of the Pakistan Artillery is the lineal descendant of 3rd LAA Battery whose traditions it cherishes.
9. Official History, p. 210.
10. During the arduous night march by 17th Division along the east bank of the Chindwin from Shwegyin, many mules could not keep their feet and the weapons they were carrying had to be abandoned. An exception was 12th Mountain Battery, who had supported us so well at Moulmein. They brought back two of their guns, a most gallant performance.
11. Mackenzie, *op. cit.*, p. 492. Fortunately few refugees used the Myittha valley and it was not until after Kalemyo that 2nd Burma Brigade came upon the dead and dying. Just south of Tamu they had to protect some Sappers engaged in dismantling a box girder bridge across a *chaung*. It was the *only* one in India and had to be salvaged if at all possible!
12. Slim, *op. cit.*, p. 107.
13. Eleven officers and twenty-one Burmese soldiers were decorated in the first Wingate expedition; twenty-seven were mentioned in dispatches. On the second expedition 2 BURIF were awarded ten MCs. It is hard to conceive of a finer record.
14. Slim, *op. cit.*, p. 111.
15. Slim, *op. cit.*, p. 113.
16. Interview, 15.6.84.
17. Slim to Lt-Col H. R. K. Gibbs, 18.11.42 (Imperial War Museum).

Chapter 17: Against All the Odds

1. *Desperate Journey* by Clifford, *op. cit.*, p. 190.
2. Dorn, *op. cit.*, p. 77.
3. General Dorn has given a graphic account of this journey in *Walkout: With Stilwell in Burma*.
4. Diary of Captain H. B. Toothill (Imperial War Museum).

5. *Last and First in Burma* by Maurice Collis (Faber, 1961) pp. 174–8.
6. Major E. H. Cooke: 9 BURIF Diary (National Army Museum).
7. Quoted in Collis, *op. cit.*, p. 175.
8. 'The Indian Exodus from Burma 1942) by Hugh Tinker (*Journal of South-East Asian Studies*, Vol. VI, March 1975) p. 10.

Chapter 18: The End of the Beginning

1. Smyth Papers.
2. Slim, *op. cit.*, p. 115.
3. Wavell, *Dispatch*, (PRO WO/106–2666). Author's italics.
4. Maurice Collis, in *Last and First in Burma*, makes out a convincing case in support of the Governor.
5. Address to the Royal Central Asian Society by Mr T. L. Hughes on 3.11.43. Hughes had been Alexander's Chief Civil Liaison Officer during the campaign and was later Secretary to the Governor of Burma (PRO 106/2693).
6. *A Matter of Honour* by Philip Mason (Jonathan Cape, London, 1974) pp. 490–1. The infantry battalions in 63rd Indian Brigade, the last formation to be landed before Rangoon was evacuated, were given their mortars *in boxes* straight from the arsenal, when embarking at Calcutta. They had a sea journey of 5–7 days in which to unbox them, learn how to put them together and, with luck, fire one or two of them. They were in action less than two weeks later!
7. PRO WO/106–2666.
8. Louis Allen, *op. cit.*, p. 96.
9. Lt-Gen Sir Reginald Savory of the 11th Sikh Regiment was GOC 23rd Indian Division when the Burma Army passed through on its way to Imphal. Despite his somewhat rigid manner, he was an innovator, a military historian and a man of remarkably wide interests. He ended his distinguished Indian Army career as Adjutant-General of the Army in India, the very last of the line.
10. Brigadier Bourke commanded 39th Division for several months in the acting rank of Major-General. Later in the war he successively commanded Jubbulpore and Vizagapatam sub-areas. He was also a member of the board that court-martialled the first three senior officers of the 'Indian National Army' – Shah Nawaz Khan, Gurbaksh Singh Dhillon and P. K. Saghal. It has since been generally agreed that these trials were a mistake but that was not the considered opinion in the Army at the time.
11. Callahan, *op. cit.*, p. 163.
12. *The Second World War* by Winston Churchill (Cassell, 1949) Vol. II, p. 109.
13. *The Oxford Book of Ballads*, ed. Sir Alfred Barton, (Clarendon Press, 1910) p. 694.

Postscript

1. Slim, *op. cit.*, pp. 109–10.
2. Allen, *op. cit.*, p. 313.

BIBLIOGRAPHY

I have a profound suspicion of long bibliographies. Nothing is easier than to obtain a book list on a given subject and reproduce it *in extenso*. All the books and manuscripts listed below have been consulted in the course of writing this book. Those marked with an asterisk are to my mind essential reading for anyone seeking to acquire an understanding of what happened during the Retreat from Burma 1941–2.

MANUSCRIPT SOURCES

Correspondence etc. in the Public Records Office: (WO/106 and War Diary 2nd Burma Brigade).

Imperial War Museum: Smyth Papers; Memoir of Brigadier L. F. Field; Diary of Captain H. B. Toothill; Tuker Papers; Miscellaneous 824 (Letters from Field Marshal Lord Slim to Lieutenant-Colonel H. R. K. Gibbs).

Liddell Hart Centre for Military Archives, King's College, London: Hutton Papers.

National Army Museum: Account of operations of 4/12 Frontier Force Regiment in Burma in 1942 by Lieutenant-Colonel I. A. J. Edwards-Stuart; Diary of Major E. H. Cooke, 9th Burma Rifles.

Rough notes made by Brigadier John Bourke during the campaign.

My own diary written up after the campaign from rough notes made during it.

PUBLISHED SOURCES

*Allen, Louis: *Burma: The Longest War 1941–45* (J. M. Dent, 1984)

*Baxter, Walter: *Look down in Mercy* (Heinemann, 1951)

Bond, Brian (ed.): *Chief of Staff: The Diaries of Lieutenant-General Sir Henry Pownall* (Leo Cooper, 1974)

*Callahan, Raymond: *Burma 1942–45* (Davis-Poynter, 1978)

Calvert, Michael: *Fighting Mad* (Jarrolds, 1964)

Calvert, Michael: *Slim* (Pan, 1973)

*Carew, Tim: *The Longest Retreat* (Hamish Hamilton, 1969)

*Carmichael, Pat: *Mountain Battery* (Devin Books, Bournemouth, 1983)

Clifford, Francis: *A Battle is Fought to be Won* (Hamish Hamilton, 1960)
*Clifford, Francis: *Desperate Journey* (Hodder & Stoughton, 1979)
*Collis, Maurice: *Last and First in Burma* (Faber, 1961)
Connell, John: *Auchinleck* (Cassell, 1959)
*Connell, John: *Wavell: Supreme Commander* (Collins, 1969)
*Dorn, Frank: *Walkout: With Stilwell in Burma* (Thomas Y. Crowell, New York, 1971)
*Dun, Smith: *Memoirs of the Four-Foot Colonel* (Cornell, 1980)
Evans, Geoffrey: *Slim* (Batsford, 1969)
Evans, Geoffrey: *The Johnnies* (Cassell, 1964)
Fergusson, Bernard: *Beyond the Chindwin* (Times of India Press, Bombay, 1945)
Irwin, Anthony: *Burmese Outpost* (Collins, 1945)
*Jesse, F. Tennyson: *The Lacquer Lady* (Heinemann, 1929)
*Kirby, S. Woodburn etc.: *The War against Japan*, Vol II (HMSO, 1958)
*Lewin, Ronald: *Slim – The Standardbearer* (Leo Cooper, 1976)
*Lewin, Ronald: *The Chief* (Hutchinson, 1980)
Lunt, James D.: *Charge to Glory* (Harcourt Brace, New York, 1960)
Lunt, James D.: *Imperial Sunset* (Macdonald, 1981)
Mackenzie, Compton: *Eastern Epic* (Chatto & Windus, 1951)
Mackenzie, W.: *Operation Rangoon Jail*
*McRae, Alister & Alan Prentice etc.: *Irrawaddy Flotilla* (James Paton, Paisley, 1978)
*Mains, Anthony: *The Retreat from Burma* (Foulsham, 1973)
*Mason, Philip: *A Matter of Honour* (Cape, 1974)
*Morrison, Ian: *Grandfather Longlegs* (Faber, 1947)
Nicholson, Nigel: *Alex* (Weidenfeld, 1973)
Oatts, L. B.: *The Jungle in Arms* (Kimber, 1962)
Oxford Book of Ballads (Clarendon Press, 1910)
*Prasad, Bisheshwar etc.: *Official History of the Indian Armed Forces in the Second World War – The Retreat from Burma 1941–42* (Calcutta, 1952)
Purton, L. H.: *The Safest Place* (Norfolk, 1982)
*Rodger, George: *Red Moon Rising* (Cresset Press, 1943)
Seagrave, Gordon S.: *Burma Surgeon* (Norton, New York, 1943)
Shaw, James: *The March Out* (Hart-Davis, 1953)
*Slim, Sir William: *Defeat into Victory* (Cassell, 1956)
*Smyth, Sir John: *Before the Dawn* (Cassell, 1957)
*Smyth, Sir John: *Milestones* (Sidgwick & Jackson, 1979)

*Stilwell, Joseph: *The Stilwell Papers* ed. T. H. White (Macdonald, 1949)

Strawson, John: *A History of the S.A.S. Regiment* (Secker & Warburg, 1984)

*Tinker, Hugh: *The Union of Burma – A Study of the First Years of Independence* (Oxford University Press, 1961)

*Tinker, Hugh: 'The Indian Exodus from Burma 1942' (*Journal of South-East Asian Studies*, Vol. VI, March 1975)

*Tuchman, Barbara: *Stilwell and the American Experience in China 1911–45* (Macmillan, New York, 1970)

Wagg, Alfred: *A Million Died!* (Nicholson & Watson, 1945)

Warner, Philip: *Auchinleck* (Buchan & Enright, 1981)

Williams, J. H. : *Elephant Bill* (Hart-Davis, 1951)

Also useful are the histories of most of the regiments involved.

INDEX

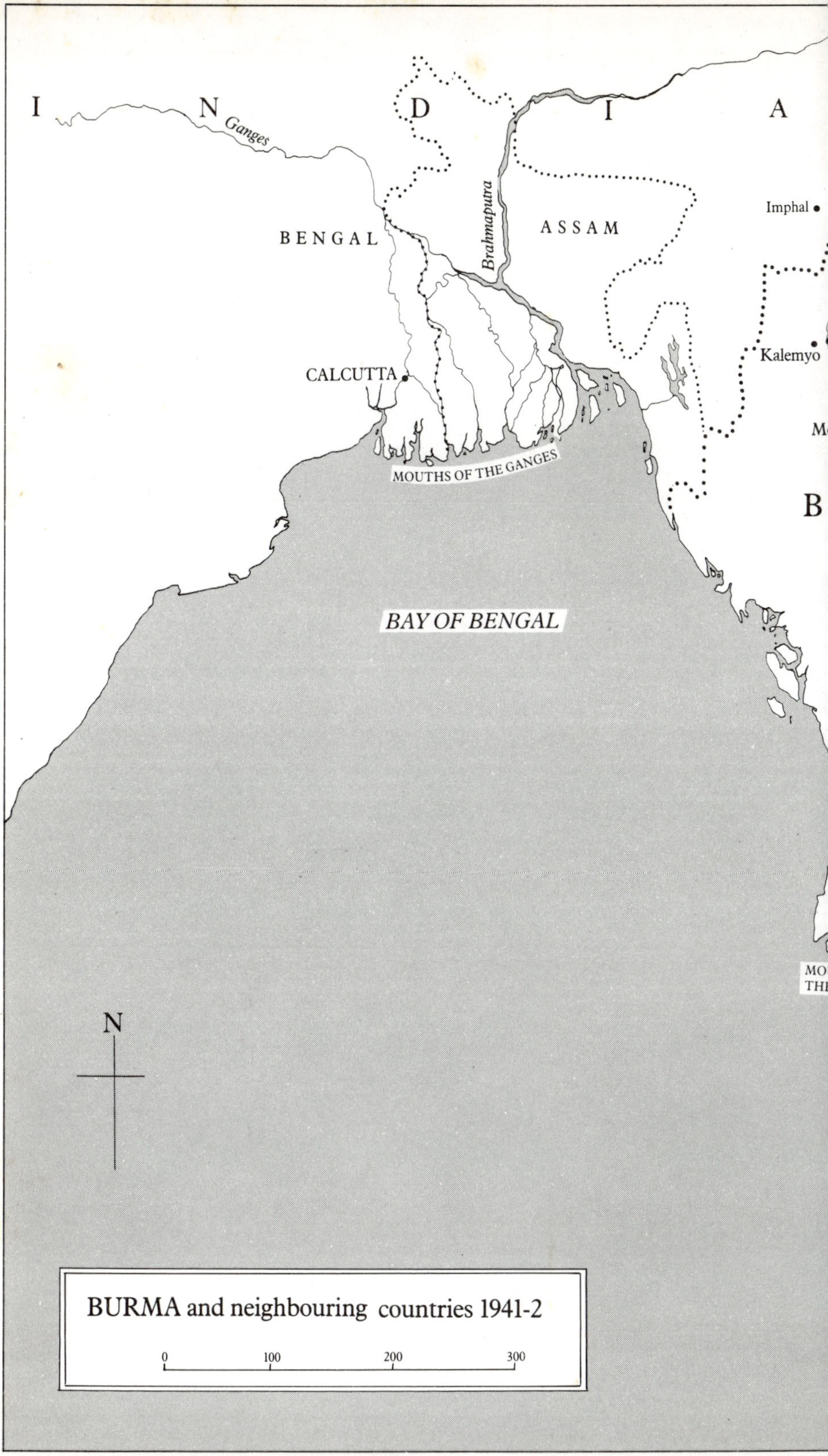
I N D I A
Ganges
BENGAL
Brahmaputra
ASSAM
Imphal
Kalemyo
CALCUTTA
MOUTHS OF THE GANGES
B
BAY OF BENGAL
N
BURMA and neighbouring countries 1941-2
0
100
200
300